A POISONED PAST

A POISONED PAST

*The Life and Times of Margarida de Portu,
a Fourteenth-Century Accused Poisoner*

STEVEN BEDNARSKI

UNIVERSITY OF TORONTO PRESS

Library and Archives Canada Cataloguing in Publication

Bednarski, Steven, 1973–, author

A poisoned past : the life and times of Margarida de Portu, a fourteenth-century accused poisoner / Steven Bednarski.

Includes bibliographical references and index.
Issued in print and electronic formats.

ISBN 978-1-4426-0477-3 (pbk.).—ISBN 978-1-4426-0771-2 (bound).—
ISBN 978-1-4426-0478-0 (pdf).—ISBN 978-1-4426-0479-7 (epub)

1. De Portu, Margarida—Trials, litigation, etc. 2. Trials (Poisoning)—France—History—To 1500. 3. Women poisoners—France—Biography. 4. Women—France—Social conditions—To 1500. I. Title.

HV6555.F7B43 2014   364.152'3094409023   C2013–906784–1

C2013–906785-X

We welcome comments and suggestions regarding any aspect of our publications—please feel free to contact us at news@utphighereducation.com or visit our Internet site at www.utorontopress.com.

North America
5201 Dufferin Street
North York, Ontario, Canada, M3H 5T8

2250 Military Road
Tonawanda, New York, USA, 14150

ORDERS PHONE: 1-800-565-9523
ORDERS FAX: 1-800-221-9985
ORDERS E-MAIL: utpbooks@utpress.utoronto.ca

UK, Ireland, and continental Europe
NBN International
Estover Road
Plymouth, PL6 7PY, UK

ORDERS PHONE: 44 (0) 1752 202301
ORDERS FAX: 44 (0) 1752 202333
ORDERS E-MAIL: enquiries@nbn international.com

Every effort has been made to contact copyright holders; in the event of an error or omission, please notify the publisher.

The University of Toronto Press acknowledges the financial support for its publishing activities of the Government of Canada through the Canada Book Fund.

Cover design: Pamela Woodland
Cover image: A Sorceress, probably Circe, with the cup of poison, from the *Nuremberg Chronicle* by Hartmann Schedel (1440–1514) 1493 (woodcut), German School, (15th century) / Private Collection / The Stapleton Collection / The Bridgeman Art Library (detail)

CONTENTS

ILLUSTRATIONS

PLATES

CHARACTERS

MEMBERS OF THE DE PORTU, DAMPONCII, AND GAUTERII FAMILIES:

Damponcii, Bartomieu	The dead man's aging paternal uncle.
Damponcii, Johan	The dead man. He was married to Margarida de Portu and has three half-siblings: a brother, Raymon Gauterii, and two sisters named Beatritz and Catarina.
de Portu, Margarida	A young woman from the Provençal village of Beaumont who moved to the town Manosque to marry Johan Damponcii. When he died suddenly, she was accused of using sorcery or poison to kill him. She has several siblings, including her brother Peire who is a cleric.
Gauterii, Raymon	Margarida's adversary, a local notary who shared a mother with the dead man, Johan. Raymon also has two full sisters, Beatritz and Catarina (mentioned above as Johan's half-sisters).
Peysoni, Boniface	The dead man's brother-in-law from his first marriage.

TOWNSPEOPLE:

Attanulphi, Nicolau	A prominent local notary who defends Margarida and acts on her behalf in court.
Baudiment, Johan	Johan's servant who comes from nearby Volx and who was with him on the fateful morning of Johan's demise.
de Selhono, Johan	Margarida's procurator in civil court.
Fossata, Bila	A local midwife who testified in court.
Sanxia	A neighbor who testified in court.
Sartoris, Johan A.	A possible excommunicate and definite supporter of the dead man's uncle, Bartomieu Damponcii.

LOCAL OFFICIALS:

Bonilis, Ugo	A court notary.
Josep, Vivas	A prominent Jewish physician and surgeon who testified in court.
Rebolli, Peire	A criminal judge.
Reynaudi, Fortunat	An appellate judge.
Savini, Johan	The leading knight of the Hospital of St. John of Jerusalem, preceptor and commander of Manosque.
Suavis, Antoni	A civil judge.

TIMELINE

c. 1378	Margarida de Portu is born in Beaumont, Provence.
14 August 1390	Raymon Gauterii makes his Testament (i.e., will).
c. spring / summer 1394	Margarida de Portu marries Johan Damponcii and moves to Manosque.
16 October 1394	Raymon accuses Margarida of murdering his brother, Johan Damponcii.
5 November 1394	Inheritance dispute begins between heirs.
12 November 1394	Raymon Gauterii presents his petition in the inheritance dispute.
17 November 1394	Bartomieu Damponcii presents his petition in the same case.
25 February 1395	Proclamation by *nuncio* seeking claims against Johan's estate for past debts.
26 February 1395 *27 February 1395* *1 March 1395* *3 March 1395*	Twenty claims by creditors submitted on these dates against Johan's estate.
18 March 1395	Judge finds Margarida innocent of murdering Johan.
2 August 1395	Margarida demands payment of a widow's pension (*alimentum*).
16 November 1395	Raymon appeals judge's verdict in favor of Margarida's request for a pension (*alimentum*).
23 February 1396	Margarida accuses Raymon of defamation.
1398	Margarida is remarried, to Antoni Barbarini, by this time.
5 May 1399	Defamation suit still unresolved.
20 June 1415	Peire de Portu, Margarida's brother, makes his Testament while of unsound body.
20 August 1450	Margarida makes her Testament.

ACKNOWLEDGMENTS

This book has a feminine spirit. It is, therefore, dedicated to all the brilliant women teachers, colleagues, and friends who supported me over the decade and a half it took me to pen Margarida's tale.

Andrée Courtemanche made the book possible. She had previously noticed Margarida during her own archival excavations and had identified some of the supporting documents used in this book. When it came time to write Margarida's microhistory, Andrée invited my family to visit hers in Québec City. There, one morning over rich black coffee and crêpes soaked in maple syrup, she generously gave me her blessing and passed me a tattered grey file folder stuffed with handwritten notes. These were indispensible as I set about organizing the evidence from Margarida's encounters with courts, tracked down original documents in Marseille, and struggled to reconstruct the Damponcii and de Portu family trees. I hope Andrée recognizes in my characterization of Margarida some of the qualities she herself would have ascribed to her own Marguerite.

One dreary afternoon at Kalamazoo, I had the good fortune to meet a truly superb editor, Natalie Fingerhut, who grasped instantly what I hoped to do with Margarida. Natalie responded to my pitch for a "pedagogical microhistory" with energy and enthusiasm and a support for my vision that has never wavered.

At St. Jerome's University and the University of Waterloo, I benefit from strong collegial support from Frances Chapman, Greta Kroeker, Tracy Penny Light, Wendy Mitchinson, Julia Roberts, Lynne Taylor, and among many others. At the University of Guelph, Jacqueline Murray offers constant support for my research agenda, as well as congenial encouragement when I need it most. At York University, Libby Cohen informed my early sense of gender history and women's agency and offered a model of the thoughtful, reflexive storyteller. At Arizona State, Monica H. Green, pre-eminent scholar of medical history, offers unfailing advice on questions of women's medicine.

In the summer of 2007, I traveled to Manosque to meet Sandrine Claude, an expert on the town's medieval archaeology. Sandrine took to me to places I had never seen before, into crumbling Renaissance buildings and up rotten wooden staircases. Later, she shared with me her stunning map of medieval Manosque, the culmination of years of primary archaeological research. A previous town map, based on a cadaster record (that is, registry of property) of 1941, was republished for scholars in Félix Reynaud's *La commanderie de l'hôpital de Saint-Jean de Jérusalem, de Rhodes et de Malte à Manosque*. Whereas Reynaud altered the 1941 plan to include the placement of towers according to references contained in the Abbot Féraud's *Histoire civile, politique, religieuse, et biographique de Manosque*, Sandrine's version added a great deal of detail and data lacking from the original survey. These details stem from her own extraordinary research, and I am indebted to her for allowing me to reproduce her map here. It allows my readers to "see" the space Margarida inhabited in a way words cannot.

Good visuals enhance all teaching, and, from the start, I wanted Margarida's tale to benefit from illumination. On a 2013 sabbatical to England, I visited the Fitzwilliam Museum in Cambridge and acquired a facsimile edition of Stella Panayotova's gorgeous Fitzwilliam Hours. In it, I found the perfect images to accompany my text. When I contacted the Fitzwilliam to request permission to replicate them, Emma Darbyshire, Image Library Assistant, responded with kindness and generosity on behalf of Dr. Panayotova and their laudable institution.

I have been blessed with talented graduate students who helped with this book. In 2011 and 2012, I workshopped, with the support of the History Department at the University of Waterloo, many of the book's ideas during a new graduate seminar on microhistory. There I benefitted from thoughtful feedback from many gifted young minds, including those of Caitlin Holton, Alex Logue, and Marjorie Hopkins. Caley McCarthy, now a doctoral candidate at McGill University, continues to support my research requests and panicked emails. Lillian Wheeler, a former M.A. candidate in Classical Studies, spent an entire summer sitting beside me proofreading my Latin transcripts. Years earlier, some of those transcripts had benefitted enormously from the skill of my brilliant friend Nancy Prior, then a doctoral student at the University of Toronto's Centre for Medieval Studies. Any errors in the Latin are, of course, mine and not theirs. None of these students understand the fundamental part they played in helping me think about how to present Margarida's tale, but I hope each of them will one day experience for themselves the intellectual rewards of teaching.

Not all the support for Margarida came from women. Chief among my masculine influences is Tom Cohen, microhistorical rogue and historical raconteur par excellence. From him I learned not only how to write but also to teach, to engage students, and to transform classroom into laboratory. His colleague, Richard Hoffmann, modelled for me the diligent scholar-gentleman who follows and documents all leads. My debt to Michel Hébert and to the Université du Québec à Montréal can never be repaid. Michel gave me Provence, the land I inhabit in my quiet moments of reverie and reflection. Though I ceased being his student over a decade ago, my *Doktorvater* never fails to make himself available to me and to support my writing. Through his intervention, I made the acquaintance of the learned Florent Garnier, Professor of History of Law and Dean of the Law School at the Université d'Auvernge. Professor Garnier provided generous commentary on some of the finer points of Roman law and helped inform my sense of legal process. Finally, I owe debts to three other gifted graduate students: Zack McDonald helped conduct secondary research into epilepsy, Andrew Moore helped prepare the book's bibliography, and Graham Moogk-Soulis made an important contribution to the book's visuals. His talent with history is surpassed only by his artistic gifts. His companion illumination to those of the Fitzwilliam Hours captures visually all the imaginative power of historical writing.

Institutionally, the Margarida project benefitted from substantial support. The friendly and knowledgeable staff at the Archives départementales des Bouches-du-Rhône in Marseille never failed to offer their willing assistance, even when I insisted on always consulting fragile originals instead of microfilmed copies. At home, Margarida would never have seen print without the support of a robust Canadian public education and public research system. My position as a tenured faculty member at a publicly funded university allowed me to write this book. St. Jerome's University and the University of Waterloo both supported me throughout this project with sabbaticals, research assistants, internal faculty research grants, and seed grants. I would be remiss not to thank Angela Roorda, Research Development Officer in the University of Waterloo's Faculty of Arts, and Thomas Barber, Manager of Grants and Government Research Contracts, for their personal and professional encouragement. The Social Sciences and Humanities Research Council of Canada (SSHRC) saw fit to award this project an Insight Development Grant, the latest in a string of SSHRC funding that has enabled me to "do" history for 20 years. Through this book, a classroom tool, I hope to give back to our system of public education.

Finally, on the home front, Leslie, Iris, and Harper shared their weekends, summers, and family vacations with a dead Provençal townswoman. Though she did not take up much space in the car, she did steal me away for many long hours. Their love and sacrifice allow some part of Margarida to live on in these pages. I hope her story, and my dedication to it, provides a good example to my beautiful wife and daughters, strong-willed women all.

LATE MEDIEVAL MANOSQUE

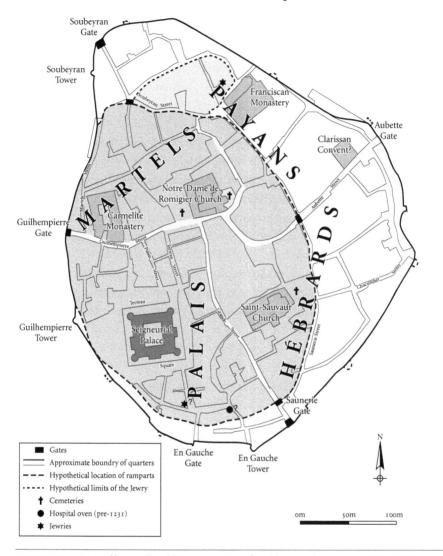

FIGURE O.I: *Map of late medieval Manosque. Reproduced by special permission of the PULM, Montpellier.*

The Microhistory and Margarida

This is the story of Margarida de Portu, a medieval woman accused of murdering her husband by nefarious means.[1] Though Margarida is the main protagonist of the story, other characters played important roles too. The most notable was her brother-in-law, who claimed she had used poison or sorcery to dispatch her spouse. Margarida's apparent tale, and the personalities it presents, comes to us through medieval court records. Her lengthy criminal trial coincided with a civil suit between her husband's living heirs, led to an even lengthier criminal appeal, and, eventually, produced a series of civil litigations. Throughout all the litigation, this remarkable young woman seems to have struggled, though not alone, to assert her legal rights. The use of "apparent" and "seems to" is deliberate. Though we have documents that record legal events from Margarida's life, the tale in this book is constructed. It is not a work of artifice, and indeed it projects verisimilitude. But Margarida's real lived experience is long lost to us, impossible to reconstruct with absolute accuracy. A modern mind has assembled the tale of her ordeal and attempted to ascribe to it some meaning. The story in this book, therefore, cannot but reflect modern interests and priorities. In that sense, the constructed tale is as much about us as it is about Margarida. This book is also different from most other histories in that it interrupts its narrative to interrogate how we know what we think we know about Margarida and her world. At times, it presents alternative visions of how to interpret the past.

---

1 I first presented this case superficially in the opening pages to my book, *Curia: A Social History of a Provençal Criminal Court in the Fourteenth Century* (Montpellier: Presses Universitaires de la Méditerranée, 2013).

The story is important not so much for what it tells us about Margarida *per se* but for how it generally illuminates a lost world. Through the depositions and accusations made in court, we learn much about women, agency, kin networks, solidarity, sex, sickness, medicine, and law. These are weighty topics for the historian and helpful as we attempt to reconstruct ordinary life at the end of the Middle Ages. Alongside these important lessons are glimpses into less weighty matters that reveal the obscure fabric of everyday life: the documents allow us to learn about shoes and clothing, travel, sleeping arrangements, breakfast foods, pets, and table settings. These details color and sharpen a distant world. They remind us that the past, though alien in many respects, is also familiar. And therein lies a tricky paradox, for the past is not the present. It is a foreign world, one we can never inhabit. In some ways, any sense of familiarity is dangerous since it can lead to false assumptions and wrong conclusions. At the same time, feelings of proximity are essential to historical analysis. At a basic human level, they render the study of the past more manageable.

I have written Margarida's story in such a way as to make it accessible to as many people as possible. I tell it as a self-conscious microhistory. Its tale is focused on a distant but instructive moment: Margarida's trial and its aftermath. But mine is equally a tale of a modern historian and his texts. Unlike most histories, this book does not purport to remove the author. Rather, it lays bare the working method of the historian and highlights weaknesses, flaws, and dangers. The aim is twofold: first, to present the reader with a good historical yarn from which to learn; and second, to show how and why historians attempt to *do* history.

The book opens with a chapter on microhistory that explains the genre's strengths, weaknesses, and inherent risks. Then follow chapters on Margarida's criminal trial, the civil lawsuits, the legal appeal, and her eventual fate. There is much I do not know about this long-dead woman. But there is much of her I do know, or at least *think* I can know. I serve it all up here, as Margarida once did her fateful dish.

PLATE O.1: A woman serves a man a meal. *Around her, another man carries a platter of food, a dog begs for scraps, and a child warms himself by the fire. Though the image comes from a Flemish manuscript of c. 1500, it captures almost perfectly the scene of the alleged poisoning described in Margarida's criminal trial. The original illumination is on folio 1 of the* Fitzwilliam Book of Hours. *Used with permission.*

CHAPTER ONE

On Microhistory and Pedagogy

"In the twentieth century we have seen a break with traditional narrative history, which, like the break with the traditional novel or with representational art or with classical music, is one of the important cultural discontinuities of our time."

—*Peter Burke*[1]

"Historians have always told stories. From Thucydides and Tacitus to Gibbon and Macaulay the composition of narrative in lively and elegant prose was always accounted their highest ambition . . . . Now, I detect evidence of an undercurrent which is sucking many prominent 'new historians' back again into some form of narrative."

—*Lawrence Stone*[2]

1.1   What is Microhistory?

This chapter reviews microhistory as a genre to situate Margarida's tale within a body of contested scholarship, that is, within its historiography. The goal is to show how microhistory evolved, to demonstrate where it has succeeded, and to present its limitations.

Among the subjects of the most famous, and infamous, works of microhistory there lurk a not-so-saintly lesbian mother superior who fakes the stigmata and bullies a younger nun into sexual intercourse;[3] a well-read Italian miller who misunderstands his readings and imagines the moon a hunk of cheese with craters

---

1 Peter Burke, "Introduction: Concepts of Continuity and Change in History," in *New Cambridge Modern History,* vol. 13 (Cambridge: Cambridge University Press, 1979), 1.
2 Lawrence Stone, "The Revival of Narrative: Reflections on a New Old History," *Past & Present* 85 (November 1979): 3.
3 Judith C. Brown, *Immodest Acts: The Life of a Lesbian Nun in Renaissance Italy* (New York: Oxford University Press, 1986).

carved out by hungry worms;[4] a sex-crazed heretical priest and his brother who rule a remote Pyrenean village through fear and bullying until the Inquisition exposes them;[5] a Basque trickster who returns from war, leads his family, makes love to his wife, renews old friendships, and then admits he is an imposter;[6] dozens of Friulian peasants armed with bundles of herbs who fly around at night to battle evil witches and save the harvest;[7] a seventeenth-century Chinese peasant woman who runs away with her lover and whose husband then strangles her and frames their neighbor;[8] and two Renaissance lovers who marry in secret before launching a spectacular lawsuit that exposes their lust and love.[9]

Microhistory is a form of historical analysis and writing, a genre. It takes a single, focused, historical "moment" and uses it to shine light on a broader world. The name microhistory evolved from a technique, originally called microanalysis, first articulated by the Italian theorist Edoardo Grendi in Bologna in the 1970s and 1980s and in the pages of a particular Italian scholarly journal, *Quaderni storici*.[10] Though originally centered on Italy, it soon leapfrogged over the Alps, most notably into France, and eventually rooted itself as far north as Iceland, where the Reykjavik Academy currently houses a Chair and a Centre for Microhistorical Research. By the 1980s, microhistory had also crossed the Atlantic into Canada and the United States, where it made a lasting impression. It remains today an intriguing if contested mode of historical writing.

---

4 Carlo Ginzburg, *Il formaggio e i vermi: Il cosmo di un mugnaio del '500* (Torino: G. Einaudi, 1976); available in English as *The Cheese and the Worms: The Cosmos of a Sixteenth Century Miller* (Baltimore: The Johns Hopkins University Press, 1980).

5 Emmanuel Le Roy Ladurie, *Montaillou, village occitan de 1294 à 1324* (Paris: Gallimard, 1975); available in English as *Montaillou: Cathars and Catholics in a French village, 1294–1324* (London: Scolar, 1978).

6 Natalie Zemon Davis, *The Return of Martin Guerre* (Cambridge, MA: Harvard University Press, 1983).

7 Carlo Ginzburg, *Stregoneria e culti agrari tra Cinquecento e Seicento* (Piccola Biblioteca Einaudi: Turino, 1966); available in English as *The Night Battles: Witchcraft and Agrarian Cults in the Sixteenth and Seventeenth Centuries* (Baltimore: The Johns Hopkins University Press, 1992).

8 Jonathan D. Spence, *The Death of Woman Wang* (New York: Viking Books, 1978).

9 Gene Brucker, *Giovanni and Lusanna: Love and Marriage in Renaissance Florence* (Berkeley: University of California Press, 1986).

10 See Edoardo Grendi, "Micro-analisi e storia sociale," *Quaderni storici* 35 (Aug. 1977): 506–20. Shortly thereafter there appeared a groundbreaking essay by Carlo Ginzburg and Carlo Poni, "Il nome e il come: Scambio ineguale e mercato storiografico," *Quaderni storici* 40 (1979): 181–90, subsequently translated as "The Name and the Game: Unequal Exchange and the Historical Marketplace" in *Microhistory and the Lost People of Europe*, ed. Edward Muir and Guido Ruggiero, trans. Eren Branch (Baltimore: The Johns Hopkins University Press, 1991), 1–10. Ginzburg and Poni's article acknowledged the dominance of quantitative, statistical history. At the same time, it pushes for an ethnographic history of everyday life by looking at tightly constrained phenomena to recreate historical relationships and to cast light on people's lived experiences. It advocates, in brief, for an analysis of the social world of those who left no intentional written testimonies of their existences.

Microhistory was, in its origins, both an offshoot of and reaction to the large-scale, quantitative, and statistical form of history characterized by what is known as the Annales School.[11] That school, founded in 1929 by the French medievalist March Bloch and by his colleague, the early modernist Lucien Febvre, came of age during World War II. It survived Bloch's assassination by the Gestapo during the German occupation of France and went on to dominate Western historical research in the postwar decades. It came to define the "new history" of the first half of the twentieth century, though, through its obsession with a "scientific" approach to the past, it was grounded in older nineteenth-century sensibilities. Historians of that previous era, led by the German Leopold van Ranke (d. 1886), reacting against a philosophy of history espoused by Georg Wilhelm Friedrich Hegel (d. 1831) and his followers, were the first to develop a method focused on the empirical treatment of new primary sources. The Rankian goal was to write history "as it really was" (*wie es eigentlich gewesen*). Though much of Ranke's method remains standard, historians today have moved beyond his simple reporting of the facts and adopted Fernand Braudel's technique of organizing their work around a central problem.

Annales history touted that all the great problems of history were solvable if only the right data were analyzed empirically. Annalistes of the 1950s and 1960s believed, for example, that they could answer why the French Revolution happened, or why society moved from a feudal mode to a capitalist one, by crunching the right numbers. This was the age when historians sought to define themselves as social scientists, and so they took up the tools of economics and demography: increasingly computerized statistics, charts, tables, and graphs. Annales history was history writ large. It was macrohistory.

Whereas Annales historians focused on total or complete history (*histoire totale*), took a big picture, long-term (*longue-durée*) approach to the past, and saw large structures and enduring processes, microhistorians of the 1970s moved in the opposite direction. Some, such as Emmanuel le Roy Ladurie, were Annalistes themselves but questioned whether sweeping macrohistorical assertions held up on a smaller, more observable scale. They came to suspect that such broad assertions actually tended to flatten past realities and projected a deterministic reading of history. Today, it may seem obvious that a history of the twentieth century based on 10 decades of census data and stock market records from four countries would not provide a particularly accurate or representative view of the past 100 years or give a sense of where the world is headed. True, it might shed light on

---

11 For a concise introduction and overview of twentieth-century historiography, see Norman J. Wilson, *History in Crisis? Recent Directions in Historiography*, 2nd ed. (Upper Saddle River, NJ: Pearson, 2005).

economic trends, elite values, and major political conflicts and changes, but, by virtue of the sources consulted, it would be largely useless in helping the reader understand the lived experience of the majority of the human population between 1900 and 2000. Today, any historian bold enough to attempt a scholarly history of the twentieth century, if indeed such a writer exists, would necessarily draw on magazines, music, films, clothing, songs, diaries, and a variety of other sources to guide the reader in understanding how most people experienced the era. Most modern historians, however, would never attempt to study an entire century. They would focus their research more tightly, on a shorter period of time, and on a much more specific topic. Finally, in addition to using different types of sources, most contemporary historians would shudder at the thought of writing a book driven by a *longue-durée* approach to history. Books of the sort produced by the great Annalistes, such as Fernand Braudel's magisterial three-volume *Capitalism and Material Life, 1400–1800*, or his sweeping three-volume history of the Mediterranean, are simply too vast in scope for a single historian to contemplate.[12] Such compendia are now normally handled by teams of scholars, each with different areas of expertise, who collaborate to produce a definitive reference text.

1.2 The Microhistorical Method

Italian and French microhistorical pioneers of the 1970s, partly in response to concerns about whether the Annaliste approach distorted reality, proposed a new method. First, they advocated for a severe reduction in scope: rather than looking for trends over great lengths of time, they preferred to isolate historical "moments." Second, instead of analyzing and quantifying huge amounts of data, they preferred a close, deep reading of a small number of texts. Third, rather than study the great men of history, they attempted to recreate the lived experiences of people who inhabited past societies' lower ranks—the little people (*petit peuple*) or, to borrow the Italian phrase, the lost people. Instead of looking for trends

---

12 Braudel was the greatest student of the Annales co-founder, Lucien Febvre. For Braudel's two major works, consult Fernand Braudel, *Civilisation Matérielle, Économie et Capitalisme, XVe–XVIIIe*, 3 vols. (Paris: Armand Colin, 1976–1979), also available in multiple English translations such as the reprinted *Civilization and Capitalism, 15th–18th Centuries*, trans. Siân Reynolds (Berkeley: University of California Press, 1992). Braudel's magisterial thesis in three volumes, written while the author was a prisoner of war at Lubeck, supposedly in notebooks from memory which he then mailed to France, is: *La Méditerranée et le Monde Méditerranéen a l'époque de Philippe II*, 3 vols. (Paris: Armand Colin, 1949). It has had several revisions and is also readily available in English as *The Mediterranean and the Mediterranean World in the Age of Philip II*, trans. Siân Reynolds (New York: Harper and Row, 1972–1973). For a nice overview of Braudel's approach to history, new readers should consult Fernand Braudel, *Écrits sur l'histoire* (Paris: Flammarion, 1977), available in English as *On History*, trans. Siân Reynolds (Chicago: University of Chicago Press, 1980).

in political movements over time, they sought to understand how interpersonal relationships structured people's lives. The overarching aim of microhistory was and is to "elucidate historical causation on the level of small groups who would be left out by other methods."[13] Microhistorians as a whole ask, "What can we know about the peoples lost to history?"[14] This goal is by no means unique to microhistory. Indeed, microhistorians share it with all sorts of other socio-economic historians who, since the 1960s, have sought "the obscure history of all the world" (*"histoire obscure de tout le monde"*).[15]

From the start, microhistorians extended this common goal—to know about the forgotten peoples of the past—not only to the shape of their physical world but also, importantly, to the content of their souls. It was insufficient for microhistorians, or indeed social historians in general, to know how much peasants in fourteenth-century England earned, how heavily they were taxed, or at what age they died. Early microhistorians expanded the search, seeking to recreate the entire peasant universe, internal and external. The layout and contents of peasants' homes was as important as the layout and contents of their hearts and minds. Such historians began, moreover, to draw links between inner intimate experiences and outer structures. The idea was to feel the holistic spirit of an age through its people. This task, of capturing what French Annalistes had first called the *mentalité* of an age, its *zeitgeist*, to use the German expression, its mindset, is so central to most contemporary historical writing that it is easy to forget that it was not always a function of it. Yet this whole project of recreating *mentalité* called out for a new way of writing the past. Historians of events (*histoire évènementielle*), to use Braudel's term, had abandoned storytelling as too fanciful and unscientific. But the new microhistorians, writing about everyday people's personal experiences, embraced it as a logical way to express their tales. They nourished a shift in the late 1970s toward a new or, more accurately, a renewed narrative.

The use of narrative in historical writing became an enduring debate for historians. In an important and prescient article that captured all the energy and excitement of the historical changes happening in the 1960s and 1970s, Lawrence Stone trumpeted the "Revival of Narrative."[16] He wrote that historians since the Greeks

---

13 Edward Muir, "Introduction: Observing Trifles," in *Microhistory and the Lost People of Europe*, ed. Edward Muir and Guido Ruggiero, trans. Eren Branch (Baltimore: The Johns Hopkins University Press, 1991), xxi.

14 *Ibid.*

15 Fernand Braudel, "Une parfaite réussite," review of Claude Manceron, *La Révolution qui lève, 1785–1787* (Paris, 1979), *L'Histoire* 21 (1980): 109.

16 Stone, "The Revival of Narrative." Stone's article was by no means accepted by all his contemporaries. No less an historian than E.J. Hobsbawm published an immediate rebuttal. See E.J. Hobsbawm, "The Revival of Narrative: Some Comments," *Past & Present* 86 (February 1980): 3–8.

had told tales, but since the rise of Rankian history in the late nineteenth century and continuing on with the purportedly "scientific" history of the Annalistes, they had eschewed narrative writing. As Stone saw it, the break with pure Annaliste strictures in the 1970s opened the door to renewed interest in narrative history. Not everyone agreed with him. Many historians preferred to keep narrative at bay or, at best, to remember it as a quaint manifestation of a pre-scientific era. Around the same time that Stone announced the revival of narrative, for example, one of the greatest historians of the twentieth century, Peter Burke, confirmed its death. The two quotations at the head of this chapter show how differently Stone and Burke viewed the appetite for narrative.

To be fair, Burke and Stone had slightly different notions of what narrative *meant* in modern historical writing. In hindsight, though, it is still obvious that Burke failed to grasp what was so clear to Stone.[17] Some historians of the 1970s and 1980s clearly did return to narrative to frame their tales. Stone eloquently explained what they meant by the term narrative:

> ... the organization of material in a chronologically sequential order and the focusing of the content into a single coherent story ... history ... that is ... descriptive rather than analytical and [whose] central focus is on man not circumstances. It ... deals with the particular and specific rather than the collective and statistical. Narrative is a mode of historical writing, but it is a mode which also affects and is affected by the content and the method ... it possesses a theme and an argument .... And finally [narrative historians] are deeply concerned with the rhetorical aspects of their presentation. Whether successful or not ... they certainly aspire to stylistic elegance, wit and aphorism.[18]

Stone attributed the revived interest in narrative to three causes. First was a pervasive disillusionment with the "economic deterministic model of historical explanation" favored by the Annalistes. This model, he claimed, had produced a decline in intellectual history since, to their detriment, Annalistes-trained socio-economic historians had cast it aside. In their quest to quantify data like economists, they had ignored the complex relationship of values and ideas to food supply, climate, currency, and population. By the 1960s and 1970s, though,

---

17 Jan de Vries labelled Stone the historian equivalent of a "weatherman" who knows which way the wind blows. See Jan de Vries, "Great Expectations: Early Modern History and the Social Sciences," in *Early Modern History and the Social Sciences: Testing the Limits of Braudel's Mediterranean*, ed. John A. Marino (Kirksville, MO: Truman State University Press, 2001), 75.
18 Stone, "The Revival of Narrative," 3–4.

historians had begun to recognize the error in setting aside intellectual history. By the time of Stone's article, historians widely acknowledged the need to reintegrate intellectual history into social history. Second was a belated acknowledgment of what Stone called personal political power, but which was essentially individual agency. By this time, historians understood that the choices people made affected demographics, currency fluctuations, and the human environment. It was not sufficient, therefore, to study these phenomena without asking first how human agency influenced them. The final cause was dissatisfaction with the Annalistes' supposedly scientific method of quantification. This, Stone claimed, was scientific experimentation that could not be replicated or verified. It depended upon a number of arbitrary factors and questionable techniques. Worse, it perplexed the vast majority of historical readers. He added that this "[q]uantification has told us a lot about the *what* questions of historical demography, but relatively little . . . about the *why.*"[19] Because historians were no longer satisfied with a deterministic model of history that set aside ideas and agency, and because the new science had left a dry taste in most historians' mouths, Stone believed the moment was ripe for a return to storytelling. Like the pioneers of microhistory, he felt the best way to recreate *mentalité* and to correct the perceived errors of pure Annaliste history was through narrative. Even historians who disagreed with Stone's assessment of the reasons for the shifts happening in their discipline at that time conceded that narrative was sometimes an appropriate option. In the words of Eric Hobsbawm, "There is nothing new in choosing to see the world via a microscope rather than a telescope. So long as we accept that we are studying the same cosmos, the choice between microcosm and macrocosm is a matter of selecting the appropriate technique."[20] For microhistorians, the technique called out for narrative.

1.3   Microhistory, Theory, and Interdisciplinarity

It is important to note that the shift to microhistory was not independent of other intellectual changes happening after 1960, many of which echoed broader social changes. Microhistorians' interest in the lower ranks of society was quite obviously influenced by Marxist theories of class structure that dominated colleges and universities at that time. An abundance of scholarship coming from the so-called New Left appeared in the 1960s to draw attention to the history of the lower classes.[21] Similarly, the Women's Liberation movement of the 1960s, the

---

19   *Ibid.*, 12. The emphasis is in the original text.
20   Hobsbawm, "The Revival of Narrative," 7.
21   See, for example, E.P. Thompson's influential *The Making of the English Working Class* (London: Gollancz, 1964).

struggle for African-American rights in the United States, and even the Gay Rights Movement—all interconnected manifestations of pervasive and ongoing Western liberalization—influenced the types of history written. Beginning in the 1960s, second-generation feminists began to write women's history, even though their doctoral supervisors often discouraged them with claims that women had left no written records and it was, therefore, simply impossible to reconstruct their history. Once women's historians proved their supervisors wrong, and demonstrated that women's history was both possible and desirable, this opened other areas of research. Histories of children and of marginal peoples (for the Middle Ages, this meant Jews, lepers, heretics, paupers, and so on) began to appear in great numbers. Women's history led to gender history (the historical study of masculinities and femininities), sexual history, and even to a substantial and important body of queer history.[22]

Once historians pioneered the first works on women and other understudied groups, the need for better analytical tools became obvious. In their quest for better methods, historians turned to other theory-based disciplines such as sociology. Throughout the 1970s, 1980s, and 1990s, there was intense interest in applying the work of social theorists such as Michel Foucault, Pierre Bourdieu, and Emile Durkheim to help historians better understand human social interactions.[23] Closely linked to this sort of non-economic social history came the evolution of cultural history, which also drew on methods offered by the sister disciplines of

---

22 Of particular note for the Middle Ages is the early work of the Princeton medievalist John Boswell and the two generations of scholars who have followed in his footsteps. Readers unacquainted with Boswell or the foundations of queer history must read his *Christianity, Social Tolerance, and Homosexuality: Gay People in Western Europe from the Beginning of the Christian Era to the Fourteenth Century* (Chicago: University of Chicago Press, 1980) and his later *Same-Sex Unions in Premodern Europe* (New York: Villard Books, 1994). For a synthesis of the methodological problem of writing history for a group that is all too historically invisible, see Jacqueline Murray, "Twice Marginal and Twice Invisible: Lesbians in the Middle Ages," in *Handbook of Medieval Sexuality*, ed. V.L. Bullough and J. Brundage (New York: Garland, 1996), 191–222.

23 Readers unfamiliar with Michel Foucault's work should begin with his *Surveiller et punir: naissance de la prison* (Paris: Gallimard, 1977), which is widely available in English as *Discipline and Punish: the Birth of the Prison*, 2nd ed. (New York: Vintage Books, 1995), and then read his important *Histoire de la sexualité* (Paris: Gallimard, 1976), which is available in English as *History of Sexuality* (New York: Vintage Books, 1978). For an excellent introduction to Pierre Bourdieu's reflexive sociology, consult the second chapter of Pierre Bourdieu, *Outline of a Theory of Practice* (Cambridge: Cambridge University Press, 2000) and Pierre Bourdieu, *An Invitation to Reflexive Sociology* (Chicago: University of Chicago Press, 1992), pp. 2–26. Emile Durkheim, along with Karl Marx and Max Weber, spurred the creation of sociology as discipline with the 1895 publication of his *Les règles de la méthode sociologique*. It is widely available in English online or in print. See, for example, the version published as *Rules of the Sociological Method*, trans. Steven Lukes (New York: Free Press, 1982). There are now several generations of later sociologists who have built upon the foundations laid by these three scholars; many of them have also filtered into historical analysis.

anthropology and ethnology. As social historians looked at ordinary people's social experiences, cultural historians interrogated people's food and clothing habits; their rituals, music, and myths; their kin structures; and even their knowledge
systems. They borrowed from great cultural thinkers such as Claude Lévi-Strauss
and Victor Turner to articulate a new mode of historical interpretation.[24] This
opened up new avenues of speculation and inquiry to microhistorians. When
Natalie Zemon Davis published her now famous account of a peasant imposter,
she attempted to explain why the real Martin Guerre's family had chosen to emi-
grate from the Basque region of the Pyrenees into the Languedoc. She wondered,
"Perhaps it was something personal, a quarrel between Sanxi and his father, the
'senior lord of the household' (the *senior echekojaun,* as he was called in Basque),
if he were still alive, or with some other person. Perhaps Martin's mother had
urged the move, for Basque women were said to be forward, making known their
wants."[25] This type of cultural speculation, grounded, after all, in Davis's intimate
and expert knowledge of early-modern Basque society, brought harsh criticism
from other, more conservative historians. For Davis, this resulted in a well-staged
public debate in the pages of a special volume of the *American Historical Review.*
There, the eminent historian Robert Finlay poked holes in the weaknesses of her
anthropological and microhistorical tendencies. She defended herself ably, laying
stake overtly to her purpose in writing as an anthropologically minded historian:

> I have the additional goal, at least as important, of embedding this story in
> the values and habits of sixteenth-century French village life and law, to use
> them to help understand central elements in the story and to use the story
> to comment back on them—that is, to turn a legend into history. Finlay
> gives short shrift to my material on Basque customs, migration, property

---

24 Claude Lévi-Strauss is often called the father of modern anthropology. In the 1940s, he conducted
   early field work with the Nambikwara Indians. His *Les structures élémentaires de la parenté* (Paris:
   Presses universitaires de France, 1949) is available in English translation as *The Elementary Structures of Kinship,* trans. James Harle Belle (London: Eyre and Spottiswoode, 1969). In it, he articulated his method of structural anthropology. For an introduction to the pioneering work on
   symbols, rituals, and rites of passage by the Scottish cultural anthropologist Victor Turner, see
   his books *The Anthropology of Performance* (New York: PAJ, 1986); *The Ritual Process: Structure
   and Anti-Structure* (Chicago: Aldine Publishing Company, 1969); *Dramas, Fields, and Metaphors:
   Symbolic Action in Human Society* (Ithaca: Cornell University Press, 1974); *The Drums of Affliction:
   A Study of Religious Processes Among the Ndembu of Zambia* (Oxford: Clarendon Press, 1968).
      It must be noted that the post-1960s push toward anthropological history was not the first of
   its kind. At least a generation earlier, during the Second World War, some historians had begun
   to acknowledge the importance of anthropology on their discipline. See, by way of example, the
   collection of essays preserved in Caroline F. Ware, ed., *The Cultural Approach to History, Edited
   for the American Historical Association* (Port Washington, NY: Kennikat Press, Inc, 1940).
25 Davis, *Martin Guerre,* 7.

and land sales, inheritance, women's work, judicial practice, and the rest as "context" and "color in historical reconstruction." Or else, when it impinges too closely on his own moral concerns, as with my discussion of religion and marriage law as elements in the mental world of Arnaud and Bertrande, he dismisses it as "exculpatory." In contrast, he is content to leave a cultural and social void . . . . [26]

By no means were anthropology, ethnography, women's studies, and sociology the only external influences on how historians thought about the past. In literary studies, the preoccupation in the 1980s with postmodernism played an equally large role in shaping historical discourse. Historians, somewhat belatedly, mimicked their colleagues in literary criticism to adopt the approaches of Jacques Derrida and Mikhail Bakhtin. The former developed the critical theory known as deconstruction; the latter focused on rhetoric and the evolution of style.[27] By borrowing from such literary theorists, historians acquired new tools to help them decode and interpret their texts. Throughout the 1980s, 1990s, and into the twenty-first century, socially and culturally minded historians have continued to transpose interdisciplinary methods.

The result of all this imported theorizing means that microhistories alternate, sometimes awkwardly, sometimes seamlessly, between narrative and theoretical analysis. An example illustrates. When microhistorian Thomas V. Cohen studied the seduction of a Renaissance Italian woman, he deliberately began his tale with this artful narrative:

> The bed had room for three. On one side lay Francesca, a governess no longer young. On the other lay her charge, Innocentia, a young woman of the house, perhaps a little innocent, but old enough to marry. Summoned by the servant, Innocentia had come last to bed. She still wore her shift.

---

26 Natalie Zemon Davis, "On the Lame," *The American Historical Review* 93, no. 3 (June 1988): 573.

27 Mikhail Bakhtin wrote during the 1920s but was only rediscovered by Soviet scholars in the 1960s. For an example of his thought, see the work attributed to Mikhail M. Bakhtin and Pavel N. Medvedev, *Formal'nyi metod v literaturovedenii (Kristicheskoe vvedenie v sotsiologicheskuiu poetiku)* (Leningrad: Priboi, 1928), available in English as *The Formal Method in Literary Scholarship: A Critical Introduction to Sociological Poetics,* trans. Albert J. Wehrle (Baltimore: The Johns Hopkins University Press, 1978). For the French philosopher Jacques Derrida, see his *L'écriture et la différence* (Paris: Seuil, 1979), available in English as *Writing and Difference,* trans. Alan Bass (Chicago: University of Chicago Press, 1978); *Marges de la philosophie* (Paris: Editions de Minuit, 1972), available in English as *Margins of Philosophy,* trans. Alan Bass (Chicago: University of Chicago Press, 1982); and the collection of essays *Acts of Literature,* ed. Derek Attridge (New York: Routledge, 1992).

"Take off your shift! The fleas are eating me!" It was the older woman who spoke and the girl who with some reluctance let the servant, naked herself, rise up and strip her to the skin. Both lay down again. But not alone. In the middle of the bed lay Francesca's ex-nurseling, Vespasiano, no longer babe at breast, but an archivist attached to city hall. Full grown, he had other things in mind than filing papers at the Campidoglio. Thus begins a tale.[28]

Later, Cohen shifted modes, revealed his approach to his reader, and explained why we must study Innocentia's seduction through a sociological lens:

. . . like athletes in the stadium, on the field of life we act with a half-informed, reflexive semi-rationality. But life is more complex than playing ball; we are, Bourdieu notes, on many fields at once. Our social instincts, which he calls *habitus,* allow us to navigate with partial information and semi-comprehension. Bourdieu's "habitus" is both individual and collective, both semi-voluntary and semi-determined. It bundles together patterns of perception and judgment, and senses of the costs, benefits, and other effects of actions. According to Bourdieu, we neither blunder blindly, nor do we calculate our moves with the precision of an intuitive chess champion, much less his nemesis, the intuition-free fast computer. Rather, we make our moves with the half-informed, half-conscious rationality of a seasoned player of the game of life. Bourdieu calls the requisite knowledge a "sense of the game." Though it lacks predictive power, Bourdieu's scheme is nicely heuristic, for it alerts historians to the likelihood of semi-conscious, reflexive strategic play. In the affair of Innocentia, our five major protagonists—the judge included—and all their partners, make best sense if seen as playing the games of friendship, courtship, seduction, matchmaking, litigation, and mediation in just such a fashion.[29]

To sum up, around the time that microhistory first appeared, there was a general broadening of historical inquiry: new objects of historical analysis, new questions to help interrogate these topics, and new theories with their own technical vocabularies to sharpen the questions. All of this spelled a new emphasis on theory and method. No longer was it sufficient to compile sweeping accounts of nation-states, human populations, geographic regions, religions, or great men.

---

28 Thomas V. Cohen, "Bourdieu in Bed: The Seduction of Innocentia (Rome, 1570)," *Journal of Early Modern History* 7, no. 1 (2003): 55–56.

29 Cohen, "Bourdieu in Bed," 80.

Historians and their readers since the 1970s cast those still important themes against a richer tapestry composed of varied people, lives, and habits. Microhistory was one of the early techniques developed to facilitate this contrast. It embraced the themes of social and cultural history and employed the theoretical socio-cultural approaches imported from other disciplines.

1.4 Critique and Defense

Despite Stone's belief that narrative would carry the day, and despite the best efforts of microhistorians, narrative remains the greatest challenge of microhistorical writing for some other historians. Microhistorians have done a compelling job over the past three decades of addressing other concerns with their methodology. Narrative style, however, continues to elicit feelings of malaise. Other social and cultural historians may have embraced the same objects of inquiry as microhistorians, but narrative writing tends to polarize history, a discipline already known for its factional divisions and internal fragmentation. Microhistorians know and accept that not all historians appreciate their culturally sensitive attempts to write elegant narratives using tightly focused case studies. Still, within the discipline of history, there lingers some tension between those receptive to microhistory and those opposed to it. This tension is not as pronounced, or overt, as it was in the 1980s, but it endures.

Early critiques of microhistory did not focus merely on the dangers of a compelling narrative; they cut to the very essence of studying a single problem in close detail. It was not unusual when microhistories began to appear for critics to question the validity of studying a single, often sensational, event. This, some said, was a flawed experiment since it took something which, by its nature, was abnormal and used it as a baseline for supposedly normal life events. How, critics asked, could the Inquisition register of Jacques Fournier, which detailed interrogations of suspected heretics, illuminate average belief? By definition, medieval heretics were a minority group, their beliefs limited to their own sect. Was it fair to use their testimonies and depositions to understand an entire world? Davis's infamous imposter Pansette, who styled himself as the missing Martin Guerre, likewise made for a fascinating story, but such a brazen act of identity theft was far from normal. Similarly, the Italian miller Menocchio may have read widely from books lent to him and drawn wild conclusions about the moon and the cosmos and God, but millers by their nature were apart from most other people. They had access to some degree of literary culture that most peasants simply did not have. The average person in the late Middle Ages and early modern period likely resented the local miller, a sort of middleman for the seigneur, an agent of taxation.

How could a miller be an example of widespread beliefs? These were the sorts of early concerns raised about the subject matter of *Montaillou, The Return of Martin Guerre*, and *The Cheese and the Worms*.

In response to concerns that their topics of study were too abnormal ever to shine light on the mundane, microhistorians insisted that by reducing the scale of observation, they were more likely to understand how people really conducted themselves as individuals or as members of groups. By looking to rule-breakers, transgressors, and those who went against supposed norms, they perceived the dividing lines. After all, to be declared an outlier implies some sense of boundary transgression. Finding the outliers lets us spot the mass of average people. Through the exceptional, microhistorians hemmed the normal. In fact, that became a guiding principle of the microhistorian—to study what is called the "normal exception." Microhistorians pushed the utility of the normal exception even further by showing that even transgressors did not transgress all the time. When Jacques Fournier interrogated the mountain peasants of Montaillou about their heretical beliefs, the stories they told him reflected masses of information about their ordinary lives. The places they met heretics, the clothes they wore, their sleeping habits, the ways husbands beat disobedient wives, the methods of contraception used in licit and illicit lovemaking, the levels of homosexuality, the movements of shepherds during transhumance, the types of cheese the shepherds made—all this and more came clear when peasants told their tales to Church authorities. The point here is that no criminal is criminal all the time. So, while microhistorians used the exceptional to see the boundaries of normality, their abnormal subjects themselves appeared to be for the most part, aside from some singular abnormality, quite usual.

Another criticism of early microhistory was that the subjects chosen all came from legal records: Le Roy Ladurie wrote *Montaillou* using an Inquisition record; Davis wrote *Martin Guerre* using a judge's memoir; Brucker wrote *Giovanni and Lusanna* using court transcripts, and so on. How, critics asked, could legal documents, intended for specific juridical purposes and shaped by legal forms, be converted to provide accurate views of everyday life outside the courtroom? Here, too, microhistorians had an answer. Court records are the richest sources that survive from the pre-modern and early modern world. In courts, witnesses spoke and told tales. No other type of archive provides such rich texture. Court records, moreover, are not normative or prescriptive. Unlike Church writings or laws, they do not attempt to portray the world in an idealized or didactic manner. They have a better chance of recording not just how people wanted the world to be, but how it actually was. Critics remained undaunted. Legal texts are complex, and to read them requires special tools and technical knowledge alien to most historians. The stories told by Montaillou peasants were not, after all, free flowing. They were structured in a question-and-answer format that limited what speakers could say. Law, furthermore, subtly reshaped and refashioned the ways lawyers presented information and court scribes recorded it. In response, microhistorians became more and more adept at reading court records. They incorporated, consciously, legal process into their analyses. And they reminded critics that even within courtrooms, there was a plurality of viewpoints: the accused, the accuser, their supporters, the judge, the law, the witnesses, and so on. It is an oversimplification to assume that the juridical was the dominant process shaping the agenda. In fact, one of the aims of microhistory is to point out the complexities, to highlight the contradictions and plurality of viewpoints within an apparently normative process.[30] According to Sigurdur Gylfi Magnusson, "To be able to illustrate this point, microhistorians have turned to the narrative as an analytical tool or a research method where they get the opportunity to present their findings, show the process by which the conclusions are reached, and demonstrate the holes in our understanding and the subjective nature of the discourse."[31]

Though early criticisms of its exceptional and overly sensational subject matter or of its handling of primary sources are now mostly a thing of the past, the nagging doubts around microhistory come back to risks of narrative form. As Guido Ruggiero put it:

> I have attempted to use the techniques of microhistory to craft . . . truths, half-truths, and evident lies into stories that reveal the underlying complexities of sixteenth-century culture and values, shared (and at times not shared) from which their tales sprang and drew meaning. Moreover, approaching the archives as a storyteller as well as a historian has helped me to better appreciate what a rich pool of insights on the human mental world past, present, and possible lies buried there overlooked, to our aesthetic and intellectual loss.
>
> I must admit, however, that attempting this mix of storytelling and microhistory also helped me to better understand the dangers of both and to appreciate that storytelling has some rather different ways of showing proximate truths. Ways the discipline of history might well reject, even if they are often to be found unrecognized in the most traditional histories.[32]

---

30 Giovanni Levi, "On Microhistory," in *New Perspectives on Historical Writing*, ed. Peter Burke (University Park: Pennsylvania State University Press, 1991), 107.

31 Sigurdur Gylfi Magnusson, "What is Microhistory?" *History News Network*, <http://hnn.us/articles/23720.html#_edn4>, accessed 17 July 2012.

32 Guido Ruggiero, *Binding Passions: Tales of Magic, Marriage, and Power at the End of the Renaissance* (Toronto: Oxford University Press, 1993), 19.

From the beginning, critics were unsure of the influence of narrative in microhistory. Around the same time Carlo Ginzburg declared that narrative was the "oldest act in the intellectual history of the human race: the hunter squatting on the ground, studying the tracks of his quarry," other well-respected historians questioned its utility.[33] As noted, Finlay famously attacked Davis's style in *The Return of Martin Guerre*, only to face her graceful rebuttal.[34] Kuehn likewise chastised Brucker's *Giovanni and Lusanna*.[35] Both critics accused their respective microhistorian opponents of being swept away by their own narrative liberties and of committing the disciplinary sins of anachronism and presentism.[36] Thomas Kuehn questioned the "motives imputed to the characters by the authors of [such] narratives." He believed that Brucker's misuse of narrative led him to cast his Italian Renaissance protagonist inappropriately as an "American heroine."[37] He went so far as to question the extent to which the historical Lusanna had any independent agency in her own trial. Finlay leveled the same sort of accusation against Davis's female protagonist, Bertrande de Rols:

Bertrande de Rols now suffers the posthumous fate of being refashioned into an assertive and principled champion, the shrewd and ardent companion of a man who transformed himself for her. No longer a dupe and victim, she has become a heroine, a sort of proto-feminist of peasant culture. This Bertrande de Rols seems to be far more a product of invention than of historical reconstruction.[38]

The situation has softened but not abated. In part, this happened because there is now a substantial body of narrative microhistory that takes up serious historical problems. In part, the situation softened because historians were forced to acknowledge the fictive nature of all human speech, action, and written text. After writing *Martin Guerre*, Davis published her artful *Fiction in the Archives*, which looked at so-called letters of remission to uncover the stories people told in

---

33 Carlo Ginzburg, *Clues, Myths, and the Historical Method*, trans. John and Anne C. Tedeschi (Baltimore: The Johns Hopkins University Press, 1989), 105.

34 Robert Finlay, "The Refashioning of Martin Guerre," *The American Historical Review* 93, no. 3 (June 1988): 553–71.

35 Thomas Kuehn, "Reading Microhistory: The Example of Giovanni and Lusanna," *The Journal of Modern History* 61, No. 3 (September 1989): 512–34.

36 In a popular university textbook from the 1970s and 1980s, historian David Hacket Fischer warned that anachronism and presentism were two of the most egregious offenses committed by careless narrators. See David Hacket Fischer, *Historians' Fallacies: Toward a Logic of Historical Thought* (New York: Harper Torchbooks, 1970), 129–40.

37 Kuehn, "Reading Microhistory," 513–14.

38 Finlay, "The Refashioning of Martin Guerre," 570.

order to be pardoned for murder.[39] Her analysis highlighted the tropes, motifs, themes, and stylistic forms common throughout her sources. This demonstrated that all written texts are fictions, narratives, calling out for interrogation and deconstruction. So historians' collective appreciation for the role of narrative, not only in their own writing but also in the texts they study, evolved.

Despite this evolution, there is still an obdurate and lingering anxiety that narrative works of history may not be entirely precise or academic. The fear, to put it bluntly, is that graceful prose may be an indicator of popular unscientific writing. Even supportive reviewers sometimes feel obliged to apologize for a narrative microhistorical structure. Take, for example, the very positive review of Nicholas Terpstra's recent microhistory *Lost Girls: Sex and Death in Renaissance Florence.* The reviewer noted that the book "maintains readability and clarity of narrative" but that this was "perhaps to appeal to a wider readership."[40] The implication is that real historians neither require nor desire readability or clear narrative. That same reviewer cautioned that Terpstra's use of "modern jargon such as 'john' and 'red light district' may strike some readers as jarring."[41] We must presume that the reviewer feared that serious historians have not encountered such terminology associated with the sex trade and may indeed be offended by it. Another positive reviewer wrote that *Lost Girls,* a book by a senior historian at a major university, based on difficult archival research, and published by a top academic press, was written in a "journalistic style" to "appeal to general readers."[42] The fact that such apologies continue to temper positive reviews of microhistories indicates a discipline not entirely comfortable with its narrative voices.

All scholarly historians undergo a rigorous peer-review process prior to publishing their works, but for narratively inclined historians, this process frequently underscores the tension within the discipline. The blind reviews I received for my previous book illustrate the problem. The first reviewer praised my vivid and arresting prose and the book's accessible use of language. The second, who reviewed the same manuscript, complained adamantly about the breezy and casual writing style. This contradiction exemplifies the difference between historians receptive to narrative and those in opposition to it. It also shows the extent to which historians disagree about the place of narrative in historical analysis.

---

39 Natalie Zemon Davis, *Fiction in the Archives: Pardon Tales and their Tellers in Sixteenth-Century France* (Stanford: Stanford University Press, 1987).

40 Holly S. Hurlburt, "A Review of *Lost Girls: Sex and Death in Renaissance Florence,*" *History* 40 no. 2 (April 2012): 52.

41 *Ibid.,* 53.

42 Anon., "*Lost Girls: Sex and Death in Renaissance Florence,*" *Reference and Research Book News* 25, no. 3 (August 2010).

Finally, the reviewers of *Lost Girls,* like my two anonymous readers, highlight a perceived link between clear writing, narrative structure, and non-expert audiences. For that reason, microhistories often find their way into the classroom as teaching tools. Since microhistories are guided by a clear story line and are set within manageable parameters, they appeal to teachers of history and, more importantly, to their students. Though some historians may feel that these two groups are not part of the scholarly audience, I argue they are its core.

1.5 Pedagogy

When historians lament that most people today do not know anything about history, they overlook that all human beings are, by nature, historical. Our internal narratives, how we define ourselves and make sense of our world, are shaped by experiences, relationships, and events sorted chronologically. Our feelings of belonging, or not, are informed to a large extent by our personal historical sense. When teenaged boys take up automatic weapons in a far-off desert to repel invaders, when men fly planes into buildings, when athletes are slain in an Olympic village, when sectarian violence leads to genocide, when two women fight for the right to marry one another, and when two rival superpowers vie to be the first to walk on the moon, the implicated actors do so out of a profound sense of historicism. Our historical sense informs who we are, where we wish to go, where we do go, and how we choose to get there. It also frames what we make of the journey. It is wrong to say that those who are ignorant of the past are condemned to repeat it. No two historical contexts are identical and no two outcomes can ever be the same. It is right to say that those who do not know the past cannot understand the present or engage the world in any meaningful way. This is why we share our historical sense with those close to us and why we use it as an important factor in interpersonal bonding and delineation. Yet we do all this reflexively.

The reflexive nature of most people's internal sense of historicity renders the study and teaching of history inherently problematic. Most people's historical sense is, on the one hand, intensely personal, innate, unconscious, and autonomic. On the other hand, because historical sense is so much a part of our internal workings, the conscious teaching of history is immensely complex. Other disciplines, such as the study of human sexuality or psychology, have developed methods to separate the object from the observer. History claims to do so, too, but does it badly.

Microhistory is one tool that allows us, through its narrative structure, to feel a connection to the past even while acknowledging that we are not of it. It exploits a core feature of historical writing that Sam Wineburg calls the "tension between the familiar and the strange, between feelings of proximity and feelings of distance."[43] In doing this, it allows the reader to hone what Jannet van Drie and Carla van Boxtel call historical reasoning, the ability to interpret past events and gain insights from them.[44] At its most general, it cultivates historical literacy and consciousness. These concepts require, among other things, that readers know and understand past events, understand continuity and change over time, grasp multiple ways of viewing the past, interpret evidence appropriately, make connections, grapple with causation and motivation, and incorporate modern debates.[45] Just as movies and novels reflect, construct, and reconstruct our sense of who we are as cultural beings, microhistory teaches lessons about the past and how we relate to it and to its people. In learning these lessons, adherents of microhistory think about how their own world, internal and external, is structured; about the narratives we use to explain it; and about the fictions we all inhabit. These, ultimately, are the benefits of all historical study. Consider the wonderful analogy offered by Fernand Braudel as he wrote to his fellow Frenchmen: "Live in London for a year and you will not know much about England. But, in contrast, in light of what has surprised you, you will suddenly have come to understand some of the most deep-seated and characteristic aspects of France, things you did not know before because you knew them too well. With regard to the present, the past too is a way of distancing yourself."[46] Microhistory, framed as it is in storytelling, is a potent tool to understand ourselves by relating to others.

This book goes further pedagogically than other microhistories in that it overtly articulates its formative processes. Throughout the tale of Margarida de Portu, it exploits the microhistorian's tendency to raise doubts by pointing deliberately to authorial choices, limitations, and liberties. It hides nothing of the techniques that went into crafting the yarn. It deliberately inserts the historian

---

43 Sam Wineburg, *Historical Thinking and Other Unnatural Acts* (Philadelphia: Temple University Press, 2001), 5.

44 Jannet van Drie and Carla van Boxtel, "Historical Reasoning: Towards a Framework for Analyzing Students' Reasoning about the Past," *Educational Psychology Review* (2007): 87–110.

45 On historical literacy, see Peter Lee, "From National Canon to Historical Literacy," in *Beyond the Canon: History for the Twenty-First Century*, ed. M. Grever and S. Stuurman (Basingstoke: Palgrave Macmillan, 2007), 48–62; C.A. Perfetti et al., *Text-based Learning and Reasoning: Studies in History* (Hillsdale, NJ: Erlbaum, 1995); M.J. Roderigo, "Discussion of Chapters 10–12: Promoting Narrative Literacy and Historical Literacy," in *Cognitive and Instructional Processes in History and the Social Sciences*, ed. M. Carretero and J.F. Voss (Hillsdale, NJ: Erlbaum, 1994), 309–20.

On historical consciousness, see Peter Seixas, "What is Historical Consciousness," in *To the Past: History Education, Public Memory and Citizenship in Canada*, ed. Ruth Sandwell (Toronto: University of Toronto Press, 2006), 11–22; Peter N. Stearns, Peter Seixas, and Sam Wineburg (eds.), *Knowing, Teaching and Learning History: National and International Perspectives* (New York: New York University Press, 2000).

46 Braudel, *On History*, 37.

into the history in an attempt to make the reader aware of the creative process. In doing this, I hope to present not only a compelling microhistory but also an example of how historians write the past. This, in and of itself, is an important pedagogical lesson.

Imagine a physician diagnosing a patient and you will come close to understanding how an historian, any historian, not just a microhistorian, interprets the past. The patient presents with a set of symptoms. Some of these symptoms, such as a fever, a rash, or cough, the physician observes directly. Others, such as queasiness, light-headedness, or a ringing in the ears, the physician notes indirectly. For them, he must rely on the patient's description. Some patients are better at describing what they feel. To make the most accurate diagnosis possible, the physician interrogates the patient by asking a series of standard questions learned through training: "did you eat anything unusual for dinner?"; "have you been traveling?"; "have you been in contact with anyone sick?" Here, too, the physician is at the mercy of the patient who may or may not respond accurately or precisely. To compensate, the physician draws on formal training and, more importantly, on personal experience of treating illness. The physician then casts all the information gathered against training to conjecture a diagnosis. The patient hopes that the diagnosis is accurate but knows it may not be. The diagnosis, however, is most certainly plausible given all the available evidence. It can happen, though, that a different physician, with different questions, experiences, or expertise, may render a completely different second opinion. In the end, medicine, like history, remains an art, not an exact science. Since, more often than not, clinical experts cannot see sickness, they must rely on evidence, training, and experience to draw their conclusions. That is precisely what historians do. Yet historians more often compare their work to that of detectives.[47] Both dig for clues, decipher them, and recreate a past reality to arrive at a deduction. Just as much as historians mirror detectives in their approach, they also mimic the process of physicians.[48]

Like medicine, history is a deductive art that aims for accuracy but can often provide only plausibility. This is the great conclusion of the postmodern era: far from writing the truth, historians can only write the possible. If the past is a foreign landscape, if all texts are fictions, if our distance from our subjects renders them alien to us, then it is all but impossible to report with certainty any historical "fact." Yet, when it comes to teaching history, despite the widely held postmodern

---

47 A book popular on 1960s undergraduate reading lists still appears in modern syllabi: Robin W. Winks, ed., *The Historian as Detective: Essays on Evidence* (New York: Harper and Row, 1968).

48 For a detailed examination of the historian as detective and clinician, see the seminal article by Carlo Ginzburg, "Morelli, Freud and Sherlock Holmes: Clues and Scientific Method," *History Workshop* 9 (1980): 5–36.

recognition that history is suppositional, students still learn history at all levels in an absolute way:

> In many history education circles there is still the presumption that if chil-
> dren blacken the appropriate circle with a No. 2 pencil they "know" his-
> tory. Such thinking is another curious holdover from behaviorist models
> that dominated educational thinking. For the behaviorist, assessing learn-
> ing was straightforward. If the proper behavior was "emitted," the child
> "knew." But in the past twenty or thirty years, we have become more astute
> about what the "correct answer" really means and how the beliefs, concep-
> tions, and assumptions students bring to instruction shape what they take
> from it.[49]

Microhistory attempts to combat the didactic obsession over "facts." It allows learners of history to digest a manageable historical problem. It then lays bare the discrepancies, limitations, and lingering questions in its analysis. It leaves learners to wonder about what really happened, even as it equips them with a good sense that they understand the various possibilities and have a good appreciation for the world in which they existed. At its best, it also leads readers to draw conclu-sions, with some confidence, about what probably happened. The beauty of mi-crohistory, though, is that it makes no absolutist claims to what really happened and offers instead an explanation of people's interior lives to support a range of possibilities. This is summed up in the concluding sentence to Davis's *The Return of Martin Guerre,* in which she considers the role of the imposter Pansette, who replaced the real Martin Guerre only to be exposed as a fraud years later: "I think I have uncovered the true face of the past—or has Pansette done it once again?"[50] In many ways, this final word is the most important notion in Davis's book, though at the time she wrote it, it caused considerable consternation. Still, for students of history, this lesson is foundational.

The way historians write changes over time. Microhistory is one genre of his-torical writing that grew out of a reaction to the heavy, quantitative, long-term ap-proach to the past that dominated Western historiography after World War II. It was, like the broader concern with social history, also a product of major cultural shifts happening in Western society, shifts that put new emphasis on women,

---

49 Sam Wineburg, "Making Historical Sense," in *Knowing, Teaching and Learning History: National and International Perspectives,* ed. Peter N. Stearns, Peter Seixas, and Sam Wineburg (New York: New York University Press, 2000), 309.
50 Davis, *Martin Guerre,* 125.

children, minorities, sex, poverty, and class structure. Its aim is to limit the scope of analysis to a single problem or historical "moment," but to read it with careful, detail-oriented eyes. In doing this, the microhistorian hopes to learn more about the larger world at that time, but most especially the world as it existed between people and groups, as well as the mental spaces and structures they inhabited. The objects of inquiry for microhistorians are usually deviants whose stories survive in court records. But, through those exceptions, the microhistorian extrapolates the normal. All of this takes shape, for the microhistorian, within a tightly crafted narrative tale.

I first discovered Margarida the poisoner in the late 1990s when I was reading hundreds of criminal trials for my doctoral thesis. Her criminal inquest was the longest contained in all the registers I examined. Its contents leapt off the page. Here was a poor woman, a foreigner, accused by her in-laws of using sorcery or poison to kill her husband. Over the years, I continued to dig for Margarida's presence in the archives. When I first wrote about her, I knew only of her criminal case.[51] With the help of a generous and supportive former supervisor who knew the archives well, I amassed a significant amount of additional information: a criminal trial that ran 64 pages; various civil law suits that covered another 45 pages, broken up across other documents; and a lengthy appeals case that ran another 53 pages. In time, I added to these court transcripts data from last wills and testaments, tax rolls, and other related documents. This constituted an enormous body of information from a single ordinary woman's life. From these pages I saw the potential to write about the status of a young, unattached woman in medieval society; about her illness and life as an epileptic; about the state of medicine and medical training; about family finances, inheritance, and patrimony among the lower ranks of society; about internal family politics; about courts, lawyers, notaries, and judges; about enmity and love; even about the breakfasts of late medieval farmers. There is no question that microhistory was the only way to make sense of the many pages of records left behind from Margarida's encounters with the law. In telling her tale, and in telling about how I wrote it, I describe a lost world as I perceive it.

---

51 I wrote, "The legal attack on Margarida by her brother-in-law was surely the product of a troubled history. Did it revolve around personalities? Money? Inheritance? Class? Who knows! Equally frustrating: once the trials end, so does our ability to observe the inhabitants. Did Margarida go on to lead a happy life? In some future attack, did her brother-in-law finally ruin her? Did she leave Manosque or remain? Did she eventually remarry? Could she? Again: who knows!" Bednarski, *Curia*, 36.

PLATE 1.1: Farm workers gather wheat and prepare it for threshing. *These two images, contained on folios 7v and 8 of the* Fitzwilliam Book of Hours *(c. 1500), depict in striking detail the physically demanding sort of agrarian field work carried out by Johan Damponcii. In the scene on the left, male workers harvest tall stalks of wheat while a woman waves at them from her home. In the scene on the right, men beat wheat stalks to separate the edible portion from the chaff. To keep cool, one has stripped his leggings, while another drinks from a flask. (Used with permission.)*

CHAPTER TWO

A Poisoned Past

Be your tears wet? Yes, faith. I pray, weep not:
If you have poison for me, I will drink it.
I know you do not love me

—King Lear, *Act 4, Scene 7*

2.1 The Poisoner and Her World: The Microhistory Begins

They ate breakfast together, wooden bowls full of piping hot stew. He complained it was too spicy, but he ate it anyway. She sat with him, surrounded by people, helpers and friends, the dog underfoot, darting between legs, eager for scraps. Then out went her man, his belly full of that stew, only to drop like a stone in the field before stumbling back home to bed. It was midday, three o'clock, when he died. And now she heard whispers that it was her stew that killed him, that she had poisoned it or used sorcery. But she was no sorceress, no poisoner, no brewer of potions. Say what they might, she had used no dark magic.

She was clever enough to connect the accusations to her malady, her curse for having been born under an unlucky star. Still, her sickness had never harmed anyone other than herself. When sometimes she fell trembling and choking to the ground, others remained unaffected. No, the illness that wracked her body could not have touched her husband. Yet still they came for her.

So she fled, running to the protection of Church and cloister. Her brother, the deacon, would know what to do. And he was nearby. But she could not stay in the convent. Even its thick stone walls and calming silence could not protect her forever. There would be a reckoning; her brother-in-law would see to it.

As if on cue, a trumpet pealed outside and a man shouted her name: "Margarida de Portu! You are summoned to appear personally before the court and the lord judge at the hour of vespers to respond to certain allegations made against you under law! Failure to appear shall result in the imposition of a fine of 100 pounds!" So it began, her trial for the murder of her husband. Her only option was to remain hidden.

The year is 1394, the place a middling Provençal town called Manosque. Imagine narrow streets twisting and turning inside strong stone battlements. Within these tall walls are houses packed tight along winding streets. Most buildings are low, usually just one or two stories, though towers and steeples break the skyline. By day, the streets and alleys bustle with life. By night, the town watch patrols with lanterns to keep away burglars and ne'er-do-wells. Looming over the streets, at the highest elevation, is an impending stone fortress, the old residence of the counts before the last heir donated the entire town to the military Order of the Hospital of St. John of Jerusalem. The Hospitallers now have their convent inside the old palace, their banners flapping noisily in the winds from the ramparts. Armored horses ride in and out and through the streets, bringing with them all the usual smells of such animals, especially in the arid summer heat. From the palace or the battlements, the town's ham-shaped form appears as a mass of red clay pottery rooftops, punctuated by gray church steeples with belfries, and surrounded by a rolling countryside. To enter Manosque, residents and visitors pass through one of the newly rebuilt gates; the two towering *portes,* Saunerie and Soubeyran, make it clear this is a fortified place, no easy picking for bandits or rebels.

Outside the defensive walls stretches the sprawling hinterland, the lower foothills of the Alps. There are still forests then, full of rabbits and other game. Bold townsmen sometimes poach on the knights' reserve. Some are caught and pay the fine; others eat for free. Forests are harder to police than streets, despite the knights' best efforts and those of their official forester. Around the forests are fields of wheat, barley, spelt, and oats through which wind groves of low, dry olive trees. Olives are an important commodity, providing salty flavor and necessary oils to the people of southern Europe. This far south, frost never touches the delicate trees, and so they thrive. Around the olive groves, the roots of grapevines pierce deep into the driest soil, drawing moisture even during the most punishing summer droughts. Thanks to those stubborn vines, decent red wine slakes the town's thirst. The knights have something of a limited monopoly on wine at certain times of year, but this does not stop the locals from making and trading it, opening makeshift taverns in their homes to compete with more permanent ones. A tall hill, the Mont d'Or, juts up from the vineyards. The yellow stone tower on its crown is in ruins, but the remnants of human settlement, largely abandoned in favor of the town's greater protection, remind climbers that people had once lived above and around the town, not just in it. Farther off in the distance, the Durance

River, tributary of the mighty Rhone, provides water for irrigation and transportation. There are conventional roads, too, in and out of Manosque. Upon them move all sorts of travelers: migrants, mendicants, and merchants, as well as journeymen and entertainers. These ways and highways connect humble Manosque to the great metropolises of the south. This is the physical landscape Margarida de Portu inhabited. This is what her world looked like.

Margarida's adoptive city was well positioned geographically. It lay between Avignon, the great papal city with its college of cardinals and the Holy Father; Aix-en-Provence, the royal capital and home to the claimant of Jerusalem's throne, the King-Count of Provence; the port city of Marseille; and, farther south, Rome. Manosque was close enough to Italy that Lombards visited regularly, and some even stayed. In the fourteenth century, the town brimmed with human activity.

Before the Great Pestilence of 1348, Manosque housed about 5,000 souls. In the generations after, that number dropped. Abandoned settlements dotted Provence and all of Europe at this time; these were places that famine, plague, and war had decimated. Survivors sought out safer living conditions, and each new day brought immigrants to the town, which fared better than some other places. Inside its strong fortifications lived many artisans, crafts- and tradespeople, and professionals—blacksmiths, cobblers, chandlers, innkeepers, seamstresses, dyers, weavers, midwives, whores, notaries, lawyers, jurists, and so on. Many, alone or with their extended families and households, operated shops and workshops. Some had separate spaces for commerce, boutiques, ateliers, and so on. Others worked out of their homes. The great oven of the Hospitallers, and their mill, lay outside the walls, but town dwellers had easy access to fresh baked bread.

All of this commercial activity drew immigrants, among them the young Margarida de Portu, a girl from a small nearby village. Her entry into Manosque came when she wed a local man, Johan Damponcii. The move from her small village to this bustling town quite overwhelmed her. The people of Manosque were more mixed than where she came from. Aside from the occasional Lombard merchant with his lilting Italian accent, there were also Jews. These men and women were foreign and familiar at the same time. In general, they lived in peace in Manosque, though, when the plague erupted, there had been a pogrom.[1] Town records preserve notes on how some Christians looted and burned the homes of their Jewish

---

1 On the pogrom in Manosque, see Bednarski, *Curia*, 50 and note 4; also Joseph Shatzmiller, "Les juifs de Provence pendant la peste noire," *Revue des Études juives* (1974): 457–80. The basic study of the Manosquin Jewish community remains Joseph Shatzmiller, *Recherches sur la communauté juive de Manosque au Moyen Age, 1241–1329* (Paris: Mouton, 1973). See also his *La Famille juive au Moyen Age: Provence-Languedoc* (Paris: CNRS, 1987). See also Danielle Iancu-Agou, "Les juifs et la justice en Provence médiévale: Un procès survenu à Manosque en 1410," *Provence historique* 27 (jan.–fév. 1979): 21–45.

neighbors, killing as they went. The Jewish community survived, rebuilt, and remained. By Margarida's time, it numbered in the hundreds. Its members supported not one but two synagogues, where boys and men learned and where the devout prayed.[2] There was also a kosher butcher to slaughter animals in accordance with Hebrew dietary laws and a separate Jewish marketplace to prevent dietary contamination. Overall, the Jewish minority, protected by its very own book of liberties, lived harmoniously with the Christian majority. This book, now lost to history, contained written rights, freedoms, and duties negotiated with the seigneur. Though there was a separate Jewish quarter, just as there were several Christian quarters, the two faiths openly mingled. They drank, played games, and, sometimes, though this was a major taboo, made love together.[3]

The Jews of Manosque, as Margarida would discover, were good neighbors who provided vital services. As in other places, they were bankers, jewelers, pawnbrokers, and moneylenders[4]—as were many Lombards and any number of Christian housewives who made small profits by lending to needy neighbors. Borrowing and lending was not the exclusive purview of the Jews in late medieval Provence. In contrast to popular mythology, they participated in a range of professional activities, not all tied to finance. Some even farmed. Others were highly educated.

It was widely accepted in Provence at this time that the best physicians and barbers were Jews.[5] Though barred from the medical faculty at Montpellier and from the great schools of Italy, some Provençal Jews studied the works of the ancient medics and their Arab heirs. Thanks to a system of learned apprenticeship, Jewish skill in medicine was second to none. In fact, Jewish physicians were so respected that they treated Christians, men and women, and served as expert medical witnesses in the Order's courts, as Margarida would soon learn when it came time to discuss the manner of her husband's demise.

---

2 M.-Z. Isnard, *Livre des privilèges de Manosque* (Paris: Honoré Champion, 1894), xvii.

3 A criminal case documents a fight over a game involving Christians and Jews (*ad stacos luderent*). See the fifth transcript contained in ADBDR 56 H 992, unfoliated, entitled "Against Guilhem Aymerici." For the case of a Jewish man who sold his daughter for illicit sex with Christians, see Bednarski, *Curia*, 70. For a trial in which a Christian woman protested the sexual advances of her Jewish physician, see Bednarski, *Curia*, 130. For more general information on crime and Jewish sexuality, see Rodrigue Lavoie, "La délinquance sexuelle à Manosque (1240–1430): Schéma général et singularités juives," *Provence historique* 37 (oct.-nov.-déc. 1987): 571–87.

4 For small-scale loans, see Andrée Courtemanche, "Les femmes juives et le crédit à Manosque au tournant du XIVe siècle," *Provence historique* 37 (1987): 545–58. For more general information, consult Joseph Shatzmiller, *Shylock Reconsidered: Jews, Moneylending, and Medieval Society* (Berkeley: University of California Press, 1990).

5 Joseph Shaztmiller, *Médecine et justice en Provence médiévale: documents de Manosque, 1262–1348* (Aix-en-Provence: Publications de l'université de Provence, 1989) and his *Jews, Medicine, and Medieval Society* (Berkeley: University of California Press, 1994).

Governance in late medieval Manosque was shared. At first, the Hospitallers ruled as co-seigneur alongside the last counts of Forcalquier. Eventually, though, they came to possess the town in its entirety (see Chapter 4). The preceptor, the highest-ranking soldier in the town, was technically the lord of Manosque, and he named one of his brethren as bailiff, a sort of chief of police. But before the town passed out of noble hands and into knightly ones, the final count bestowed upon his Manosquin subjects certain rights and privileges. In some senses, these rights seem unusually liberal and modern: the right to elect a kind of municipal council from local worthies, the right to choose men to perform certain civic tasks, the right to levy certain forms of taxation, and the right to benefit from a criminal and civil court. The town council ensured that the criminal judge appointed by the Order adhered to the negotiated penalties contained in the municipal *Book of Privileges*.[6]

The knights maintained the old comital system of justice, that is, the old system used by the Counts of Forcalquier and Provence. When Manosque was still ruled by the Counts of Forcalquier, they provided criminal and civil courts to govern their subjects. These courts followed the rule of Roman law, reconstituted in Italy in the twelfth and thirteenth centuries. The knights who inherited the comital courts named a criminal judge, a civil judge, and an appellate judge. By the fourteenth century, instances of second appeals went to the court of the King-Count in Aix-en-Provence. Thousands of pages of judicial records survive from this era. They reveal a complex judiciary, sensitive to local needs, drawing people into its workings to legitimize the knights' regulatory authority over the town.[7] By the late fourteenth century, as Margarida sat huddled in the convent avoiding arrest, the courts had become a convenient place to air enmities. Neighbors routinely took satisfaction in denouncing one another and dragging their opponents before a judge. Gossip and scandal, as much as formal denunciations, initiated criminal inquests, which were judicial investigations that produced verdicts and sentences. In Margarida's case, it was rumor, not formal denunciation, which began a criminal inquest into her involvement in her husband's death. His family, led by her antagonistic brother-in-law, began to spread the word that she was a wicked killer. The court responded to the local rumor mill.

Margarida de Portu was a very young woman from the nearby village of Beaumont who came to Manosque to marry into the local Damponcii clan. Her natal family, like many others, was in the process of integrating into the urban world of Manosque, and the marriage was advantageous. Johan Damponcii was not rich, but he had property and connections. Margarida's brother, Peire de Portu, was a

---

6 The book is available in edited French and Occitan. See Isnard, *Livre des privilèges de Manosque*.
7 This is one of the central arguments of my book *Curia*.

deacon in a local religious community, and her cousin was a nun in the cloister where Margarida first hid. Her family, thus, was already in the process of migrating from Beaumont to Manosque.[8] Through her marriage, Margarida gained not only a husband and a new home but also a brother-in-law and two sisters-in-law. Johan's half-brother, Raymon Gauterii, was a busy notary in Manosque. When Johan died, Raymon wasted no time in using his legal connections to prosecute Margarida. He was her greatest adversary and enemy, threatening her reputation, her financial security, even her bodily health.

To ruin Margarida, Raymon provided the court with rich details of her perfidy. The criminal charges against her are laden with rhetoric, far more eloquent and poetic than other inquest records from this time (see Appendix III). Rather than make a formal accusation against her, which would have earned him the legal classification of denouncer and, thus, barred him under law from offering direct testimony in the case, Raymon chose stealth. He whispered in the judge's ear. He passed notes to court scribes. He ground the public rumor mill. This public rumor, called *fama publica* in the Middle Ages, was itself legal grounds to initiate a criminal inquest.

Raymon's public-relations campaign worked well. He stoked the fire enough that Peire Rebolli, the criminal judge, moved quickly to make an example out of Margarida. In order that the "examples of transgressors not be an indication to other evildoers" and because sometimes it is not "love of virtue but fear of punishment" that prevents people from acting wickedly, Rebolli indicted Margarida and launched a formal investigation.[9]

2.2   The Criminal Charges

According to the information Raymon provided, Margarida

> handed her husband, to whom she stands forth espoused through the matrimonial knot, on account of a false and harmful suggestion in her damnable soul, over to the defeat of death suddenly and, moreover, through the use of sorcery or venom, since venom is more painful to slay than with the sword.

---

8 For an explanation of immigrant strategies and integration, see Andrée Courtemanche, "De Bayons à Manosque: Une expérience migratoire en Provence à la fin du Moyen Âge," in *Prendre la route: L'expérience migratoire en Europe et en Amérique du nord du XIVe au XXe siècle,* ed. Andrée Courtemanche and Martin Pâquet (Hull, QC: Les Éditions Vents d'Ouest, 2001), 55–80.

9 For the original, consult the Archives Départementales des Bouches-du-Rhône, series 56 H, register 1001, folio 32 (henceforth noted simply as ADBDR 56 H etc.). To assist the reader, I have transcribed the entire criminal inquest and attach it as Appendix II. Appendix III contains selected English translations of the original Latin. For this reason, throughout the book, when I quote in English from the criminal inquest, I do not provide the Latin text in the footnotes, merely a pointer to the appropriate place in the Appendix. Later, when I quote from other original documents, I do provide the Latin in the notes since I do not append those other texts at the back of the book.

Raymon then told the court it was his brother's habit to eat before going out to work. He said Margarida prepared a "certain harmful potion or dish or some other wicked and evil sorcery" and fed it to Johan. His brother, heavily laden and realizing he had been poisoned, returned home to bed. Once there, he promptly died.

Raymon cast Margarida as a fickle woman and a devious killer. He told the court that she and Johan had had a terrible fight after which she ran away to her native Beaumont, where she lingered for eight days. Eventually she returned to Manosque—and Johan died the very next day. The coincidence was too great. Johan was healthy the whole time she was away, so clearly there was a connection between Margarida's sudden return and his death. What else could be expected of a woman of Beaumont? Everyone, Raymon said, knew that Beaumont was a place of scandal. If common knowledge were insufficient evidence of her guilt, her behavior after Johan's death spoke volumes: she had fled immediately to a convent for safekeeping and hidden within the cloister. Any decent woman would have returned to her husband's house to tend to the corpse, but Margarida did no such thing. Raymon also told the court that Margarida sensed the cloister could not offer sufficient protection so she moved into St. Anthony's chapel, throwing herself on the general mercy and protection not only of the Church but also of its patron saint. Eventually, Raymon told the court, his brother was buried in the Church of the Holy Saviour. There, priests chanted masses and lit candles for his soul. Margarida never heard them, never smelled the burnt beeswax. She never even attended the funeral, nor did she mourn. No widow's tears fell from her eyes; no wails escaped her throat. No honest wife behaved like this when her husband died! Margarida behaved as if she had never met the man. Finally, Raymon noted, when the court herald went to the cloister to summon her to court, she refused to come. Her contumacy, her refusal to attend a legal summons, was further evidence of guilt. Raymon concluded his informal accusations by noting, as was quite typical in criminal inquests of this type, that there was universal knowledge and agreement about all these matters.

Three days passed, then more accusations. When Margarida failed to heed the judge's summons, Raymon was there in her place. He offered up a helpful paper schedule of her offenses, a supplemental legal document with additional information, in case the court had missed any of his insinuations. His schedule claimed she blasphemed and cursed those who had negotiated her marriage: she did not want the union, resisted it, and swore against it. When she saw her husband, she called him a whiner, a dour man; she never had anything good to say about him. She threatened to run away to Beaumont several times, until, at last, her brother the deacon said he would whip her if she did not behave. She said it was wicked of him to have given her to Johan in marriage. She refused to bring her wedding dress into Johan's house, alienating property that by rights belonged to her husband. When she did eventually return to Beaumont for eight days, she took with her three pairs of boots, three pairs of socks, and her jewels. The night she returned from Beaumont, she slept with the nuns instead of her husband. The next morning, rising early, she told her brother that she had asked Johan for money to buy some honeyed treats (*menudetos*), but he had refused, saying he didn't want to eat sweets. And so that morning they made a meal with garlic. After he ate it, Johan went off to work in a field belonging to Lady Antonieta Savine, outside the town's upper gate. When he came to the Albeta spring, he complained to his servant that his whole tongue burned.[10] He asked who the devil made the meal and the servant replied he did not know.[11] When they began to sow seeds, the servant noticed Johan turn completely black, then completely red, and then tremble violently. Johan told the servant he felt ill in his heart and stomach. The servant, worried, told Johan to return home, and Johan limped blindly back. When he crawled into bed, he could neither speak nor move. Raymon said that, at that point, his poor brother gave up his spirit and ended his earthly days.

Raymon's schedule claimed to be submitted on behalf of all Johan's friends and family. Since this was a serious, indeed capital offense, he requested that the court pay immediately to have Margarida bound in iron shackles within the church. That way there was no chance she could flee, which Raymon certainly insinuated she might. Raymon, the court transcript tells us, made this last request humbly and through tears. This, though, was stout legal rhetoric. It aimed to demonstrate his grief at the loss of his beloved brother while acknowledging his own impotence.

2.3 The Witnesses

The Midwife: Bila Fossata

Bila Fossata testified first. She was a prominent local woman, known if not universally respected throughout the town. At some points in her life, the court ascribed to her the title *bajula publica,* public midwife. She worked at the fringe of women's health care and had access to male authority figures. When she fumbled, as in a prominent adultery case that involved an illegitimate birth, the court reminded her of the responsibility Manosquin society had invested in her.[12] Perhaps because

---

10 ADBDR 56 H 1001 fo. 36 v.
11 *Ibid.*
12 Bednarski, *Curia,* 96.

of her role as a quasi-public official, perhaps because of her strong personality, Bila had experience with and was undaunted by the patriarchal court system. Nowhere is this written down, but there are clues in the documents. To begin with, she had a written surname, a remarkable thing in the fourteenth century. Aside from prostitutes, vagabond women, and, very occasionally, widows, women in late medieval Manosque were typically represented in official documents in relation to their fathers or husbands. So, it is normal, for example, to read that a woman was called Sanxia, wife of Bernardo Bermundi, or that she was Sanxia, daughter of Johan Savini. Whores and homeless women had no male protectors and guardians and so received feminized surnames. Bila, though married, appears with her own name and only sometimes in relation to her husband. She is simply Bila Fossata, or else Bila Fossata, the wife of Peire Galhardi.

Bila's autonomy and fearlessness, or at least feistiness, come through in her dealings with the law. In 1403, she told the court *nuncio*, among other things, that she would break his neck if he came to her home.[13] For a short time during Margarida's criminal trial, Bila was also on the wrong side of the law for an unrelated matter and was arrested.[14]

Given all this, it is no surprise that Bila was not afraid to speak against Raymon's charges. The judge asked what she knew of the case. Very little, she said. It was true that Johan and Margarida sometimes fought, but he was as much to blame as was she. It was true, too, that when Margarida returned to Manosque from Beaumont before her husband died, she had slept in the home of a neighbor, Antonieta Olivarie. Bila explained, though, that this was on account of Margarida's illness. This is the first indication in the records that Margarida was unwell, a fact used by her defense to explain much of her allegedly erratic behavior, but one that Raymon pointedly left out of his accusations. Bila said that when Margarida was staying with Antonieta, another woman, a nun called Sister Maria, led the suspect to the monastery. There, Margarida's brother, the deacon, took her and a friend first to the cloister, then to one of his rooms. The judge asked why Margarida retreated to the church. Bila responded drily that she could think of only one cause: the threats Raymon Gauterii had made against Margarida. After all, she reminded the judge, Raymon had just accused Margarida of murder.[15]

---

13 ADBDR 56 H 1008 fo. 94 dated 8 January 1403 reads that she said that *si ipse nuntius iret . . . ad domum suam frangeret sibi collum, et multa alia verba que ad injuriam reputavit.*

14 ADBDR 56 H 1001 fo. 38 reads *Item fuit interrogata dicta testis super contentis in / sexto indicio dixit eius juramento se nil scire de contentis / in eo quia erat tunc temporis infra presentem curiam arrestata.*

15 ADBDR 56 H 1001 fo. 37 v.

Bila also spoke at length about the rumors about Margarida. Specifically, the judge asked Bila whether there were rumors going around that Margarida had enchanted or poisoned Johan, and Bila more or less pinned their source on Raymon. She said that when Johan died, Raymon went around yelling and screaming, "how did this happen?" He said other things she could not recall, too.[16] Her point was clear. Though she did not state overtly that Raymon was the source of the rumors, when asked about them, she pointed out that he was the only one agitating that Johan's death was unnatural.

Having moved through the formal list of charges, the judge next asked Bila about the accusations in Raymon's paper schedule. First, the judge wanted to know whether Margarida had cursed the people who arranged her marriage. Bila said she did not know about that, but she told the judge Johan had once told her that anyone who harmed him was cursed.[17] This was a neat trick. In answering the judge's question, Bila turned it around on him to imply that husbands cursed their enemies as often as wives did. In and of itself, cursing an enemy proved nothing. Bila did not think Margarida a thief. When Margarida went to Beaumont, Bila noticed she had on a pair of sandals but that she was not carrying any other shoes. Margarida had also told Bila that she did not make the supposedly deadly stew and that she herself had eaten it. Finally, Bila mentioned that a servant who lived with her had contradicted one of Raymon's other allegations about the stew. Overall, Bila, a public expert in womanly secrets, testified that she did not believe the food was enchanted or poisoned.

Without calling Raymon a liar, Bila cast serious doubts on his allegations and pinned him as the source of malicious rumors. Her testimony points to a number of other single women who seemed to be keeping an eye on Margarida: the woman in whose home she slept while ill, the nun who brought her to the convent, a friend who went with them, Bila's servant, and Bila herself, the strong-willed midwife who snorted at the thought that Margarida's curses or stew had killed anybody. On the whole, Bila's testimony was a frustrating way for Raymon to begin his case against Margarida.

The Neighbor: Sanxia

The court next interrogated Margarida and Johan's neighbor, Sanxia, the wife of Moneto Sarelherii, whose greatest contribution to the trial were comments about Margarida and Johan's physical health. Sanxia emphasized that Margarida

---

16 *Ibid.*
17 ADBDR 56 H 1001 fo. 38.

claimed to be unwell and to have difficulty standing. She was the first to expound on the nature of Margarida's illness. She said that Margarida told everyone she suffered from an illness that the court notary translated into Latin as the *morbum caducum,* literally "the falling sickness." This was a usual medieval term for epilepsy. Because of it, Margarida claimed, she had difficulty standing. When the judge asked about the accusations in Raymon's paper schedule, Sanxia said she knew nothing except that she once heard Johan say to Margarida, "get up," and heard Margarida reply, "I can't. I'm not well."[18] Sanxia said that Margarida believed her epilepsy began when she relocated to Manosque.[19] Sanxia had other health-related information, for she had spoken to Johan as he lay dying. He told her he had returned from his work because of an intense pain in his heart.[20] In other matters, Sanxia claimed ignorance or else agreed with Bila. Sanxia's testimony clarified the situation around Margarida and gave the judge enough evidence to justify further investigation about the state of Johan's health. Like the midwife's deposition, it did nothing to advance Raymon's case against Margarida.

The Servant: Johan Baudiment of Volx

Johan's servant, a man from the nearby village of Volx, offered insights into Johan and Margarida's marital relations: sure, they fought, but they also joked! And Margarida only went to Beaumont with Johan's okay, and even then only because she was sick. The servant did not think her illness contagious or that Margarida's husband suffered from it. At any rate, Johan had been suffering from regular chest pains. He had a big appetite and carried ginger with him to chew on whenever the pain bothered him. In the Middle Ages, as today, ginger was a common remedy for acid reflux, or heartburn. The servant's information alerted the court that Johan had suffered from burning pains in his chest after he ate, and was attempting a folk remedy.

Concerning Margarida's behavior as an absent wife, the servant confirmed that Johan had given her his blessing to travel to Beaumont and to take some possessions with her. He added that when Margarida returned to Manosque, she had tried to return home to sleep with her husband. Johan, however, had instructed her to sleep at the convent, saying he had asked another man named Ugo Gardilini to "come and sleep with me."[21]

---

18 ADBDR 56 H 1001 fo. 39.
19 ADBDR 56 H 1001 fo. 38 v.
20 ADBDR 56 H 1001 fo. 39.
21 ADBDR 56 H 1001 fo. 40 v.

The servant's greatest contribution to the investigation, though, came when he described the supposedly enchanted or toxic meal, a meal he had shared. He claimed it was he and Johan who cooked the stew that day, along with Margarida's little brother Bartomieu. When they were done, Margarida appeared and, in front of everyone else, added some oil.[22] Everyone, including Margarida and another young woman, then ate the stew. The servant later added that Margarida always ate at the same table with Johan.[23] Then came a revelation. Normally, court scribes took pains to record witnesses' answers to directed questions. In this case, though, the scribe was careful to make one additional note. He wrote that "the witness said one more thing without being asked." The servant wanted the court to know that, when Johan had finished eating his stew, there remained a bit in his bowl. He fed it to his dog.[24] That dog was still alive and well.

The servant gave other details about the meal. Johan complained it was too spicy and that the garlic burned his tongue. He was annoyed that yesterday he had found a whole almond in his food. But, it was absolutely not true, as Raymon had claimed in his schedule, that Johan had ever asked "who the devil made this meal?" or, perhaps, "what devil made this meal?" Johan knew quite well that he himself had prepared it with them.

Before dismissing the servant, the judge asked whether he had been bought or bribed in any way:

> Item, that witness was questioned and diligently examined whether he had been instructed, taught, advised, or aided in any way that he might make his previous statements in such a manner. Under oath, he replied that was not the case.
>
> Item, the witness was questioned whether or not he was given, promised, or in some way obligated for something in return for his deposition as it was given. Under oath, he said that was not the case.

Raymon was becoming frustrated. He must have complained to the judge that the witnesses had been suborned. In criminal cases, Manosquin judges rarely asked already sworn witnesses to reconfirm their objectivity. This was the legal reason that formal denouncers could not give evidence: their bias was already known.[25] Everyone

---

22 ADBDR 56 H 1001 fo. 40 v.
23 Later, on folio 49, Margarida's sister-in-law confirmed this fact and said that Margarida happily ate with Johan on a daily basis.
24 ADBDR 56 H 1001 fo. 40 v.
25 The impediments to testifying in courts of Roman law are summarized neatly in Bernard Schnapper, "*Testes inhabiles:* Les témoins reprochables dans l'ancien droit pénal," *Revue d'histoire du droit* 33 (1965): 576–616.

else, prior to making a deposition, swore to God upon the Holy Gospels to speak only the truth. Unless someone in court had reason to suspect otherwise, it was redundant to ask for a declaration of honesty. Raymon must have objected loudly.

Beatritz: The Sister-In-Law

When he was done with the servant, the judge heard from another neighbor who added only that one time Margarida had wanted to go back to Beaumont, and Johan had asked her to wait since there were not enough people to accompany her. The witness said that Margarida had gone anyway. Though this speaks to a disobedient streak, it also indicated Johan's concern for his wife, her safety and physical health, and her good reputation.

The next witness after this was Beatritz, wife of Peire Rufferii, and the dead man's half-sister. This was the first time a family member took the stand or acted in an official capacity in the criminal inquest. Thus far, everything Raymon had submitted had been for information only. Beatritz's testimony was an official legal statement, recorded by a notary public, and, like the other testimonies described so far, was given evidentiary weight in determining Margarida's innocence or guilt.

Beatritz thought Margarida honest. She said that Margarida had gone to Beaumont with her husband's blessing. She also said it was true that Margarida was ill and that other women were worried about her health.[26] Once, Margarida had wanted to go back to Beaumont but Johan and another man had stopped her. Beatritz said that Margarida was desperate to return because she felt she would never recover from her illness unless she went back home, where her brothers could care for her, and make certain that she did not fall into the hearth and burn, as had already happened once during a fit.[27]

The bedroom where Johan died was a crowded place. Beatritz was there with her brother, along with several other neighbors and relations. She heard Johan say that he had never felt such a pain in his heart. Hearing this, she told the young Margarida to go to her house to fetch some eggs for her brother.[28] When Margarida returned with them, Johan was dead. Was Beatritz hoping to make something with the eggs to relieve her brother's pain, or was she simply sending the frail Margarida on an errand to spare her the impending death? It is impossible to know for certain, except that before she ended her testimony, the judge asked if she had any suspicions about anyone possibly involved in Johan's death. Beatritz said she did not.

Raymon learned that membership in a family or kin group does not guarantee unanimity. By now the judge knew there was a problem with the case Raymon had

---

26 ADBDR 56 H 1001 fo. 48v.
27 ADBDR 56 H 1001 fo. 49.
28 A fact Margarida confirmed on folio 47 v. in her own deposition.

insinuated against Margarida. The witnesses all painted a picture of a relatively normal, happy marriage. Margarida was ill, but so too was Johan. She was young and he allowed her to return to her family home where her brothers might care for her. She had already had a scare when she fell into the hearth and was burned. Otherwise, the couple laughed together, shared meals together, and had a wide circle of friends, neighbors, and associates. Beatritz's testimony undermined her brother's case. It aired the fissures in the Damponcii clan openly and signaled to the judge that, though young and epileptic, Margarida, a foreigner, had earned the support of many local women, not the least of whom was her sister-in-law.

While the judge interrogated the witnesses, Margarida's supporters wasted no time. Her brother, the deacon Peire de Portu, appeared in court armed with his own paper schedule. Peire the deacon was an able opponent to Raymon the notary. Both men were literate; both knew legal culture. Peire's schedule was an elegant appeal to dismiss the case. It urged the judge to acknowledge what was obvious to a man of his skill, that almost all of the deceased man's friends and neighbors had excused Margarida of any wrongdoing, and none bore any suspicions against her.[29] The judge considered the deacon's request, but Raymon must have exerted considerable pressure. He pointed out that the process was not yet complete and must be allowed to play out. And so, almost one month after he had launched his murder investigation, the judge summoned Margarida to speak.

2.4 The Accused Woman

Margarida spoke for herself. She had a lawyer by then, technically a *procurator,* and her brother was with her. But she herself requested a copy of the proceedings, which the judge conceded, to help her team prepare her defense. She then answered questions directly, wholly denying the accusations leveled against her.

– WHO MADE THE STEW?
– *Johan, along with some others.*

– WHAT WAS IN IT?
– *Dried almonds, oil, garlic.*[30]

– DID YOU EAT IT?
– *Yes, but not very much since it was still morning and I wasn't hungry.*

---

29 fo. 43: . . . *omnes afines et amici dicti Johannis Dampons ipsam Mar- / garitam excusent nullamque se dicant habuisse seu / habere suspectionem contra eandem* . . .

30 Later, on fo. 47, she admitted that she added the oil in the presence of several other people.

– DID YOU PLACE ANYTHING INTO THE EGGS OR THE WINE THAT WOULD
   RESULT IN YOUR HUSBAND'S DEATH?
– *I swear I did not.*

– WHAT DID HE DO AFTER HE ATE?
– *He went out to work with his servant.*

– DID YOU RECEIVE ADVICE OR HELP OR ANY OBJECT FROM ANY FRIENDS
   OR FAMILY TO KILL HIM?
– *I swear I did not.*

– WHAT DID HE SAY WHEN HE RETURNED FROM WORK?
– *Nothing, except that he had a great pain in his body and his heart was
   failing him.*

And then the most striking question of all, one that cut to the most intimate aspect of her marriage:

– HAD YOUR HUSBAND KNOWN YOU CARNALLY?[31]
– *No . . . because whenever he lay beside me in bed, I trembled so badly that
   nothing could happen.*

The seizures that marked Margarida as different, that earned her the protection of other women, that so scared her, and that once caused her to fall into the hearth, were exacerbated by Johan's sexual advances. Publicly, Margarida and Johan's friends and neighbors attested to a normal marriage. Privately, the couple was impotent.

Celibacy was no impediment to marriage. By the fourteenth century, the Catholic Church was clear that couples could opt to refrain from sex and still remain married. After all, to deny this fact would undermine the foundation of (the Ever Virgin) Mary's marriage to Joseph, and throw into question the entire validity of Jesus' earthly family. So medieval theologians were more or less obliged to agree that celibate marriages were still marriages.[32]

Impotence caused by sexual dysfunction was another matter and cause for considerable discussion among medieval thinkers. To begin with, theologians and jurists went to pains to develop tests to discern whether a man was indeed

---

31 ADBDR 56 H 1001 fo. 45 v.
32 For more, see André Vauchez, "Conjugal Chastity: A New Ideal in the Thirteenth Century," in his *The Laity in the Middle Ages: Religious Beliefs and Devotional Practices* (Notre Dame: University of Notre Dame Press, 1993), 185–90.

impotent. English lawmakers prescribed savvy crones to inspect a man's genitals for problems and to test whether he could become aroused and ejaculate. A man who could withstand such tests and prove he could not become aroused had valid grounds to seek a legal annulment to his marriage, an act that effaced the union.[33] The very concept of female impotence, however, was almost inconceivable within the learned discourse. Since woman was the passive sexual partner, the experts assumed impotence was purely a male problem. Marital duty worsened this situation. Theologically, within a marriage, if one partner desired sex for procreation, the other owed it. This was called the marital debt. On the surface, the marital debt appears as the great sexual equalizer of the Middle Ages, since it openly acknowledged that women had a sex drive.[34] In practice, the concept greatly favored men's urges and limitations over women's. It was difficult for a woman to deny her husband sex if he wanted it, since she was, theoretically at least, the passive partner and owed the debt. No medieval law code, therefore, ever developed a concept of marital rape. Wives simply could not, legally at least, refuse their husbands sex. Husbands, however, because theologians deemed their role active, might legitimately deny sex if they were exhausted, if they were fasting, if they were spent from prior sexual activity, if they were temporarily impotent from an injury, and so on.[35] Were Margarida a man who suffered from epilepsy, the disease may have excused her from her sexual duty. As a woman, however, at least according to the learned theologians, it did not. Theologically, and, by extension, to some degree culturally, her debt remained unpaid.

After sex, the interrogation turned to love and curses and threats. Despite their lack of sexual intercourse, Margarida claimed to bear a great love for her husband.[36] This flew in the face of Raymon's allegations—he claimed he had heard her curse her union. So the judge asked whether she had in fact said anything negative about the people who arranged her wedding and whether she had cursed them. Quite the opposite. What she did say was "cursed was the day and hour I was born!"[37] And she only said that because, having married Johan and come to

33 Jacqueline Murray, "On the Origins and Role of 'Wise Women' in Causes for Annulment on the Grounds of Male Impotence," *Journal of Medieval History* 16 (1990): 235–49.

34 This was the opinion expressed by the great scholar of medieval sexuality and law James Brundage, "Sexual Equality in Medieval Canon Law," in *Medieval Women and the Sources of Medieval History,* ed. Joel T. Rosenthal (Athens: University of Georgia Press, 1990), 70–72.

35 See Dyan Elliott, "Bernardino of Siena versus the Marriage Debt," in *Desire and Discipline: Sex and Sexuality in Premodern Europe,* ed. Jacqueline Murray and Konrad Eisenbichler (Toronto: University of Toronto Press, 1996), 168–200.

36 ADBDR 56 H 1001 fo. 45 v. For more on love in medieval marriage, see the classic article by Michael M. Sheehan, "*Maritalis affectio* Revisited," in *Marriage, Family, and Law in Medieval Europe,* ed. James K. Farge (Toronto: University of Toronto Press, 1996), 262–77.

37 ADBDR 56 H 1001 fo. 45 v.

Manosque, she was afflicted with the falling sickness. What about the supposed scandal in Beaumont, the judge asked. Was there any truth to that story? Yes, Margarida admitted. There was a wanton woman in Beaumont, but she was not a local. Still, she was a source of scandal and had suffered temporal punishment. Licentious acts committed by other women in Beaumont were not, however, evidence against Margarida.

The judge shifted tactics and asked Margarida about her travels to assess her wifely character. Young wives simply did not leave their husbands to travel about, even if they did return home. It was improper.[38] "Ah, but my husband made arrangements for me, sir! He even sent me a letter to arrange for an escort back to Manosque!" The judge was at a loss. He shifted again. Why, he asked, did she flee to the church when her husband died? "On account of the miseries that master Raymon Gauterii inflected on me, sir! He shouted at me, 'Get out! Get out! You killed my brother!' And I was so scared I fainted twice while Johan lay dying!" And so Margarida's brother, the deacon, and her relative Maria, the nun, and some friends arranged to move her to the cloister. Later she retreated deeper, into the chapel, out of fear of the preceptor. She worried he would seize her because of Raymon's agitations. True, she said, she did not emerge even for the funeral, since she had no one to go with. But, oh, how she had wept and mourned![39]

In frustration, the judge asked then why she had not appeared when summoned. She said her brother had forbidden it. If he had allowed it, though, she would have gladly come to prove her innocence![40] What about the allegations that she stole some of her marriage goods from Johan's house when she traveled to Beaumont? Johan, she said, told her to take a portion of her marriage goods with her. She traded them for 18 bundles of hemp and 3 small chickens, which she brought back to him. Johan, in short, took advantage of his wife's travels to acquire goods. Margarida denied taking extra shoes or sandals or anything else with her when she went. She wore her good belt, she said. And she brought it back. The judge pressed on with other questions, but Margarida said nothing else new. Her two brothers, Ugo and Guilhem de Portu, and another male relation, Laugier Montaguti, all gave bond for her and agreed to pay 100 silver marks should she flee or disobey the court. Normally this would have sufficed: three honest men

---

38 For an example of a traveling woman suspected of witchcraft and, possibly, sexual impropriety, see Andrée Courtemanche and Steven Bednarski, "De l'eau, du grain et une figurine à forme humaine: Quelques procès pour sortilèges à Manosque au début du XIVe siècle," *Memini: Travaux et documents* 2 (1998): 75–106.

39 ADBDR 56 H 1001 fo. 46.

40 ADBDR 56 H 1001 fo. 46 v.

placing their worldly goods as bond. But Raymon exerted his influence. The judge accepted their bond but still ordered that Margarida be held under house arrest in the local Clarissan convent. Although the case did not require it, this was done expressly at the command of the preceptor, the Lord of Manosque, a man who never interfered in criminal matters. Raymon had friends in high places.[41]

The judge and his officials came to her again in the convent to see if she would change her testimony. She stood by it.

> . . . she claimed in every way that she said only the truth in the deposition, and she wished to stand by each and every thing from point to point and intended neither to deny nor remove anything. And through this present deposition, she did not intend to disagree with the previous deposition in any way, but confirmed it in every way possible.[42]

She remained nonetheless a prisoner. Ten days later, while Margarida was still under house arrest in the convent, her faction made a bold move. They brought in an expert.

2.5   The Jewish Doctor

The judge, at the behest of Margarida's brother, ordered the court *nuncio* to summon master Vivas Josep, a Jewish physician. Peire de Portu offered Josep up as an expert to testify about the cause of Johan's death. Over the course of his career, Josep was no stranger to this court. In 1395, a judge had summoned him to testify to the extent of an injured man's wounds.[43] Five years later, Josep offered expert testimony in the matter of a young boy beaten to the brink of death.[44] In the former case, the court notary styled Josep *medicus et surgicus:* physician and surgeon. In the latter, he was simply *surgicus:* surgeon.

Medical titles pose something of a problem. Provençal notaries were careful to distinguish between different classes of medical practitioners. One might be a barber (*barberius, barbitonsor*) or a barber-surgeon (*barberius et sirurgicus*), a physician (*phisicus*), a surgeon (*sirurgicus*), or even a "physician and surgeon" (*medicus fizicus et sirgicus*).[45] These distinctions doubtless held meaning, since

---

41 ADBDR 56 H 1001 fo. 47 v.
42 ADBDR 56 H 1001 fo. 48.
43 ADBDR 56 H 1001 ff. 183–184 v. dated 25 May 1395 against Guilhem and Johan Fulconis.
44 ADBDR 56 H 1005 fo. 31–31 v. dated 27 July 1400 against Stephanus Rufandi.
45 ADBDR 56 H 986 ff. 204–206 v. contains a lovely criminal inquest in which four medical experts appear, each with their own specific title.

notaries were not sloppy about professions. Unfortunately, the subtle distinctions between a physician, a surgeon, or a physician-surgeon are today difficult to recapture. We know for certain that barbers and barber-surgeons were mechanical health-care providers of a lower rank than the rest. They were probably not university-trained and learned their craft through apprenticeship with a master.[46] At the end of their training, master barbers presented pupils with their own sets of razors, the tools of the trade. Barbers cut flesh to let blood, employed leeches and other topical remedies, set bones, pulled teeth, and performed rudimentary surgeries. When necessary, they may even have performed more complex operations or dissections.[47] Physicians, in theory, prescribed these treatments. Their knowledge came from books, mostly Greek or Arabic in origin, and their understanding of human health was grounded in the Hippocratic theory of the humors. The notion was simple: in order for a body to be healthy, its internal elements must be balanced. Sickness and disease were the result of humoral imbalance. The ancient and medieval body was supposedly composed of four humors: black bile, yellow bile, blood, and phlegm. Each had different qualities or temperaments, roughly analogous to the four elements: cold, dry, hot, and moist. To remove excess or restore depletions, learned physicians studied the humoral properties of plants, animals, and minerals. They also considered environmental pressures, including the qualities of heavenly bodies. When a physician diagnosed an ailment, he based his diagnosis and prescribed treatment on his learned knowledge. Though Jewish physicians were barred from attending the great Christian universities and their medical faculties, such as the one at nearby Montpellier and those of Italy, such men still had ample access to erudite book culture. Through a system of apprenticeship, they studied the same books as learned Christian physicians. Josep's testimony makes this abundantly clear.[48]

---

46 For a documented case of a barber's apprenticeship contract see the case study contained in Steven Bednarski and Andrée Courtemanche, "'Sadly and with a Bitter Heart': What the Caesarean Section Meant in the Middle Ages," in *Florilegium: Essays in Honour of Margaret Wade Labarge*, Vol. 28 (2011): 33–69. For more on apprenticeship contracts and the ways in which boys acquired trades, see Steven Bednarski and Andrée Courtemanche, "Learning to be a Man: Public Schooling and Apprenticeship in Late Medieval Manosque," *Journal of Medieval History* 35, no. 2 (June 2009): 113–35.

47 This was the case in the caesarean section described in our article "Sadly and with a Bitter Heart."

48 Vivas Josep's scientific knowledge and expertise in this case is already the subject of an article that proves he had read the relevant medical sources and was able to cite them fairly accurately from memory in court. See Andrée Courtemanche, "The Judge, the Doctor, and the Poisoner: Medical Expertise in Manosquin Judicial Rituals at the End of the Fourteenth Century," in *Medieval and Early Modern Ritual: Formalized Behavior in Europe, China and Japan*, ed. Joëlle Rollo-Koster (Leiden: Brill, 2002): 105–23.

Here is what the doctor said after he swore with his hand upon the Torah, the sacred texts of Judaism, to tell the truth.[49] Josep had gone with the judge and the court notary to the dead man's home to inspect the corpse. Now, Johan had died before 16 October and there had been a funeral. This was now 24 November. Was the corpse exhumed for Josep's examination? Do the documents misrepresent the date of his inspection? Both are possible. Regardless of this mystery, Josep did conduct an examination. He studied the limbs to see if a cause of death was apparent on them. He looked closely into empty eyes, prodded dry lips and tongue, made note of the face's complexion, the color of the nostrils. In his own warm hands he held the body's cold, stiff hands and manipulated them to inspect the nails, which were particularly important to his investigation. He took samples of the dry hair and scraped the scalp. When he finished his examination of the corpse, he interviewed the household servants. They told him the dead man had eaten some stew of garlic and almonds before he went to work in the fields, returned with a pain in his heart, and then died. Josep asked if the dead man had vomited and, when he learned Johan had indeed thrown up, inquired whether they had saved it. This may not have been cutting-edge science by modern standards, but it was thorough. There was a method to Josep's inquiries.

Having explained his forensic examination, Josep went on to deduce a cause of death. There are many types of poisons, he explained. According to Albucasis's chapter on poisons, they can be divided into three categories: first, those contained in inanimate things such as metal; second, vegetal poisons such as those found in herbs; third, animal venoms, which come in two forms, hot and cold. Each type of poison presents with different signs.[50] Josep lamented that he could not examine the dead man's vomit, since the leading Arabic medical authority, Avicenna, wrote that a poison's nature is revealed in the composition of a victim's vomit. But, said Josep, Avicenna also wrote that those who drink poison will have

---

49 Oaths were important things in the Middle Ages. They were the cement that bound feudal relations and underpinned political structures. They were also necessary formalities before speaking in court. In Manosque, Christian witnesses swore by touching "the holy evangelists of God" (*juravit ad sancta Dey evangelia*), the Christian Gospels. Jews routinely swore upon the "holy laws of Moses" (*juravit ad sancta legem Moysi*). In this case, fo. 51 notes that Vivas Josep swore by touching the Hebrew letters in the Jewish custom (*Qui / juramento suo per eum corporaliter prestito super / litteris ebraycis more judayco, dixit...*). Physical contact with a sacred object was always necessary to render an oath valid. One scholar of this region claimed to have found evidence of a Jew, in the absence of a copy of the Torah or Pentateuch, swearing upon the court notary's robes; see Camille Arnaud, *Histoire de la viguerie de Forcalquier* (Marseille: Etienne Camoin, 1874), 435–36. Speakers in court swore all their oaths *in vulgari*, in the common tongue, to ensure that everyone knew what they were doing.

50 ADBDR 56 H 1001 fo. 51 v.

swollen lips or tongue, that their eyes swell and protrude. Since Josep did not find the lips inflated, neither the tongue nor eyes swollen, nor any blackness in the nails or elsewhere, he could find no signs of poison.[51]

There was further evidence, the doctor said, that Johan was not poisoned. The dead man had eaten a breakfast made of garlic. According to Lo Circasitans, in a chapter on the properties of garlic, garlic weakens venom. Galen's book of *Good Digestion* states that milk, garlic, wine, vinegar, and salt dilute all venoms. Galen's *Regiment of Good Health*, moreover, asserts that garlic is a medicine that weakens and stops bodily inflammations. Since Johan had eaten a stew made with garlic, it was categorically impossible that he died from poison.[52]

Josep offered alternatives to the poison theory. There are diseases, he said, that strike men down quickly. He noted that Galen explains in chapter 30 of his *On Therapies* that when Syncope strikes it is very dangerous and potentially lethal. Elsewhere, Galen teaches that Syncope destroys the spirit of life. Josep also knew people to die suddenly from epilepsy. Avicenna, Josep told the court, wrote that epilepsy came and went quickly; those who have it are sometimes strong, sometimes weak. It was no accident that Josep shifted his lesson from poison to epilepsy. He saw a definite connection between Margarida's affliction and her husband's death.

Margarida, according to the documents, suffered from *morbum caducum*, the falling sickness, and though we often translate this expression simply as "epilepsy," it remains a problematic term for medical historians for two reasons. First, historians are never entirely certain whether and when the term referred to actual epilepsy, as defined by modern medicine, and when it pointed to other ailments, especially those with seemingly epileptic symptoms such as seizures. Second, by the late Middle Ages, "epilepsy" referred both to a specific attack characterized by seizures, foaming at the mouth and nose, memory loss, etc., and to a spectrum of ailments that medieval doctors believed were somehow linked to that cerebral ailment.

In his still foundational history of the falling sickness, famed medical historian Owsei Temkin noted that by the later Middle Ages, medical writers, loosely following the first-century Roman doctor Galen, linked three forms of pathological ailments under the rubric "epilepsy."[53] These medieval authorities used the term

---

51 ADBDR 56 H 1001 fo. 52.
52 ADBDR 56 H 1001 fo. 52 v.
53 Owsei Temkin, *The Falling Sickness: A History of Epilepsy from the Greeks to the Beginnings of Modern Neurology*, 2nd rev. ed. (Baltimore: The Johns Hopkins University Press 1971). See especially p. 120 *et passim*.

not only generically to refer to all three forms but also sometimes more precisely, to refer only to its first form that attacked the head or brain. Those same writers, though, also distinguished secondary and tertiary forms of the disease: analepsy, which originated somewhere in the stomach and which may have led to intestinal disorders such as dysentery or to attacks of other internal organs such as the kidney, liver, spleen, uterus, etc.; and catalepsy, wherein the attack struck other body parts. To confuse matters further, the term catalepsy had originally referred to a distinct medical disorder characterized by a high fever, but one that never presented symptoms such as a foaming mouth or nose. By the later Middle Ages, however, medical writers abandoned that other usage and subsumed catalepsy entirely as the second or third form of epilepsy.

Beyond the medical discourse, medieval epilepsy was a significant cultural concern in a number of ways. Slave traders, for instance, were especially wary of its health implications.[54] Though there was no slavery in late medieval Manosque, ordinary townspeople likely worried about epilepsy for other reasons related to religion and cosmology. Temkin was careful to point out that since antiquity, Europeans of all sorts associated seizures with supernatural possession, a fact reinforced in the Christian Middle Ages by biblical stories of Jesus and the apostles driving out unclean spirits. Mark 1:21–28 relates that

> Just then there was in their synagogue a man with an unclean spirit, and he cried out, "What have you to do with us, Jesus of Nazareth? Have you come to destroy us? I know who you are, the Holy One of God." But Jesus rebuked him, saying, "Be silent, and come out of him!" And the unclean spirit, *throwing him into convulsions and crying with a loud voice,* came out of him. They were all amazed, and they kept on asking one another, "What is this? A new teaching—with authority! He commands even the unclean spirits, and they obey him." At once his fame began to spread throughout the surrounding region of Galilee. [Italics added]

The Christian Gospels and the book of the Acts of the Apostles are full of exorcisms. Medieval people knew these key Bible passages since preachers routinely preached them and artists often depicted them. The link between seizures and

---

54 On slavery and epilepsy, see Francisca A.J. Hoogendijk, "Byzantinischer Sklavenkauf," *Archiv für Papyrusforschung* 42 (1996): 225–334, esp. p. 229; and chapter 5, "The Process of Selling a Slave," in Hannah Katherine Barker, "Egyptian and Italian Merchants in the Black Sea Slave Trade, 1200–1500," doctoral dissertation, Columbia University (forthcoming 2014); finally, Carmel Ferragud Domingo is preparing a forthcoming article for the *History of the Bulletin of Medicine* in which he analyzes doctors' legal testimonies about the slave disease known as the *mal de caure.*

demonic possession, however, was reinforced by the most popular of these biblical tales. It appears in Mark 9:14–29 and is repeated in Matthew 17 and Luke 9:

> When they came to the disciples, they saw a great crowd around them, and some scribes arguing with them. When the whole crowd saw him, they were immediately overcome with awe, and they ran forward to greet him. He asked them, "What are you arguing about with them?" Someone from the crowd answered him, "Teacher, I brought you my son; he has a spirit that makes him unable to speak; and *whenever it seizes him, it dashes him down; and he foams and grinds his teeth and becomes rigid;* and I asked your disciples to cast it out, but they could not do so." He answered them, "You faithless generation, how much longer must I be among you? How much longer must I put up with you? Bring him to me." And they brought the boy to him. When the spirit saw him, *immediately it threw the boy into convulsions, and he fell on the ground and rolled about, foaming at the mouth.* Jesus asked the father, "How long has this been happening to him?" And he said, "From childhood. It has often cast him into the fire and into the water, to destroy him; but if you are able to do anything, have pity on us and help us." Jesus said to him, "If you are able!—All things can be done for the one who believes." Immediately the father of the child cried out, "I believe; help my unbelief!" When Jesus saw that a crowd came running together, he rebuked the unclean spirit, saying to it, "You spirit that keep this boy from speaking and hearing, I command you, come out of him, and never enter him again!" *After crying out and convulsing him terribly,* it came out, and the boy was like a corpse, so that most of them said, "He is dead." But Jesus took him by the hand and lifted him up, and he was able to stand. When he had entered the house, his disciples asked him privately, "Why could we not cast it out?" He said to them, "This kind can come out only through prayer." [Italics added]

For medieval Christians, there was a definite link between convulsions, foaming at the mouth, falling down in a fit, and demonic possession.

Temkin was quick to point out, though, that demonic possession was not the only popular association linked to the falling sickness. The ancients had made the association between epilepsy and lunacy, literally the madness that descends on people through the influence of the moon (*luna*) or a moon deity. Ancient Greek and Roman astrologers postulated that those born under the conjunction of the moon and sun, or the moon and some planet (usually Mars or Saturn), would be variously afflicted: they were doomed to madness, prophecy, and fainting but also particularly susceptible to poison, always near to death, and particularly prone to falling fits.[55]

Finally, Temkin noted that premodern people linked epilepsy to mental or moral weakness. The well-known medieval abbess and medical writer Hildegard von Bingen (1098–1179) believed that there were two causes of epilepsy, both the product of a weak soul unable to maintain control over its body. For Hildegard, and other medieval writers, the devil could exert influence on human bodies only when something internal was off balance, when the humors were agitated and the brain affected. The devil could influence such susceptible people but not force them to act since he himself had no physical body. His greatest opportunity for influence came when, as Temkin puts it, "psychic organs are in a pathological state. This was one of the prevalent theological explanations of the interplay between physical disease and demoniac power."[56]

All these learned and popular assumptions around the falling sickness undoubtedly had real consequences for Margarida. To begin with, her own form of the *morbum caducum* was quite obviously the primary one, the one historians tend to associate loosely with clinical epilepsy: she suffered from seizures (and not some intestinal disorder, or disorder of the extremities). Those seizures, according to her own words, jeopardized her life. When they struck, she lost control of her body and often fell shaking, once even into a fire. Since medieval women spent a great deal of time preparing food, this makes sense. It was why she preferred to be back in her family home, where her brothers could watch over her and save her if she fell in a dangerous place.[57]

Margarida, like learned astrologers, theologians, and medical writers, also made an explicit association between her disorder and the cosmos. While she did not explicitly link her sickness to a heavenly body, such as Saturn or the moon, she did say she was born on a cursed day at a cursed hour. In modern popular terms, her zodiac sign influenced her temperament. In court and under oath, Margarida twice directly linked the time she was born to her falling sickness.[58]

Common perceptions of epilepsy also informed Margarida's accuser. It was no accident that Raymon accused her of using deathly poison or sorcery to kill his half-brother. Epileptics, as noted, were commonly associated with poison. They were thought to be its victims, yes, but also people who were prone to its effects. The medical writer Bernard of Gordon, moreover, explained that epileptic

---

55 Temkin, *The Falling Sickness*, 94.
56 *Ibid.*, 98.
57 ADBDR 56 H 1001 ff. 46 v. and 49.
58 ADBDR 56 H 1001 ff. 37 v. and 46 v.

seizures were caused by rancid vapors that ascended to the brain and blocked normal functions. These toxic vapors stank because of their "poisonous, horrible, and fetid character."[59] The epileptic body, therefore, was something inherently unclean. It was possessed of a unique toxin that impeded normal functioning of the organs. To what extent this learned diagnosis and explanation penetrated popular thinking in late medieval Manosque is unclear. But it is interesting to note that there was an association between epilepsy, seizures, and the presence of a toxin within the epileptic body. The coincidence between Raymon's accusations and contemporary explanations for Margarida's ailments is striking.

The nature of Raymon's other accusation, that Margarida used sorcery to kill Johan, is even more obvious. Since learned and popular opinions held that epileptics were morally weak and prone to demonic possession, as attested to in the Bible, there was a certain cultural logic to the notion that Margarida had supernatural powers. All the popular prejudices—that epileptics were capable of prophecy, that they communed with spirits, that they were influenced by the moon, and so on—supported Raymon's notion that Margarida could have used magic to kill. This was at least culturally plausible. Fortunately for her, the court found such extra-judicial notions unconvincing or, at the very least, unacceptable as forms of proof.

Josep was not immune to all these cultural implications, nor was he above medieval assumptions about women's sexual duties. Though his medical expertise exonerated Margarida legally, it inculpated her culturally. Josep explained that Johan had married a tender virgin with whom, after two months, he still could not copulate because of her illness. He was, therefore, extremely worked up by his unspent passion. Since he could not have his way with Margarida, his lust generated in him an evil melancholy. His pent-up sexual passions accumulated and produced a Syncope, which turned his hot passion cold and singed him. Unhealthy humors formed and twisted around his heart, changing its complexion. Josep again cited Avicenna and Galen to prove this point. The doctor's bottom line: Johan's sexual frustration led to tendrils of unhealthy humors that wrapped themselves around his heart and constricted. Johan died, literally, of a broken heart. In modern medical parlance, this was cardiac arrest, a heart attack.

According to the most learned science of the day, Margarida was no witch, no poisoner. She was a sick young woman who suffered from epilepsy, something she considered a curse sent by God. While Margarida's party could use Josep's

---

59 Temkin, *The Falling Sickness*, 129 and particularly note 236. For the original, see Bernard of Gordon's *The Practice or Lily of Medicine* (*Practica sive Lilium Medicinae*).

expert testimony as legal proof she did not poison her husband, the burden of
Johan's death remained, indirectly at least, with her. Innocent though she may be
of a crime, she remained guilty in the eyes of medieval society. She was a woman
who had failed to pay the marital debt. Through her illness, she had prevented her
husband from relieving his natural procreative urges. This was no secular crime,
but it was a stinging moral, cultural, and social condemnation. Because she did
not have sex with her husband, he died in terrible pain.

2.6 Lessons

Margarida's criminal trial allows us to glimpse a strange yet familiar world. Beyond courts and crime, we see a tale of immigration: a teenaged girl removed
from her familiar rural home to a bustling new town full of strange sights, sounds,
and people. She married a good man, laughed with him, fought with him, shared
meals, and contributed to his household. They did not live alone. There were often
blood relations, in-laws, neighbors, and servants in their modest house, laughing
and fighting with them. Even Johan's deathbed was crowded, giving us a sense of
how differently medieval people treated the end of life. Though Margarida had
close kin in Manosque, and her baby brother may have lived with her or close
to her, she still longed for her father's house and for the comfort of her other
brothers. They took care of her and protected her. Her husband was not so cruel
as to deny this reality. He even provided the means to help her travel modestly,
arranging for escorts. Sometimes he took advantage of her trips to acquire goods
for their household. Margarida's inquest shows something about the material texture of married life. In our minds' eye, we see on display, as in a museum, the
leather belt she wore, her sandals, the wooden bowl from which he ate the spicy
stew, even the greedy dog peeking out from under the table, tongue lolling for a
treat. We know Johan and Margarida slept in a bed and that he died in it. These
are some of the historical objects we see clearly through the testimonies provided
to the court. None of them speak to deviance. All help us understand better the
everyday lives of men and women at this time.

    The firsthand testimony of a sick person is an invaluable historical record.
It corroborates learned theory and shows that there was a definite relationship
between what elite theologians, astrologers, and physicians wrote in their Latin
manuscripts and what common people believed about disease in their hearts and
minds. The relationship was not always direct, nor was it necessarily top-down.
There was a bilateral cultural dialogue between patients and physicians, between
authorities and sufferers of illness. Like all knowledge, medical knowledge was

broadly and culturally constructed. It relied in part on observation; in part on Greek, Roman, and Arabic traditions that were hard to break; and in part on understandings of the natural universe, which, in the Middle Ages, unfolded according to an intelligible divine plan.

There are other historical objects to seize, less sharp, more difficult to grasp. These are of mental or spiritual dimensions. Margarida was an anxious woman, that much is clear. We cannot ever know exactly why. On the one hand, she stated she worried because she feared harm, possibly burning, during a seizure. On the other, when pressed about her sex life, she admitted that one definite cause of her seizures was her husband's sexual advances. The judge was fascinated by this fact; the doctor pinned Johan's death on it. Margarida's sexual dysfunctionality mattered enormously, perhaps more so than any other aspect of her trial. What we cannot know is whether this masks a deeper underlying cause of her anxiety and seizures. True epilepsy is not normally triggered by intimacy. It is tempting to wonder why Raymon worried, and others noted, that Margarida sometimes slept at the convent and not in Johan's bed. May we appropriately read sexual orientation into their relationships and sleep patterns? Johan's alleged invitation to another man to sleep with him, offered through the servant, and its accompanying order for Margarida to stay away, may tempt us. May we, thus, wonder whether there was perhaps some aspect to her husband's sexuality that scared her, something she sensed but could not openly admit? Did Johan forgive her need to wander and return home out of a sense of guilt? Was this guilt over his own sexual predilections or because he knew she was still young and inexperienced? It was not unusual for young women to marry older men, but this did not mean they were sexually compatible. All of this provides a tempting framework to recast Margarida's microhistory: a young woman married to an older homosexual, or perhaps a young woman terrified of losing her virginity, or even a young woman who suffered some previous sexual trauma. Certainly, microhistories have moved in that direction on far scantier evidence.[60] In the end, though, it would be dishonest to pull the tale in those directions. The documents may raise questions in our minds, but they offer no firm answers. Despite these limitations, there are deeper truths we can more safely excavate from Margarida's criminal trial.

Ordinary women formed networks of solidarity. Margarida was a new arrival in Manosque, but her trial proves that she benefited from the support of many

---

60 This was the case with Brown's much-criticized *Immodest Acts*, whose title purports to be the tale of a lesbian nun when, in fact, the evidence of lesbianism is scant. The story actually revolves around her fraudulent miracles.

local women, some prominent, such as the midwife, others more common. At least one of Margarida's supporters was her sister-in-law, who defied her own brother and supported Margarida. So networks of support were placed over and throughout kin networks. But kin networks still mattered. Though Margarida was married, and had technically left her natal de Portu family to join the Damponcii clan, she did not sever links with her kin. They remained close at hand. When she was threatened by Johan's brother, her own brother swept her away to the safety of the Church. He sheltered her until he and his supporters could formulate a plan. We can deduce that it was he who located a lawyer and the means to pay that man. Margarida's team drew up costly legal instruments, schedules, and petitions. This ordinary young woman acted with considerable support, material and emotional.

The material support Margarida received must not be ignored. Though the trial transcript prevents us from knowing exact costs, there were several and they must have been significant. Few defendants could afford to hire procurators to represent them. Few could pay the fees for expert witnesses, notarized documents, and so on.

All of this informs our sense of Margarida's agency. Though the trial transcript makes it appear as if she acted alone, speaking for herself and appearing in person before the judge, reality was more complex. Her actions, words, and deeds were recommended, prescribed, and proscribed by her supporters. Though Raymon was Margarida's enemy, his greatest opponent was really her brother. The deacon was a man of the cloth, literate and powerful in his own way. While Raymon may have been able to incite the preceptor to place Margarida under house arrest, she remained under arrest within church walls. The deacon's ecclesiastical power allowed Margarida a temporary respite while the trial erupted. This, in turn, meant time to think and plan. Part of this plan entailed the deacon locating the Jewish doctor and delivering him to court.

This criminal trial thus allows us to recapture the material and the immaterial in a way that prescriptive medieval sources—texts that dictate norms of behavior, such as sermons, confessional manuals, law codes, or theological treatises—cannot. The criminal trial teaches us its lessons, even while reassuring us that they are knowable, that we are not so different, that our world has roots in theirs. Sometimes this is a false sense of security, and we must not lose sight of the differences. The accusation of sorcery was real, if not legally actionable.[61] The demand to have Margarida shackled was also legitimate. Accusations of impropriety based solely on freedom of movement were grounded in cultural norms different

---

61 See Courtemanche and Bednarski, "De l'eau." In that article we present all the late medieval sorcery trials from Manosque to show that no woman was ever convicted.

from our own. Their scientific and medical "knowledge," founded on ancient Egyptian or Greek philosophy, is not ours. Yet we recognize in the Jewish doctor the kernel of something familiar. We accept that he had authority because of his training and nod our approval that a court relied on him for his expertise. We take for granted that Christians would accept the word of a Jew over a successful Christian notary. Finally, through Margarida's exceptional murder inquest, we grasp much that was normal.

CHAPTER THREE

The Notary's Inheritance

"I had an inheritance from my father,
It was the moon and the sun.
And though I roam all over the world,
The spending of it's never done."

—*Ernest Hemingway*, For Whom the Bell Tolls

3.1 Contested Family Wealth

Vultures circled Johan Damponcii's corpse. These scavengers were not the feathered variety, but the familial sort. They vexed Peire Rebolli, the judge at the heart of the lengthy civil lawsuit over who should inherit the dead man's estate. Inheritance was a problem because, at the time Johan collapsed, he had made no final arrangements for his passage to the next life. He died intestate, with no last will or final testament. He had not professed in writing before a notary public who should inherit his worldly possessions. Worse, Johan's genealogy was complicated: he had no clear heir. And it was unclear who were his closest living blood relations.

Such matters concerned rich folk and commoners alike. Johan was not rich, but his estate certainly comprised more material wealth than the ephemeral moon and sun alluded to by Hemingway at the top of this chapter. And although the exact value of Johan's earthly goods at the time of his demise is lost to history, it was enough to cause family, friends, and acquaintances to bicker. Vultures squawked in the ears of the court.

First came a long line of creditors. Because Johan died intestate, Judge Rebolli mandated a judicial proclamation (*praeconizatio*). In early November 1394, he commanded Ugo Javelle, the court *nuncio,* whose position shares the same Latin root as the English word "to announce," to trumpet the following message throughout the town, in all the usual places:

> The Lord Preceptor of Manosque and his bailiff declare that any person who claims to have rights to the goods and inheritance of Johan Damponcii's estate shall present themselves and their petition to Ugo Bonilis, the court notary, within ten days, and there to have their name inscribed so that the court officials might mete out justice.[1]

Immediately, the prior of the convent of Notre Dame appeared to place a lien on the estate. He wanted to make certain he was paid the five *gros* owed for the funeral, plus another five *solidi,* or shillings, for masses sung in the dead man's memory at the request of the widow Margarida. Over the coming months, 20 individuals submitted claims to the court. First, though, before he began to pay creditors, the judge wanted to sort out the question of heirs.

And so the most pressing and vicious quarrel over Johan's possessions came not from unrelated friends and acquaintances to whom the dead man owed money, but from kin. We know there was trouble in the extended Damponcii clan because the quarrel over who would inherit Johan's estate boiled over in civil court. The dispute did not play directly into Margarida's criminal trial, but it was intimately connected.

A lengthy civil docket outlines the struggle to control Johan's estate.[2] This quarrel, to use the medieval legal term, lasted from November 1394 to February 1395. At its heart were two factions. On the one hand was Raymon Gauterii, Margarida's adversary, the notary who was her dead husband's half-brother. Raymon was in cahoots with his two sisters, Catarina and Beatritz, who also made claim to the estate. Together the three siblings stood firm in their belief that they should inherit shares of Johan's wealth. On the other hand, there was the dead man's paternal uncle, Bartomieu Damponcii, who denied their claim. It was Bartomieu who launched a civil lawsuit to protect his claim and deny the siblings theirs.

Raymon appears first in the court record, armed with a paper "schedule" (*cedula*) outlining his and his sisters' claim. It revealed to the court that the siblings (Raymon, Beatritz, wife of Peire Rufferii, and Catarina, wife of Guilhem Fulconis) were Johan Damponcii's "uterine brother and sisters." This meant the four of them

---

1 ADBDR 56 H 936 dated 5 November 1394.
2 The civil suit is 19 pages long and is unfoliated but contained in the Archives départementales des Bouches-du-Rhône, Series 56 H 936.

had shared a uterus but not a common father: they were Johan's half-brother and half-sisters through their mother. The schedule goes on to say that the siblings' close blood relationship rendered null and void any claim made by Bartomieu. The half-siblings asked the judge to name them sole heirs and to silence their uncle by nullifying his rival claim. The siblings acted in haste, they claimed, because Bartomieu had made a move that jeopardized their inheritance. He planned to hire a steward to take care of Johan's possessions, and that man planned to draw a potentially ruinous salary from the estate. Finally, the siblings petitioned, since their claim was so self-evident, the judge should grant them immediate possession of the estate without any further legal wrangling. Time was of the essence, they warned, since the estate was without an executor and each day its value deteriorated. (See Appendix I for the Damponcii and Gauterii family tree.)

Bartomieu considered his response and submitted his own schedule. In it, he said he was full uncle to the deceased, a fact acknowledged by Johan's friends and relatives, and so he had the most direct blood claim to inherit Johan's assets. Since the siblings claimed relation to his nephew only through their mother, and Bartomieu was related to the dead man through his father in the patrilineal line, he argued he should inherit. The judge received Bartomieu's schedule and declared a recess, technically a "prorogation," on the grounds that the defending party was unavailable.

Raymon was unavailable because he was in jail. Though the civil suit between the men was separate from Margarida's criminal inquest, it was not unrelated, and both courtroom dramas overlapped. In mid-November, the criminal court prosecuted Raymon for a contempt charge stemming from Margarida's murder trial.[3] The court treasurer (*clavarius*) had denounced Raymon for defamation because Raymon had said that Margarida accused him of something that was untrue. This led to a disagreement between Raymon and the judge over recordkeeping. When Raymon did not get his way, he said to the court treasurer, "By Saint Mary! I see what kind of people you are, that you take sides!" This was a serious insult to the court's honor. The treasurer accused Raymon of defamation on the legal grounds that court officials must be free of corruption (*libera de falsa subornacione*). The criminal judge summoned three witnesses to confirm they had heard Raymon's insult; Raymon himself admitted to it. And so the judge condemned him for defamation. He was subsequently incarcerated, an exceptionally rare occurrence in Manosque. The town housed no formal prison, and, in typical medieval fashion,

---

3 The criminal trial against Raymon is contained in ADBDR 56 H 1001 ff. 93 v.–94 dated 16 November 1394 and is entitled *Contra magistrum Raymundum Gauterii notarium*.

most people condemned by the criminal court simply paid a fine for their offense, and then went on their way. Corporal punishment was virtually non-existent, though implicitly threatened in the town statutes and almost always reserved for foreigners. Incarceration was equally rare. The only reason Raymon would have been incarcerated was if he were obdurate, refused to pay a fine for his slander, and opted instead for jail.

Knowledge of the Manosquin court and penal systems enables me to make assumptions about character and motivation. In the following pages, it will become clear how writers familiar with historical context may use it to flesh out their subjects' motives and personalities. Keep an eye out for how Raymon's character appears and assess to what extent context supports the description. Is the assessment subjective, objective, or somewhere in between? Does it ring true? Does it convince? Does it hinder historical inquiry or support it?

Raymon's incarceration speaks to his stubborn, vindictive, and obsessive personality. These traits shine through even old, dry legal records. Though court scribes recast people's words and deeds to conform to legal norms, and though court officials offered no direct observations on Raymon's character, to anyone reading the records his personality is evident. For whatever reason, Raymon had an axe to grind. As a notary, he knew the law and court systems and used that knowledge to vent his frustrations. First, he attacked Margarida as a poisoner and feckless wife, doing his best to ruin her through a criminal trial. Then, he fought bitterly against his uncle to secure Johan's estate for himself and, nominally at least, for his sisters. Later, he provoked other legal quarrels in his grudge against his former sister-in-law. So it comes as no surprise that he lost his temper, slandered the court, admitted it, and then refused to pay a fine. It also comes as no surprise that the judge seized the opportunity to jail him and teach him a lesson.[4]

As the civil suit progressed, both sides used whatever legal tactics they could to bring about a speedy and cost-effective resolution, but to no avail. Raymon appeared in court one week after his incarceration to ask the judge to acknowledge his and his sisters' claim without any further legal fuss or bother (*sine strepitu et figura judicii*). Two days later, Bartomieu appeared and complained about the cost of the ongoing litigation. Both parties grieved constantly about legal expenses and the estate's anticipated losses. Raymon, knowledgeable in the law, attempted a legal maneuver he hoped would abort the proceedings and compel the judge to rule in favor of the siblings. He claimed that Johan Sartoris, a man whom Bartomieu had summoned repeatedly to support his claim, was technically incompetent

---

4 Though the court took pains to indicate that it did not abuse or mistreat Raymon during his arrest. A marginal note beside the slander case, written in the judge's own hand, suggests the judge had Raymon arrested gently (*et mite aresto que incarcere stetit*).

to give evidence in a court of law because he was bound by the chains of excommunication and, therefore, ineligible to speak in a Christian court (*sit vinculo excommunicationis innodatus*). His status as an excommunicate, Raymon said, was patently obvious to the judge, to the court officials, and to many people present in the court. Raymon asked that Johan Sartoris's testimony be stricken, that the court refund Raymon his expenses, and that Bartomieu be held in contempt (*contumax*). Bartomieu, in good legal fashion, responded with a counterattack. He asked the judge to rule whether or not Raymon and his sisters were truly half-siblings of the deceased.

Judge Rebolli was unimpressed. Raymon had already slandered the court's honor in the parallel criminal process by implying official bias. Now that same plaintiff in this civil suit alleged a gross irregularity: that the judge had knowingly allowed an excommunicate to give evidence. Since Raymon had accused Bartomieu of bringing an excommunicate to court, and since Bartomieu questioned the siblings' blood relation to the deceased, the judge ordered Bartomieu to swear the oath of calumny. This ancient ritual required a plaintiff to swear that he was not prompted by malice or trickery and that he was sincere in his action, believing he had a bona fide case.[5]

Bartomieu balked and refused to take the oath. The trial states that he felt disgraced and appealed immediately aloud (*viva voce*), later in writing. The trial dates are vague, a feature of these civil records where notaries copied fragments of proceedings after the fact on single folios, sometimes out of chronological order, and later bound them for storage. But it appears that all this happened in the last week of November. By early February, the case had progressed no further. That month, Judge Rebolli noted in the record that he still needed to sort out the family relationships before he could determine which party could inherit. By then, though, Bartomieu had had enough. He renounced his appeal and switched tactics.

Manosque, as noted previously, was the seigneurial property of the military Order of the Hospital of St. John of Jerusalem, who inherited with it the right to dispense all forms of justice: high justice, which included the right to prosecute treason or murder, as any king's court could, as well as middling and lower forms of justice. So a single court prosecuted treason, murder, arson, adultery, assault, theft, property damage, and so on. But the people of Manosque had received from the last count the right to negotiate fixed punishments for all these offenses. So when a judge convicted a local of a crime, he knew exactly what the maximum sentence could be. Sentences were usually light and always came with

---

5 Poth. Pand. lib. 5, tt. 16, 17, s. 124. See *Black's Law Dict.*, 4th Rev. Ed., p. 1221.

the option of paying a fine in place of suffering bodily punishment. The local statutes also protected Manosquins in two other important ways. First, the townsmen elected two judicial overseers (*probi homines*) to monitor verdicts and ensure that they conformed to the negotiated penalties. Second, there were strict rules put on judges' terms of office and living arrangements. All judges, moreover, had to swear to uphold the municipal freedoms and privileges.

All of this matters because when Bartomieu withdrew his legal appeal, he did something extraordinary. He attempted to circumvent the entire court system by making a direct and humble supplication to the preceptor, the highest-ranking knight in the Order. It is important to stress that the court system operated at arm's length from the knights. Though the Order owned and operated the court and named its officials, including a local bailiff, the preceptor almost never interfered directly with justice, which was the court's sole prerogative. Bartomieu's abandonment of his legal appeal and his supplication for preceptorial intervention risked short-circuiting all the usual channels of justice and throwing Manosque back to a feudal time before its inhabitants had a functioning local judiciary, a time when princes dispensed justice beneath a tree unilaterally.

The judge acknowledged that Bartomieu had withdrawn his appeal and had made a formal written supplication to that "magnificent and potent man, lord preceptor of Manosque to abbreviate this trial and prevent the devastation and destruction of the goods and inheritance."[6] This was something new. Raymon, the notary, fell back on the law to prevent it.

Five days after Judge Rebolli acknowledged Bartomieu's tactic, Raymon presented yet another written schedule to the judge. In it, he recalled that this quarrel had, after all, been instigated by the other party and held up by the court for a very long time (*detenta et arrestata . . . dyu*). He noted that the judge's desire to determine closest kin had resulted in the estate's deterioration because of the perpetually hanging litigation. He also noted that this had cost him and his sisters considerable time, effort, and money. He pressed the judge to know when they might expect a sentence, clearly preferring to trust the court over the preceptor. He reminded the judge of the agreement made between the Order and the men of Manosque that held sway and must continue to hold sway. That agreement instituted a judge in Manosque for the precise purpose of trying and resolving cases, whenever possible. Raymon also reminded the judge that his oath of office required him to uphold the privileges of Manosque. The quality of local justice hung in the balance.

---

6 Batholomeo made a supplication to the *"magnifico et potenti viro domino Manuasce preceptor directam et cum per quemcumque inter est lites abreviare et fugere attenta devastationem et destructionem bonorum seu hereditate . . ."*

Raymon's protests failed; the preceptor took action. In his humble supplication, Bartomieu had written that he was a poor, decrepit, and impotent old man, close to his senility, but nevertheless uncle to the deceased Johan. Bartomieu pled for benign grace at the hand of his magnificent lord. He asked that if the preceptor was not prepared to rule immediately, then, by way of compromise, he name two local wise men (*probi homines*) to settle the question of who was the closest blood relation. The preceptor, Brother Johan Savini, the powerful military and spiritual leader of the knights, was shrewd. It was no accident that he was the longest-serving administrator of the Order in fourteenth-century Manosque. He responded to Bartomieu's supplication and named a formal commissioner to settle the question, without a formal trial, of who was the closest living blood relation to the dead man. His choice of commissioner accomplished several things all at once. First, it upheld rather than negated municipal privileges and freedoms. Second, it respected the office of judge and the spirit of local justice. Third, it allowed for a mechanism to truncate a lengthy and costly process. It did all this by making Peire Rebolli, the judge in both the criminal and civil cases involving Johan, the preceptor's informal commissioner.

Bartomieu had begun his civil challenge to the siblings in the autumn, and the newly recast judge-commissioner finally ruled in an extra-judicial sentence in late February. He pronounced his sentence, which was duly recorded by the court notary. It emphasized the importance of impartial justice by using a popular Latin formula of the time: that justice should not lean more to the left than the right (*non declinantes plus ad dextrum quam ad sinistram*). It also noted:

> . . . we proffer and declare the said master Raymon Gauterii and Beatritz, wife of Peire Rufferii, as well as Catarina, wife of Guilhem Fulconis, uterine brothers and sisters of the deceased Johan Damponcii, dead intestate, to be nearest and closest in relation to the said Johan the deceased than is the said Bartomieu Damponcii, who claims to be the paternal uncle of the former Johan Damponcii, the deceased. And so we say as a consequence, and we determine and declare, according to the law that all the possessions of that same Johan the deceased shall go in totally equal parts to the said master Raymon Gauterii, and Beatritz, wife of Peire Rufferii, as well as Catarina, wife of Guilhem Fulconis, uterine brothers and sisters of the deceased Johan Damponcii . . .

The siblings were to inherit the estate exclusively, and Bartomieu Damponcii was barred under law from succeeding the deceased.

After months of legal wrangling and odd maneuvering, Raymon's stubbornness paid off. He succeeded in securing control of his brother's estate and in silencing any further claims from his uncle. But in a sense the judge was lenient with Bartomieu. He added, almost as an afterthought, that he condemned neither party to pay the expenses of the other. Though he found for Raymon and the sisters, he did not insist that Bartomieu should be punished for making his claim.

No sooner had the judge pronounced his sentence than Raymon asked when he could take control of the estate. The judge personally handed over a set of keys. As he did so, he reminded Raymon that the estate question was not fully settled. After all, he had issued an announcement that anyone with a claim against the estate should present themselves within the next two weeks. Raymon may have squawked the loudest, but there were still neighborly vultures overhead.

3.2   Community Debts: Clues about a Dead Man's Life

The fight between Johan's half-siblings and his uncle is interesting because it suggests the value of inheritance even among non-wealthy people and the family tensions inheritance sometimes caused. The quarrel also provides fodder for my narrative structuring of Raymon's character: it allows me to paint him as tenacious, ruthless, and willing to use the law to his own advantage. Clues about his behaviors survive because the court forced him to settle his half-brother's debts. To do this, the judge ordered the herald (*nuncio et praeco*) to proclaim again that the preceptor ordered anyone with a valid stake in the estate to contact the court notary. Johan's debts to outsiders are equally instructive, though in a different manner, for what they reveal about the dead man's life.

The notary drew up a long list of creditors that is interesting for two reasons. First, it indicates the kinds of people to whom Johan owed money and the causes of his many debts. This allows us a glimpse into the sort of life he lived. Second, the list provides a valuable, if limited, sense of the scope of his wealth. There is no itemized inventory of his estate, but Raymon and his sisters clearly bickered with their uncle at great length and significant expense over something; the surviving records are simply mute on the material details. This was perhaps because everyone involved in the litigation knew what they were fighting over. Many things obvious in the past were never written down simply because they were apparent at the time. A claim made by master Johan Autrici, though, suggests that there was an inventory, now lost. Autrici sought to be paid for drawing up a notarized inventory (*facere inventarium et instrumentum*) to help the judge assess the value of the estate. Still, in the absence of this document, the surviving list of creditors is our best way to reconstruct what Margarida's husband owned. Through this reconstruction, we gain a sense of what her material surroundings must have been.

TABLE 3.1   *Claims against Johan Damponcii's Estate*

NAME	OCCUPATION	DEBT CLAIMED	PAID / OWED FROM ESTATE
Ugo Merle	Tailor (*sartor*)	2 shillings for a certain garment (*quondam raupam*) he made	
Nicolau Attanulphi	Notary (*notarius*)	6 shillings in change owed because his wife had given Johan 1 florin to buy some meat	
Johan Desderii		7 shillings for some meat	4 *deniers*
Antoni Barduchi		Owed for some spelt that Nicolau Attanulphi had purchased on Johan's behalf	4 *deniers*
Johan Autrici	Oblate of the Hospital	3 florins he lent Johan	
Guilhem Montanerii		3 shillings salary for his kin	
Peire Gauterii		A bushel of wheat	
Peire Garnerii		2 shillings for rental of ploughing beasts	2 *deniers*
Samiletus		7 florins for some linens sold to Johan, plus 3 florins for a sickle	
Saletus Jacep	Jewish cobbler?	4 shillings for a pair of boots (*caliga*)	4 *deniers*

Many other townspeople claimed that Johan owed them money, and through these claims we gain glimpses into a rather ordinary life. Table 3.1 illustrates some of these claims.

These debts speak to an ordinary man who borrowed money from friends to help make ends meet, who hired journeymen to work for him at harvest time, and who engaged in the usual agrarian and mercantile activities of a late medieval townsman: he commissioned clothes and shoes from garment makers; he sold shares in slaughtered animals to friends and acquaintances; and he had dealings with knights, notaries, and farmers. Like most townsmen in the later Middle Ages, he relied on an informal system of credit to get by. Neighbors helped one another out, and everybody knew what was owed.[7] Eventually people settled their

---

7 There have been some excellent studies into gendered small-scale lending and borrowing in Manosque. See, for example, Courtemanche, "Les femmes juives et le crédit à Manosque," 545–58 and the unpublished thesis by her student, David Bergeron, "Le prêt à crédit juif et chrétien à Manosque de 1303 à 1326" (M.A. thesis, Université de Moncton, 2002). See also the unpublished M.A. thesis by Francine Michaud, "Crédit, endettement et patrimoine féminin à Manosque au milieu du XIIIe siècle" (M.A. thesis, Laval University, Québec City, 1984).

debts. A sudden death, however, upset the system. Aside from his unscheduled departure and the ensuing wrangling over his property, though, every indication is that Johan's life was quiet and unremarkable.

Even the ghost was not unusual. The list of creditors reveals that Margarida was not Johan's first wife, whose specter still lingered. Buried in the list of lenders and tradesmen seeking compensation are some monks who tended to the dead woman. The prior of the religious community of Toutes Aures appeared before the court notary to claim that Johan owed three shillings for tapers (*pro cereis*) that the brothers had lit over the tomb of this first wife.[8] The prior, moreover, sought repayment for a florin one of the brothers had lent Johan so he could offer alms when the monks received his wife's fresh corpse. The prior also wanted the seven measures of wheat agreed upon by Johan to cover the costs of her funeral. And Johan had borrowed more money from some of the other brothers. At least a portion of this debt was recorded in the cartulary, or record book, of his friend Peire Gausi. The monks were not the only ones to whom Johan owed money on account of his previous wife. Peire Rufferii (see Appendix I, Figure A.2) sought two florins that he claimed this wife had bequeathed in her last will and testament to his daughter. And, finally, Johan's first wife's brother, Boniface Peysoni, claimed that Johan still owed him a florin he borrowed when she died.

Sifting through these debts reveals that Johan was married to a Peysoni woman before Margarida de Portu. Moreover, it seems that his first wife had not been dead long since he had yet to repay the costs of her funeral, a burden that now fell to Raymon and his sisters. Margarida, in contrast, had not been married before; this was a second marriage for him, but a first for her. There is a fairly good chance, therefore, that he was older than she. Her entry into the Gauterii household as a younger second wife may explain some of the resistance expressed by her brother-in-law. Was it hard for her to live up to the dead woman's memory? Did Raymon find Margarida lacking when held up to the ghost of his previous sister-in-law? Anything is possible. Though we cannot know for certain, the existence of a first wife offers avenues for conjecture about family dynamics.

The list of creditors also confirms that Johan owned property, a house for his ghost to haunt. This home was, no doubt, his most significant urban asset. He likely owned fields outside the town, since he hired migrant workers at the harvest and

---

8 The hill called Toutes Aures lies to the west of Manosque and contained a fortified satellite village whose population eventually fused with Manosque proper. The earliest written reference to the village is in a charter created by Guiges, Count of Forcalquier, in 1149. Today two walls of a great stone tower still adorn the hill and loom above the town.

rented animals for plowing. But there was definitely a house. We can piece together indirect evidence of its existence in two ways. First, the judge handed a set of keys to Raymon. But were these keys to the house or to a barn? To a lockbox? The records do not say. They call them simply *claves*. Chief among the list of creditors to the estate, however, was Margarida's brother, Ugo de Portu. The de Portu clan continued to look after its material assets even as Raymon sought to keep as much as he could for himself and his sisters. Within the list of creditors, Ugo sought restoration of a saddle and a small chest (*unam selam ronsini et unam budam*[9]), stored in Johan's house ever since his wedding to Margarida (*que sunt in domo dicti Johannis ex post que sua soror uxor dicti Johannis maritata fuit*). These items did not figure into Margarida's dowry. If they had, they would have been protected as her personal property. They were de Portu possessions, on loan to Johan. And Margarida's brother, sizing the greedy Raymon up, wanted them back from the house.

The list of creditors also shows that Raymon and his sisters had to pay off costs associated with Johan's death. First, there was the criminal trial against Margarida. Vivas Josep, the Jewish physician who testified as an expert witness in it, noted that he was still owed two florins for his examination of Johan's corpse. He also wanted four florins for the report (*relatio*) he made to the judge and bailiff. Then there was the cost of Johan's burial, for which the prior of Notre Dame de Pentecôte sought payment of five *gros*. As confirmed executors of Johan's estate, Raymon and his sisters were obliged to settle all Johan's debts, those incurred in life and in death. Duty and sentiment, however, are two different things. Johan's siblings did not want to watch their inheritance whittle away, so Raymon took steps to shore up some assets.

Near the bottom of the list of outside debts owed by Johan, Raymon submitted his own claims against the estate. He told the court notary that he had lent Johan a florin and an agricultural pick and that he wished to recoup two franks, the value of six legal documents (*instrumentorum*). Were these notarized documents he redacted, or drew up, for his brother in life? Probably not. More likely, Raymon wanted to be paid for drafting the various schedules he had submitted on his own behalf during the civil trial against his uncle. This was a canny way to offset some of the external claims being made against his inheritance.

Raymon and his sisters did what they could to protect their inheritance. Few creditors received anything from them, at least not according to the court records. Marginal notes beside the list of creditors indicate that no one received the full amount they requested. Most received nothing at all. Those who did were lucky

---

9 The Provençal word *boudo* is the equivalent of the Latin *boda,* meaning small chest or case. The notary here substituted a "u" for an "o".

to receive a fraction. On the whole, Raymon paid out very little. Whatever strategies he employed to inherit his dead brother's assets, and then retain them, were effective.

3.3 Legal History

There are many ways to interpret these documents. The tale of a greedy and stubborn notary and his family tensions is supported by 19 pages of civil trial record stored in the departmental archives in Marseille. These events actually happened. But the way I tell the tale is subjective. Another historian, reading the same documents, would have written a different story. When summarizing these pages of dense, repetitive legal text, replete with formulae, amendments, and insertions, written on damaged old paper, with missing sections and unclear vocabulary, I made choices about what to tell and what not to tell. I framed the conflict as one of family rivalry. I emphasized the notary's nastiness. What I chose not to say is, in many ways, as illustrative as what I did say. Normally, in a history book, most readers remain blissfully unaware of the documentary choices made by the author.

To illustrate how another historian might approach the civil court records, I want to emphasize now some of my omissions. There were many ways I could have framed the tale other than as greed or family tension. Consider some of the issues that may have appealed more to a legal historian than to a social microhistorian.

a. Roman Law as Context

First, I presented the struggle between the siblings and the uncle as a dispute over family inheritance, which it was, but I provided no context as to the legal framework that allowed this struggle to play out before a judge. The fact that this record exists at all is thanks to the robust system of late medieval Roman law in the northwestern Mediterranean.

Roman law, as its name implies, is the legal system that in antiquity governed the Roman Empire. Over the course of Roman history, a massive body of legislation grew and grew until, in the first quarter of the sixth century, at the very end of what we consider the ancient world, the eastern emperor Justinian put together a committee headed by the jurist Tribonian. Its task was to edit, condense, and revise this unwieldy body of law into a definitive and workable set of books. The result was the so-called *Corpus iuris civilis*, the Body of Civil Law, sometimes referred to as the Code of Justinian, drawing its name from the emperor who commissioned the work and from one of the books in the collection, the Code. In fact, though, the sixth-century *Corpus* contained several volumes: the *Codex,* or Code, which contained previous imperial laws; the *Digesta,* or Digest, also called the *Pandectae,* a collection of writings from the greatest Roman jurists; and the *Institutes,* which was a sort of textbook for law students. Later in Justinian's reign, the emperor proclaimed a fourth volume, the *Novellae,* or Novels, so named because it contained "new" laws he put forth.

As the Roman Empire gave way in Europe to the barbarian migrations and as various Germanic peoples forged new kingdoms, these immigrants merged their oral legal traditions with Roman institutions. Roman legal traditions gave way to the so-called barbarian law codes. In Italy, though, Roman law never disappeared completely.

In the late eleventh and early twelfth centuries, Italian jurists set about reconstituting and re-implementing Justinian's *Corpus.* Though some historians have labeled this a "rediscovery" of Roman law, that term is inaccurate; Roman law had continued to inform many local Italian customs prior to its full recovery, and whole or partial copies of the *Corpus* survived, tucked away in Italian monasteries, throughout the early and high Middle Ages. Still, around the 1080s, a law teacher known as Irnerius, called the *lucerna iuris,* the shining "lantern of the law," led his students to re-establish and reconstitute the bulk of the *Corpus.* From that point on, Italian law schools began to teach the slightly reorganized but otherwise intact *Corpus* of Justinian.

This legal reform figured into much broader social reforms happening in the late 1000s and throughout the 1100s. The so-called Gregorian Reformation, led by papal bureaucrats, saw a comprehensive review of canon law, the legal system of the Catholic Church. While popes sought to streamline Church processes, kings faced a similar challenge. This was the age when the great monarchies of Europe consolidated their kingdoms and began to centralize their administrations. Royal governments, therefore, also had need of educated, literate men trained at universities in legal processes. Even in the lower ranks of society, a similar need took hold. As people flocked to towns and cities, and as human population levels climbed, urban centers became once more focal points for commerce and trade. This gave rise to a larger merchant class and more artisans, shopkeepers, and tradesmen. These drove the demand for better systems of recordkeeping, for more paper records, and for places to settle disputes. The restoration of Roman law, therefore, happened alongside the Church's desire to recodify its legal system and its courts, the royal need for more efficient and centralized bureaucracies, and the urban revolution that was taking hold.

This historical context matters enormously, since almost everything we know of Margarida's life in Manosque comes to us via court records, which are the direct result of the implementation of Roman law across southern Europe. Legal reforms that started in Italy around the year 1100 continued to spread throughout the 1200s. By the thirteenth century, Manosquin jurists were making a deliberate effort to adapt the procedures used in their local court to conform to newer Roman trial processes. They divided their court into two branches—civil and criminal—though the distinction was not always clear and criminal judges heard cases that we today would consider civil disputes. The criminal court in Manosque was operational in the 1200s, but it functioned according to what is called the accusatorial procedure. In that system, one person accused another and the burden of proof fell to the accuser. Courts that used such a system, in theory, operated as bodies of arbitration. In the thirteenth century, however, the Manosquin court shifted from the accusatorial process to the Roman inquisitorial process.[10] This was not the Inquisition made famous in Spain, directed against heretics and renowned for its use of torture. Rather, it was the Roman system of inquests (*inquisitiones*), criminal investigations that led to a judicial verdict and sentence. The newly reformed criminal court in Manosque continued to accept denunciations against wrongdoers, but the criminal judge, beginning in the thirteenth century, also had the power to conduct criminal investigations on his own initiative (*ex officio*). Criminal judges in the inquisitorial procedure, in theory, had the power to seek out wrongdoers and enforce the law.

When Raymon denounced Margarida to the criminal court, he set in motion an investigation driven by Roman law. When Bartomieu complained that Raymon prevented him from achieving control of his nephew's estate, he launched a civil lawsuit, another process inherited from Roman law. All the direct information we have about Margarida and her world comes to us through the records churned out and shaped by Roman legal process.

b. Paper Documents

It should already be apparent that Roman law generated vast amounts of paper records. During trials, criminal and civil, a court scribe wrote detailed notes about

---

10 For the transformation away from accusatorial procedure and toward inquisitorial, see Patricia MacCaughan, *La justice à Manosque au XIIIe siècle: Evolution et représentation,* Histoire et Archives, hors-série, 5 (Paris: Honoré Champion, 2005), which grew out of an earlier Ph.D. thesis entitled "Les transformations de la justice au XIIIe siècle: l'exemple de Manosque (1240–1320)" (Ph.D. Thesis, Laval University, Québec City, 2001). The same author also produced a summative article in "La procédure judiciaire à Manosque au milieu du XIIIe siècle, témoin d'une transition," *Revue historique de droit français et étranger* 76 (1998): 583–95.

all happenings. This scribe was always a licensed notary public.[11] He recorded accusations, interrogations, depositions, and testimonies; copied schedules, judicial proclamations, and legal arguments; and made duplicates of records for interested parties. His writings served the same purpose as a modern stenographer's transcript. In Manosque, criminal and civil judges reviewed court transcripts prior to rendering their final decisions. Often, judges made marginal notes in notaries' transcripts about verdicts and sentences.

One of the challenges facing historians is that court notaries did not record words and deeds verbatim. First, they made all their records in Latin, the language of Roman law and learned society. But the men and women who appeared before them spoke Occitan, the language of the troubadours. Provence was not yet part of the French Crown, so there was little French spoken this far south. This meant that notaries made *in situ* translations of the words they heard, from vulgar Occitan to learned Latin. Sometimes, though, the notary did not have an equivalent Latin word at his disposal, and so he simply Latinized a local word. This poses challenges for historians who read notarial records, since they routinely encounter Latin-seeming words that never existed in that language. Second, notaries had to reconfigure words and deeds to fit legal norms. So, instead of writing "he said to me . . .," the notary wrote "the said witness responded that the aforementioned accused person told the said witness . . ." This made for lengthy and repetitive text. To compensate for all this repetition, to save time, and to conserve precious paper and ink, notaries used a highly abbreviated system of writing. In point of fact, all scribes throughout the Middle Ages employed paleographic abbreviations to cut out common letters or endings and to replace them with diacritics or special strokes. But in their functional recordkeeping, notaries used a particularly great number and variety of abbreviations. Thus, instead of writing the Latin word *per* (through), a notary wrote 𝄞. But if he wanted to write the Latin word *pro* (for), then he wrote 𝄞, and if he wanted to write the Latin word *propter* (about), then he wrote 𝄞. To read these documents, historians spend considerable time and effort memorizing abbreviations and learning to distinguish between them.[12] Third, because of this manufacturing process, and in the absence of sophisticated writing technologies, notaries actually wrote out messy short-hand copies of transcripts, called briefs, *imbreviatura*, that

---

11 This was the norm throughout Provence. In her study of Marseille, one historian noted that "La plupart des notaires dont on conserve la production ont été à un moment de leur carrière élevés à la charge de greffier de l'une des cours civiles de la cité." Francine Michaud, *Un signe des temps: accroissement des crises familiales autour du patrimoine à Marseille à la fin du XIIIe siècle.* (Toronto: Pontifical Institute for Mediaeval Studies, 1994), 15.

12 There is a tool appropriate to the task. Medievalists use Adriano Cappelli, *Lexicon abbreviaturarum: dizionario di abbreviature latini ed italiani,* 6th ed. (Milano: Hoepli, 1961). The "Cappelli," as it is referred to, is a compact 531-page reference tool that is absolutely essential to anyone working with primary medieval documents.

they later recopied in fuller form, *in extenso*, into the tidier records used by judges. Eventually, Manosquin notaries bound their finished documents into leather cartularies (*cartularia*). In most cases, their original rough copies are lost, and all that survives for historical study are the formal, edited, final versions.

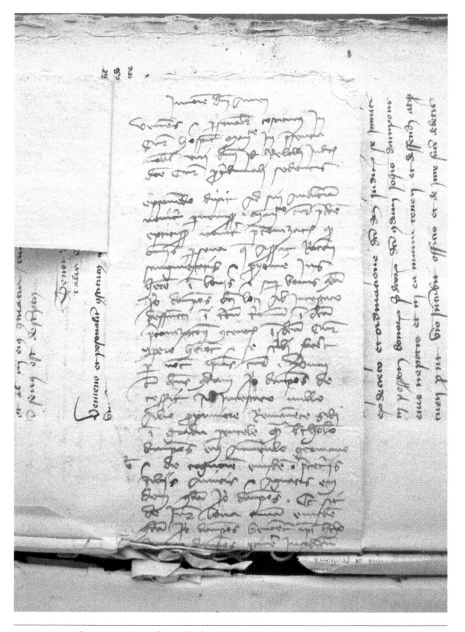

FIGURE 3.1: *Court notary's rough copy* (imbreviatura)

Legal historians would note that, in the case of Raymon and Bartomieu's civil quarrel over Johan's estate, a few rough pages remain, stuffed into the leather-bound registers containing the final good copies of the records.

Here is the same passage copied out in full in the final copy contained in the bound register:

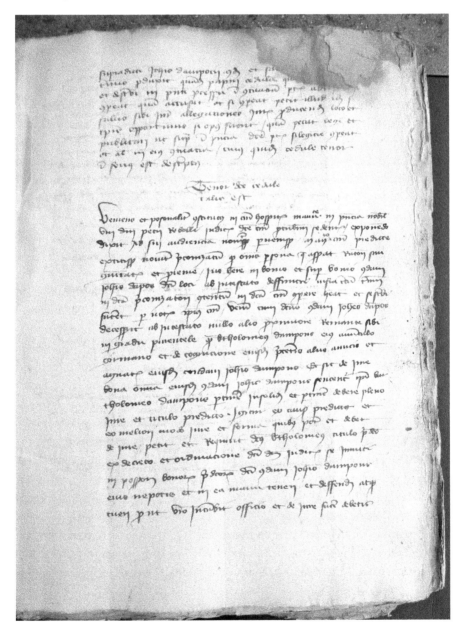

FIGURE 3.2: *Notarial act written* in extenso

One of the questions surrounding tidily bound court registers is the extent to which they were edited. We know that notaries made rough copies, corrected and amended them, and then recopied them into their final cleaner versions. What we do not know is the extent to which scribes altered their originals. Did they attempt to cover up procedural mistakes made by the court? Did they recast events in a different light after the fact? These nagging questions undermine our ability to know what happened in a trial.

In the civil dispute between the uncle and the siblings, legal historians would be delighted to draw attention to the fact that whenever a rough copy survives it agrees *word for word* with the final copy. The difference between the two versions lies in the quality of the hand and the types of abbreviations. The rough copy was sloppy, evidently written in haste, and uses a greater number of abbreviations. The final copy is tidier, written much more carefully, and uses only standard abbreviations. This confirms that very little changed in the document between its original draft form and its final "published" version. Aside from writing quickly, notaries maintained legal conventions and formulae even in their early drafts and did not attempt to alter records after the fact.

c. Legalese

Legal historians would also make note of particular terms or conventions used in the civil trial. In particular, this quarrel highlights several interesting medieval legal turns of phrase, each with its own idiomatic history. The three most noteworthy idioms are *sine strepitu et figura judicii, jurare de calumpnia,* and *viva voce.*

The first legal idiom, meaning "without the noise or bother of a trial," allowed for summary process. The *sine strepitu* phrase originates in canon law, Church law circa 1300, though it passed quickly into Roman civil law and even into English common law. Its purpose was to settle matters quickly and in a summary fashion without having to resort to all the formalities of Romano-canonical process, the so-called judicial order (*ordo judiciarius*). In Provence, summary process appealed to fourteenth-century lawmakers who dealt with pilgrims and paupers. They could ill afford the length and cost of the *ordo judiciarius* and deserved a truncated, cheaper, yet still fair alternative. Even in summary process, the great legal historian Kenneth Pennington remarked, "a judge must [still] preserve the equity of the law of nations and natural equity."[13] *Sine strepitu* was so useful to European courtrooms that it endured beyond the Middle Ages. During the English

---

13 Kenneth Pennington, *The Prince and the Law, 1200–1600: Sovereignty and Rights in the Western Legal Tradition* (Berkeley and Los Angeles: University of California Press, 1993), 200.

Reformation, for example, around the time of the death of Henry VIII and the ascension of his daughter Mary, *sine forma et figura judicii* allowed that

> . . . the forms of the court are not exactly observed. For instance, when evidence is admitted against those who are not upon the spot to defend themselves; but here nothing ought to be done to prejudice the parties, nor bar them from bringing cause to a farther trial. The process is said to be managed, *"de plano et sine strepitu judicii,"* when the judge neither sits on the bench in the customary place, nor observes the stated days for hearing, but received the libel, or appeal, or any other thing [. . .] out of the customary method. And, lastly, the process is said to go on, *"sine forma et figura judicii"* when the supplemental methods of the civil or municipal laws are omitted, and nothing made use of, but what results from the law of nature.[14]

Mary, the sixteenth-century very Catholic Queen of England, used summary process to punish bishops who had married. She empowered her commissioners to strip such clergy of property and office *de plano, sine ullo strepitu et figura judicii.*

A legal historian who commented on the universality and endurance of *sine strepitu et figura judicii* would be pressed to explain how, exactly, a canon law formula came to influence Roman civil law and, eventually, even English common law. The legal historian would necessarily trace the first appearance of *sine strepitu* in Church councils and papal decrees and explain when it permeated the civil law. Next, the legal scholar would be pressed to comment on the wide-reaching influence of Roman law. Though in Europe Roman law courts only ever operated in the northwestern Mediterranean and in the south of what is today France, the influence of Roman law extended to transalpine Europe.[15] Beginning with Bologna, the greatest of the medieval universities to teach law and the home of Irnerius and his protégés, southern Europe became famous for its law schools. Students from across the continent risked their lives and fortunes to travel to Italy or southern France to obtain degrees in law. Once at school, of course, the form of law they studied was either Roman or canon or both. When northern students completed their studies, they returned, degrees in hand, to their homes in France, Germany, England, or elsewhere. When these young jurists began to practice law, at a royal court, Church court, municipal court, or wherever, the form of law they practiced was whatever

---

14 Jeremy Collier, *An Ecclesiastical History of Great Britain, Chiefly of England, from the First Planting of Christianity to the End of the Reign of King Charles the Second* (London: Printed for Samuel Keble, 1714), vol. 6, book v, p. 65.

15 See chapters 3 and 4 of Manlio Bellomo, *The Common Legal Past of Europe: 1000–1800* (Washington, DC: Catholic University of America Press, 1995).

happened to be local to that region. This is what the legal historian Manlio Bellomo calls the *jus proprium*, the local law. But jurists trained in Italy and southern France never forgot the lessons they learned during their cisalpine studies. They relied on the vocabulary, logic, norms, and forms of Roman law to help them interpret and enact the *jus proprium*. This explains how Renaissance English lawmakers relied on the *sine strepitu* formulation. In that sense, to borrow Bellomo's other famous term, Roman law became the *jus commune*, the law that was communal to all Western civilization. There was, moreover, a hierarchy of laws. If a judge in northern France, operating according to what is called customary law, *droit coutumier*, wanted to apply legal rules, he looked for guidance first to the local statutes of his town or city or region, then to the royal law put forth by the king, and then, finally, to Roman law.

The fact that a small-town lawyer such as Raymon Gauterii, or the counsel for his uncle Bartomieu, knew to frame a legal request according to the formulation *sine strepitu et figura judicii* helps situate their legal formation in a much wider context. Jurists in Manosque shared a common training and understanding of the law that transcended local customs. Even in a middling place like Manosque, there was a standard of European justice.

A legal historian faced with the trials surrounding Margarida would, no doubt, also be compelled to comment upon the other formulations used in the records. Judge Rebolli's insistence that Bartomieu swear the oath of calumny, for example, merits explanation.

The ancient Roman jurists Marcian and Paulus expounded that calumny is a sort of intentional fraud perpetrated in a civil or criminal proceeding.[16] When a judge determined that an accuser acted out of malice, and not sincerity, that person was guilty of calumny. The ancient Roman jurists took calumny seriously. Cicero tells us that the perpetrator of the fraud could be exiled or, worse, branded on the forehead with the letter K, for *Kalumnia*, though this may be a fiction.[17] The ancient jurists all agree that defendants in legal actions could avail themselves of the *calumnia judicium*, the trial of calumny. If, through this trial, a judge

---

16 Marcian limits it to criminal matters in Dig. 48 tit. 16 s1: *Calumniari est falsa crimina intendere, praevaricari vera crimina abscondere, tergiversari in universum ab accusatione desistere.* Paulus extended calumny to both criminal and civil cases in Sentent. Recept. I. tit. 5: *Calumniosus est qui sciens prudensque per fraudem negotium alicui comparat.* For more on the ancient concept see L. Charvet, "Les serments contre la calomnie dans la procédure au temps de Justinien," *Revue des études byzantines* 8, no. 8 (1950): 130–42.

17 See Cicero, *Pro Sext. Roscio Amerino Oratio*, c57: . . . *si ego hos bene novi, litteram illam cui vos usque eo inimici estis ut etiam Kal. omnis oderitis ita vehementer ad caput adfigent ut postea neminem alium nisi fortunas vestras accusare possitis.* See John Murray, "Calumnia," in *A Dictionary of Greek and Roman Antiquities by Various Writers*, ed. Sir William Smith (London: John Murray, 1895), 235. Smith's *Dictionary* is widely available in full-text format on the Internet and is a useful resource.

determined that the plaintiff, in our case Bartomieu, was knowingly and willfully guilty of calumny, then he was obliged to pay the defendant one-tenth of the value of the suit and the defendant was deemed innocent of the action.

In lieu of the trial of calumny, however, defendants in the civil law could simply require plaintiffs to swear an oath of calumny upon the Gospels.[18] This oath did not mean that what a person said was true, merely that they believed it in good faith. Judges could dismiss suits launched by plaintiffs who refused to swear the oath and condemn defendants who refused to swear it. In some types of legal actions, the oath was a necessary step to launch the lawsuit. In general, the Digest devotes significant attention to the types of trials that require evidence of calumny.

In the dispute between the siblings and the uncle, Raymon, through his insinuation that Bartomieu relied on an excommunicate for evidence, prompted the judge to require the oath of the plaintiff. Bartomieu balked, fearful the judge intended to dismiss his suit and force him to pay Raymon one-tenth of the cost of the trial. With stakes that high, it is little wonder he appealed.

Bartomieu made his appeal *viva voce*, literally "with the living voice," an odd turn of phrase but one clearly defined in the Roman law on appeals. Throughout this civil lawsuit, both parties submitted their prepared petitions and schedules in writing. When one party was faced with an unexpected written submission, it routinely asked the judge for a delay, or recess, so that it might adjourn to prepare a formal written response. This was the normal course of events. Roman law, however, made it clear that appeals were so serious that they could be launched instantly and verbally. The Digest specifies that during a lawsuit, all one had to do to launch an appeal was to say aloud "I appeal!" After a lawsuit was done, the parties still had two or three days to call for an appeal.

These are the sorts of technical issues that would occupy historians of law and probably lead them to frame an analysis of Margarida's life story very differently, if at all. Legal historians would also tend to caution against the danger of reading a single trial record in order to draw broader conclusions. This, in fact, was the criticism leveled by Thomas Kuehn against Gene Brucker. Brucker wrote a microhistory of a Renaissance love story gone bad, based on a few trial records.[19] Kuehn reviewed the book and noted:

> The plurivocality of legal language cannot be grasped fully by reading a handful of documents relating to a single case. As that case is typified (reduced

---

18 The words of the ancient oath were simply *"se non calumniae causa agere." Ibid.*
19 Brucker, *Giovanni and Lusanna.*

to a type) in legal terms, the peculiarities can be too easily taken as elements of the type, or vice versa. A much greater range of cases and texts has to be called on to form the hermeneutic experience of the historical interpreter who would delve into an intriguing, complex, and ambiguous case.[20]

In framing my tale, I heed Kuehn's cautionary words. To determine the significance of the trials pertaining to Margarida and the death of Johan, I have cast them against a systematic study of 1,644 other cases preserved from the court of Manosque between 1340 and 1405. I tracked these cases using a computer database, reducing each one to its constituent elements. I tracked individuals as accused persons, denouncers, witnesses, plaintiffs, or defendants, and noted their place of origin, current citizenship, sex, and marital status, as well as their craft, trade, or profession. Finally, I tracked specific charges, verdicts, and sentences. In addition to the database, I transcribed 873 typed pages of trial records. This material provides the filter through which I read Margarida's trials and informs my conclusions. It also provides me with wider familiarity about the characters who populate her tale.

Were I to write a legal history of Margarida's court records, I would tell what I know about the players based on my knowledge of hundreds of other records that do not concern her. For example, I know that Raymon had extensive experience with the criminal justice system in Manosque. His actions in persecuting Margarida were not his first experience in a criminal trial, nor were they his last.

Raymon was the object of about a dozen criminal inquests. Three took place in 1394, the same year he persecuted Margarida. One, the slander case dated 16 November 1394, occurred when he accused the court officials of taking Margarida's side against him.[21] On 7 December 1394, the criminal court also proceeded against him over an instance of a man breaking into a tavern with his servants to drink a pot of wine.[22] And on 11 January 1394 (which is actually 1395 in our calendar), the court prosecuted him for arson, despite the fact that he had made reparation to his neighbor for accidentally damaging some olive trees.[23] But Raymon was the subject of at least nine other criminal trials between 1394 and 1405. Seven of them involved verbal offenses. Granted, this is one of the most common types of offenses in this series of documents; in fact, one-third of all criminal trials involved some sort of verbal offense. Provençal culture was blustery

---

20 Kuehn, "Reading Microhistory," 519.
21 See ADBDR 56 H 1001 fo. 93 v.–94.
22 See ADBDR 56 H 1001 fo. 112–112 v.
23 See ADBDR 56 H 1001 fo. 119.

and verbose. Colorful insults, curses, and profanities often preceded kicks and punches. Slander and defamation were routine worries in a culture bound up in honor. Women, in particular, worried about their sexual reputation and took their enemies to court for having called them whore or slut (*puta*). So Raymon was, in a sense, not so very different from the other Manosquin men and women who populate the court records. Except that he was. He was a notary, a trained jurist, a man licensed and sworn to uphold the law. He should have known better. At the very least, he should have known he could not escape punishment if he allowed his tongue to wag the wrong way. During Margarida's criminal trial, he suffered time in jail because of his slander. But if Raymon was too stubborn to pay a fine for his insult during Margarida's inquest, he was also no stranger to fiscal punishment. Over a 10-year span, the court repeatedly fined him for various other verbal offenses. This was a man who routinely slandered neighbors and who even once publicly and libellously accused his colleague, the notary Nicolau Attanulphi, of fraud. The negative way in which I cast Raymon's personality within Margarida's tale, therefore, is derived not solely from the documents pertaining to her life but also from a much broader knowledge of all the available records. A comprehensive and scholarly analysis of 1,600 records leads to one inescapable conclusion: Raymon had a temper, a history as a troublemaker, and a loose mouth.

d. Raymon Gauterii and Notaries Public

A legal historian would not have made that last comment, though a narrative microhistorian may do so. A legal historian would still, however, have interrogated how a man like Raymon came to interact with the law. To do this, the legal historian would draw on knowledge of the office of the notary public (*notarius publicus*). Notaries were another idiosyncratic manifestation of Roman law. Through an examination of their historical profession, a legal historian could offer some insights to explain how and why Raymon acted the way he did.

Notaries were trained and licensed to redact, or draw up, official acts (*acta*) or instruments (*instrumenta*). In Ancient Rome, they worked for the imperial senate, courts, and private citizens. Their official documents had special evidentiary status under law as certified records of events. Ancient Romans relied on notarized documents to officially capture words, deeds, and intentions, and to formulate them in a way that was consonant with the law. With the twelfth-century renaissance of Roman law in Bologna, notaries again spread across the southwestern portion of Europe and began to divide into sub-specializations. There were medieval imperial notaries, apostolic notaries, notaries tied to liege lords or seigneurs, notaries who worked for bishops and archbishops, and even, in Italy, notaries created by certain municipalities.[24] Specialized Italian schools began to train men in the Latin formats and formulas required by various types of records. For notaries public, this meant land transfers, deeds, commercial contracts, marriage contracts, last wills and testaments, legal acts, and so on. Great masters appeared who wrote learned textbooks about their profession to provide examples for their pupils. Chief among these learned experts were men such as Raynerius Perusinus, also called Rainerius of Perugia, "an imperial notary, professor of law, and judge of Bologna."[25] Raynerius was active in Bologna in 1219 and composed his *Ars notaria*, the Notarial Art, sometime around 1230. It provided comprehensive examples of sales contracts, rental contracts, adoption agreements, apprenticeships, and so on. Generations later, Bologna remained the apex for notarial formation. Seventy years after Raynerius, for example, the great master Rolandino of Bologna, who died around the year 1300, composed his magisterial *Summa Artis Notariae*.

By the fourteenth century, the French Midi also boasted several prominent legal schools that taught the notarial arts. Some were close to Manosque, along the Rhône valley, in towns such as Valence or Die. But modern experts also suspect that a good deal of Provençal notaries public learned their craft through apprenticeship (unlike imperial or canonical notaries). Regardless of how they trained, historians all agree that Provençal notaries public made important, and lasting, contributions to society. Many were leaders of their communities, and it was not unusual for the local notary in a town to own one of the best libraries or art collections.[26] Great towns and cities had a surplus of notaries, but even poor villages often had one or two.[27] But perhaps precisely because there were so many of them, not all of them were great men. In Manosque, the tax rolls show that some notaries were rich, others humble.

In Provence, *notarii publici* such as Raymon were laymen who had completed training, either through apprenticeship or a school, and passed some form of

---

24 It was lawful for notaries to accumulate qualifications. Thus, one man could be licensed to work as an imperial, apostolic, and comital notary. For more on this and the individual categories of notary, consult Chapter 1 of Roger Aubenas, *Étude sur le notariat provençal au Moyen Age et sous l'Ancien Régime* (Aix-en-Provence: Éditions du Feux, 1931).

25 Cited in Kiril Petkov, *The Kiss of Peace: Ritual, Self, and Society in the High and Late Medieval West* (Leiden: Brill, 2003), 83. Raynerius is mentioned (as Rainerius Perusinus) in detail in Harry Bresslau, *Handbuch der Urkundenlehre*, II, 2nd ed. (Leipzig: Verlag von Veit & Comp, 1915), 256–57. The great medievalist Charles Homer Haskins comments on Raynerius in his "Orleanese Formularies in a Manuscript at Tarragona," *Speculum* 5, no. 4 (October 1930): 411–20.

26 Aubenas, *Étude sur le notariat provençal*, 104.

27 Roger Aubenas notes that a century after the re-emergence of notaries, there were complaints about the excessive numbers of notaries. *Ibid.*, 73.

qualifying examination to earn a license. The authority to invest notaries public rested in the hands of the Count of Provence.[28] As in late antiquity, medieval notaries wrote qualifying exams to prove that they knew Latin. In Marseille, for example, the notaries of the royal court or the cathedral conducted these examinations. In Avignon, home to the papacy throughout most of the fourteenth century, a jury composed of municipal judges conducted them. Though we know a little about who administered exams, it is unclear how rigorous the accreditation process was for notaries licensed by the Count of Provence. Regardless, all notaries took oaths of office and loyalty and paid a fee to receive patent letters of qualification, which conferred on them the so-called notarial privilege (*privilegium notariatus*).[29]

There were limits to who could become a notary. In Provence, only legitimate Christian natives under the jurisdiction of the old Count of Forcalquier qualified. Men of illegitimate birth, Jews, and foreigners need not apply. Eligible men had to be of a sufficiently advanced age, financially independent, and legally competent (*sui juris*). All notaries created by the counts of Provence and Forcalquier were barred from civic office and had to be honorable men. This prohibited excommunicates and those convicted of fraud. Finally and, for our purposes, most importantly, a Provençal notary public had to be a layman. He could not have taken ecclesiastical vows, could not be tonsured, and could not be a cleric. Which is odd, because Raymon was a man of the cloth.

Despite the absolutely hard and fast rule that public notaries could not be clerics, Raymon confirmed his religious status during the criminal inquest that ended with his arrest. At the bottom of his deposition, the court notary wrote:

> And in the present inquest, he responded as a layman not, moreover, as a cleric and he promised in this case not to rejoice in the clerical privilege he has, on the contrary in this case he expressly renounces it, and promises to remain at the mandate of the present court.[30]

Clerical privilege, called in Latin *privilegium clericali*, was a legal benefit that existed throughout the Middle Ages. It effectively removed avowed clerics of various ranks from non-canonical and secular jurisdictions. Understandably, notaries

---

28 *Ibid.*, 49.

29 All of this information comes from *Ibid.*, Chapter 2.

30 *Et in presenti inquisitione respondit ut laycus non autem ut clericus et promisit in hoc casu se non gaudere privilegio clericali quod habet ymo expresse in hoc facto eidem renunciavit, et promisit stare mandatis praesentis curie etc.* ADBDR 56 H 1001 fo. 94.

public, men who served civil society, had, by definition, to be subject to the civil justice that they served. Clerical privilege protected from secular prosecution all the ecclesiastical ranks, not just priests and monks but even, in some places, university students who bore the tonsure. Clerical privilege meant that any cleric who committed an offense was subject solely to Church justice. In many places, this meant lighter punishments. It is no surprise, therefore, that all over Europe men accused of a crime shaved their heads and laid stake to clerical privilege in the hopes of being remanded to a bishop's court. This certainly happened from time to time in Manosque. But Manosquin judges were no fools. They sometimes wrote to the local bishop of Sisteron for proof of the privilege.[31] In Raymon's case, the court required no proof since he waived his clerical protection. The question, however, still lingers: how is it that Raymon was both a notary and a cleric when, under law, he could not be both?

The only possible solution to this problem is that Raymon was not a notary public but rather a bishop's notary. In that case, his profession should be listed in Latin as *notarius episcopi*.[32] Instead, his title and profession were always consistent with those used for public notaries. Nine criminal inquests intended against him are "Against master Raymon Gauterii, notary of Manosque" (*contra magistrum Raymundum Gauterii notarium de Manuasce*). The title of "master," akin to the modern day mister, was always accorded to notaries public. Court scribes, moreover, almost always noted their colleagues' profession as *notarius* in inquest records. So, Raymon's textual appearances in the criminal documents consistently present him as a notary public, not as a bishop's notary.

Whatever his status, Raymon benefitted from his familiarity with the law. It gave him a legal edge in driving a criminal inquisition against Margarida. That same edge allowed him to experiment with questionable juridical tactics, pushing the limits of what was allowable in court, as we shall see in the next chapter. It also helped him outmaneuver his uncle and seize through the courts, but without a full formal civil trial, his dead brother's estate. In short, Raymon's knowledge of the law and of systems of justice was a weapon he used to pursue those whom he opposed or who opposed him.

When I wrote the story of Johan Damponcii's untimely death and the struggle to claim his estate, I made narrative choices: what to tell and what to omit. Now, though, I have suggested how another historian might dwell on the same

---

31 This was the case, for example, in ADBDR 56 H 1009 ff. 103–103 v. For some other examples of suspects claiming clerical privilege see ADBDR 56 H 1009 ff. 58–58 v., and ADBDR 56 H 986 ff. 44 v.–45.

32 Aubenas, *Étude sur le notariat provençal*, 52 et passim.

documents. Through my consideration of the broader legal context, I have also pointed to other viable avenues of investigation. Too often, historians have used legal records without engaging the juridical culture that produced them. The format of my sources, the actions taken by the actors within them, and the force driving their primary antagonist, Raymon Gauterii, were all inherently juridical. While I certainly could have presented the story as a family conflict, without highlighting legal contexts, as I have done with other court tales, this would have obscured the complex legal and cultural realities that allowed me to access the tale in the first place. Though historians are detectives in as much as they sleuth and reconstruct, they have an added responsibility. They must ground interpretation in methodology. In this case, that means learning to read not just the language and paleography of court records but also their internal structure, generative processes, and formulae. The estate battle between the siblings and the uncle contributes to an appreciation of how Roman civil law actually functioned at this time. But legal history is not the only way to deconstruct these texts, and other approaches shine light on different aspects of medieval culture. All historians, to some extent, would begin with similar foundational questions: what does this passage mean; why did the medieval scribe write it this way; how does this connect to the big issues; and so on. Beyond foundations, though, historians diverge. Consider, for example, the sorts of questions an historian of women might put to this case. What about an economic historian interested in gender theory? The quarrel over Johan's estate was inherently gendered. Margarida was entirely absent from the wrangling over her dead spouse's possessions. Everyone who made a claim in court was a man, though Raymon did act on behalf of his sisters. This does not mean, of course, that Margarida's part in all this was done.

PLATE 3.1: The road to Manosque. *Artist's conception of the road to the town showing it surrounded by fields and hills and, in the distance, the foothills of the Alps. Within the town's walls are the former count's palace and its two prominent churches. By the fourteenth century, the palace was the seigneurial home to the Knights of the Hospital of St. John of Jerusalem. Image courtesy of Graham Moogk-Soulis / PostScript Comics.*

CHAPTER FOUR

A Good, Decent, True, and Honest Woman

By this reckoning he is more shrew
than she.

The Taming of the Shrew,
Act 4, Scene 1

4.1   The Verdict

By mid-February, Raymon was running out of options in his quest to ruin Margarida. Judge Rebolli asked him whether he had any further evidence to bring, but he was unprepared and stalled for time. Meanwhile, Ugo de Portu, Margarida's brother, wasted none in petitioning the judge to dismiss the case and to indemnify his sister of Raymon's insinuations. By late February, the judge summoned Raymon's sisters, Beatritz and Catarina, to see where they stood. He also called Johan's paternal uncle, Bartomieu Damponcii. The judge asked if they knew of any evidence against Margarida and whether they intended to take further part in the trial. All responded unanimously and in agreement that they were taking no part in the case, nor did they intend to produce or proffer anything against her, nor did they intend to accuse her of anything. Rather, they held her, and would hold her, as a good, decent, true, and honest woman.[1]

It is no surprise that Bartomieu stood against Raymon. This was the same man whom Raymon had deprived of the inheritance. There had already been a whiff

---

1 ADBDR 56 H 1001 fo. 55 v.

that at least one of the sisters was also not in complete alignment with Raymon, since she had testified to Margarida's good character. The break in the Gauterii and Damponcii clan was now public. Raymon was by this time operating in complete isolation from his family members, all of whom denied him support. Worse still, they endorsed Margarida openly. If Raymon had sought to present himself as the *paterfamilias,* the dominant male in his family whose task it was to protect his dead sibling's interests, the sham was up. His siblings spoke against him and his isolation was now a matter of public record.

In a fit of desperation, Raymon played his last card: he tried to have Margarida tortured. If this final, wild gambit succeeded, he would carry the day. Margarida would be strapped to a wooden horse, her body pulled and stretched, its sinews and muscles torn painfully.

What happened next is a testimony to the political influence of both parties. Somehow, Raymon managed to have the Lord Preceptor of Manosque, Brother Johan Savini, send a copy of the court docket to Aix-en-Provence for a legal opinion on whether Margarida was guilty and whether she could be tortured. We cannot know whether Raymon's influence extended directly to Savini or whether he convinced the judge to ask the preceptor to do this. Either way, the preceptor sent the file to Aix, the royal capital of Provence and home to the most learned jurists in the realm. Savini noted that he still had complete faith in Peire Rebolli, his criminal judge, but he wanted to put to rest any lingering suspicions about Margarida's guilt. For that reason, he wrote to a venerable Aixois jurist, Gaufrido Ganhomini, to ask him to inspect Rebolli's records and to weigh the merits of the case against Margarida. Ganhomini accepted the task and wrote back quickly. His response was blunt and scathing.

Ganhomini's response indicates that he studied the proceedings carefully. He noted that Margarida had not been proven guilty, nor had she confessed. He wrote that in the absence of damning evidence, it was impossible to find for the sentence of torture, since the witnesses for both sides had testified far more in her favor than against. At that point, Ganhomini inserted a dry reminder to the preceptor that witnesses of either party ought to speak only the truth. The implication was that since even the witnesses for the prosecution had upheld Margarida's good character, he was bemused about why the case lingered. Bemused shifted to impatient, though, as Ganhomini became more didactic. He admonished the preceptor as he would a beginning law student and reminded him that the only way for a judge to render a guilty verdict in the absence of a free confession was through the testimonies of two irreproachable witnesses, which this case clearly lacked. Since this was so, and since Margarida came from an honest family (*ex bonis parentibus*), and since she had lived properly with her husband as man and wife, and since she did not prepare the stew but only added some oil in front of several people and with her husband's permission, she must be absolved. Ganhomini instructed that Rebolli must absolve her without any conditions or opposition from anyone, including her husband's relatives (*affines mariti*). On receiving this response, Rebolli duly read it aloud in court. Margarida's agent immediately asked for a copy. Raymon, true to form, filed a motion for a delay.

Raymon had now exhausted all his options. He had tried every juridical tactic possible, pulled every string within reach. To carry on any further would have been a serious insult to the court's honor. The judge refused his request for further delays and summoned Margarida. On 17 March, five full months after the trial began, the court *nuncio* again visited her, this time in the Clarissan convent where she was prisoner, to command her to appear in court the following day to hear the judge's final sentence.

It was mid-afternoon when the judge cleared Margarida's name. He announced that there was insufficient evidence to warrant torture. He confirmed he had taken her good reputation into account, as well as the testimony of Vivas Josep, the physician and surgeon who had examined Johan's corpse and found no evidence of foul play. Rebolli confirmed he had spoken to all the dead man's relatives and that they all, with the exception of Raymon, were inclined to remove Margarida from suspicion. The judge noted that Raymon had presented all his information and evidence and, despite repeated delays, proven nothing. Finally, the judge noted that the case against Margarida had been given grave deliberation and was considered by a council of skilled men. He, therefore, absolved her, declaring her innocent. He instructed the court notary to draw a large X through the record's folios to cancel it. This was the traditional way court scribes signaled that a matter was done. The case was closed.

Just to be safe, Margarida asked for a copy of the official records. This may have been standard legal practice. As it turned out, it was also wise. Though the criminal inquest was complete, Raymon and Margarida were not yet done with one another.

In this chapter, I chose to write the final part of Margarida's adventures before the criminal court in a very direct manner, while still interjecting my own voice and priorities into the telling. I emphasized the breakdown in Raymon's support network, the way he was abandoned by his family, and supposed that this isolation made him frantic. I interpreted my sources to argue that Raymon was the source of the attempt to put Margarida to torture after all the witnesses agreed she was an honest woman, and that these attempts reeked of desperation. For me, as a social historian interested in how people maneuver through society, the relationship and potential tensions between Margarida and Raymon offer an interesting point of departure. I can use them to explore family dynamics, networks of solidarity,

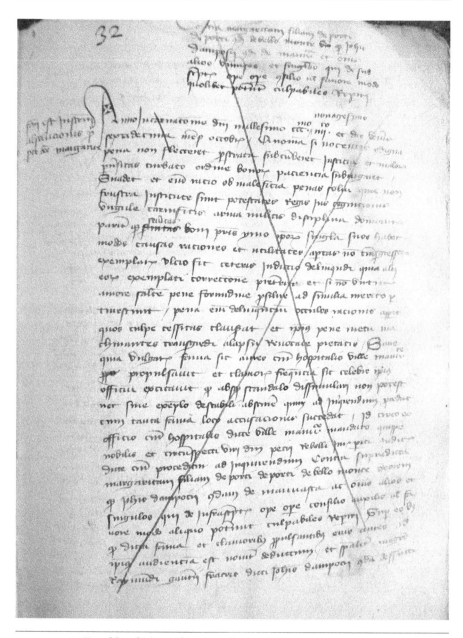

FIGURE 4.1: *First folio of Margarida's criminal inquest. ADBDR 56 H 1001 ff. 32–60, begun 16 October 1394.*

gender norms, and much else. Were I to expand upon this tale, I would draw on language and techniques developed by anthropologists to explain kin structures. This would situate Raymon's family tensions within a pattern of human behavior and give it meaning and relevance.

Were I a political historian, or an historian of crime, there are other elements I would have chosen to stress. Politics and crime might lead me to focus not so much on Raymon's mental state but on other historical factors. Two examples illustrate how subtle choices made by the historian drive the lessons derived from primary sources. First, I begin with the breakdown in established governance structures to show how Margarida's case could frame a discussion on late medieval municipal administration. Second, I use the question of judicial torture to contextualize her trial within a broader discussion of medieval crime, punishment, and bodies.

4.2   Governance

Margarida's case points to an alarming and unusual breakdown in municipal governance. This was a sure sign, no doubt, that hers was a *cause célèbre,* one that prompted the involvement of powerful players normally removed from such affairs. Manosque was a middling town, no large city but equally no small hamlet. Although it had no real visible nobility, outside of some Hospitallers, it did have its potentates and politicos. Most, however, rarely appear in its rather banal criminal trial records. Still, there were people who held power. To understand their position, it is necessary to provide some background. Manosque had a lengthy and convoluted history that shaped how its men shared political power.

There is a long tradition of human settlement in and around Manosque.[2] There were people living there before even the Romans began to cobble together their empire. When Muslim invaders crossed the Straits of Gibraltar in boats in 711, settled Iberia, and gradually made forays across the Pyrenees, Manosque, like other communities, fell victim. We know that sometime around the year 900, Saracen raiders sacked the town. The first written record mentioning *Manoasca* dates from the late tenth century, when Count Guillaume I of Arles expelled the Saracens from Provence. There must have still been Christians in need of shepherding at that time because, by the first quarter of the eleventh century, monks from the great Marseillaise abbey of St. Victor arrived. They came with the blessing of the counts of Toulouse and Provence and with the support of the viscounts of Marseille. There were other sources of religious influence in the town, too: the bishop of Sisteron, into whose diocese Manosque fit, had his local representatives, and clerics from the religious chapter of nearby Forcalquier also settled in Manosque.

It is no surprise that local lords chafed at all this monkish and priestly influence and worked to establish non-religious dominance in the region. The twelfth

---

2 I take it up in fuller detail in Bednarski, *Curia,* chapter 2 *et passim,* and merely repeat the broad lines of the story here.

century saw a redistribution of regional secular power and the creation of a new county, Forcalquier, ruled by a displaced noble house named Urgel that had abandoned Avignon and resettled in the region around Manosque. To complicate matters further, lords from Avignon, Marseille, and even Toulouse shared secular power for decades in Manosque. These noble rulers competed with the Church for municipal influence.

By the first decades of the twelfth century, two brothers shared the title Count of Forcalquier. One, Guigues, had no heirs; the other, Bertrand, had two sons. When Bertrand died, Guigues became sole count. In his last will and testament of 1149, he bequeathed Manosque and some other lands to the Order of the Hospital of St. John of Jerusalem. The Hospitallers had arrived in Provence relatively recently and earned significant respect due to their crusading successes in the Holy Land. Guigues's donation made the Hospitallers seigneur of Manosque and, thus, direct vassal to the Count of Provence. Guigues knew that his family members would not tolerate the alienation of Manosque from their fortune. He maneuvered his brother's sons into accepting the loss by offering them other choice lands. In so doing, he underestimated his brother's widow. As soon as Guigues died, that woman did all she could to contest his will and keep Manosque for her sons. The Hospitallers fought back with an appeal to the pope. Ultimately, they were forced to share power with Guigues's nephews: Manosque now had co-seigneurs. Tensions between these two brothers and the knights endured. In a move that may have been partially retaliatory for a humiliation he suffered at the hands of the Hospitallers, one of the brothers bestowed two unusual privileges upon his subjects.

In 1207, Count Guilhem II, one of Guigues's two nephews, liberated the citizens of Manosque. He elevated them from basically a traditional state of serfdom to the effective status of full burghers, free townspeople. Thanks to his donation, they were now free to buy and sell land and to transmit goods and property to their heirs. Guilhem also bestowed on them important political powers, notably the rights of assembly, representation, and oversight. Then, having empowered the people, he surrendered Manosque entirely to the Hospitallers. He handed them a poisoned apple, content in the knowledge that while the Order now held the town fully, its people were freer than ever before.

At once, the knights attempted to undo what Guilhem had wrought. Though they succeeded in abolishing the consular model of civic governance that had arisen thanks to his gift, they were forced to concede other privileges. Community leaders, hungry for liberty, pushed for even greater concessions, which they obtained in 1234, 1293, and 1316. By 1334, the community was strong enough to re-establish its consuls and assume a greater degree of self-governance.

By the time of Margarida's story, all of this was ancient history, and governance of fourteenth-century Manosque had become a matter of routinized and institutionalized compromise. The knights retained the traditional rights of seigneurial taxation.[3] They also held the old comital rights to dispense high, middle, and low justice.[4] The key, though, was that the knights agreed to administer justice at arm's length. In a formal written agreement with the community of inhabitants, the knights promised to appoint a secular (i.e., non-religious) judge to hear criminal and civil matters. That judge, the *judex ordinarius*, was to hold his office for a period of one year and then vacate it. In 1315, the community pressured the knights to appoint an appeals judge, too. The agreements stipulated that both judges must live outside of Manosque, presumably to retain their neutrality and not become enmeshed in neighborhood or factional politics. This was also the logic behind their one-year terms of office. The principle at play here was simple: the community obtained a promise from its seigneur that judges would not be religious, not directly attached to the Order, and neutral.

All of this political background matters because it explains that when Preceptor Johan Savini, the highest ranking member of the Order, interfered in Margarida's case by writing to see if she could be tortured, he broke with tradition. Interference from the top-ranking administrator in the judiciary constituted a serious rupture with how things were supposed to go. It was highly irregular. Because of this, it must have rankled the town's citizens, especially the more prominent burghers who were accustomed to judicial impartiality. All the signs point to the fact that Raymon made this happen. This shows two things: first, that he was well connected; second, that he overreached. By forcing the preceptor's hand and meddling in justice, community observers must have leapt at the opportunity to thwart him. They did this through a system of checks and balances built into the system precisely to prevent this sort of seigneurial meddling in justice.

Just as the inhabitants of Manosque had the right to elect a municipal council, they also had the right to elect two judicial overseers, called in Latin *probi homines*, literally wise or prudent men. The overseers' task was to ensure that judges adhered to a negotiated list of penalties linked to certain offenses. Manosque was not unique in this regard. One historian of the former county of Forcalquier

---

3 For a full list of taxes owed to the Hospital, see Bednarski, *Curia*, 149.

4 The division of justice into high, middle, and low forms is an old feudal convention. High justice meant high crimes, such as murder or treason. Courts empowered to dispense high justice were originally administered by princes and could mete out death sentences. Over time, important towns and cities earned the right to dispense high justice. Middle and low justice are blurrier terms. Low justice almost certainly referred to the right to prosecute delicts, minor offenses, and so on.

concluded that this type of bicameral governance was a common feature of the county, where

> Syndics [judicial overseers] assisted in simple police matters, but they also enjoyed higher privileges. They were tasked with assisting in tax collection and the publication of *parlements,* and in tribunals, to help guide the judge in the correct application of penalties.[5]

The Manosquin list of negotiated criminal penalties survives today in a document called simply the "Agreement Concerning Wrongdoings" (*Compositionis super maleficiis*).

The day before he read his verdict, Judge Rebolli consulted the two overseers, as he was required to do. Isnardo Teralhi and Isnardo Samoelis were the two community designates, selected as *prud'hommes* and tasked with verifying every judicial sentence. Normally, their role was simply to ensure that judges did not deliver punishments that did not agree with the *Livre des privilèges.* In this case, though, Rebolli actually asked them what they thought about Margarida's case, about the evidence he had gathered, and about the depositions he had collected. The two Isnardos swore a "strong oath" and spoke according to their consciences. They agreed that Margarida was in no way culpable and ought to be acquitted.

Raymon had underestimated how his ploy would play out with the rest of the community. By involving the preceptor, he had invited judicial meddling of the sort intolerable to other community politicos. These players must have leapt at the chance to set things right. There was no way the two overseers could have done anything but confirm emphatically that it was a mistake to consider torturing Margarida.

In my initial synthesis of the events, I glossed over this entire political context. Another historian, though, one interested in making an argument, for example, about the impartiality of medieval justice, could have shifted the focus of the tale away from Raymon and his family problems and made a good case using the political context. This could, in turn, have resulted in a very different tale, one focused on lords and lawyers, not siblings and squabbles.

4.3 Bodies and Torture

There are other paths through which to redirect Margarida's story, and one of them fits into what historians now call the history of bodies. Raymon requested

---

5 Camille Arnaud, *Histoire de la viguerie de Forcalquier,* 360. The translation is my own. In volume 2 of his work, pp. 370–72, Arnaud again states that it was normal for syndics to advise judges throughout the county.

that Margarida be put to bodily torture in the hopes that she would confess to murder. The expert Aixois jurist consulted on this matter replied categorically that she could not be tortured. There were several legal and cultural reasons why this was so.

Legally, torture was a legitimate tool in inquests, though it was rarely used in Manosque. In a sampling of some 1,600 criminal registers, I found five cases where a judge threatened torture and only three where he carried it out. The most striking of these cases involved a female cat burglar. During her interrogation, she admitted she also worked as an unregulated prostitute. To make matters worse, the judge in her case caught her lying under oath. Since, in the judge's eyes, that suspect was a person of ill-repute and dishonest character, she was liable to torture.[6] In Margarida's case, though, all evidence pointed to an honest life. Honesty—more accurately, honor—was key to preserving bodies.

Justinian's Digest preserves the opinion of the ancient Roman jurist Ulpian on torture. In Book 48, Title 18, Ulpian opines that it is customary for torture to be used to uncover crimes but only within limits. First, he says, the Emperor Augustus instructed that judges should not begin their inquests with torture. Second, he says, the Emperor Hadrian decreed that judges ought not to rely solely on torture for evidence. The Roman emperors principally limited torture to slaves and, more specifically, to slaves whose guilt was already suspected. This was because slaves, by definition, had no honor against which to assess their character. They could lie with impunity. Even still, torture of slaves was supposed to be reserved for cases when its absence was the only element hindering conviction. There were various other limitations on the torture of slaves, notably that a slave could not, at least in most cases, be tortured to condemn his master. For the Romans, confessions under torture were less compelling forms of proof than evidence established through investigation. This was because it was rightly thought to be less reliable. Some men, Ulpian noted, would say anything to make the pain stop.

In the Middle Ages, Christianity rendered slavery technically illegal. Far from eliminating torture from courts, though, medieval Christian jurists picked up on honor as the actual determinant of who could be tortured and who could not. Since Margarida was proven, through diligent legal investigation, to be honorable, she was legally protected from torture.

By the late Middle Ages, at least in Manosque, it was far more likely for strangers, or for those who were socially disconnected, to be tortured since their honor

---

6 For the case of Huga Aliberta, cat burglar and prostitute, see Bednarski, *Curia*, 99–101, 104–8, and 174.

was less certain. Anthropologist Julian Pitt Rivers famously wrote that "honour is the value of a man in his own eyes, *but also in the eyes of his society.*"[7] When a person traveled outside his or her "society," it was much more difficult for the natives to evaluate that person's honor. Historian Daniel Lord Smail notes, "the kinless, the foreigner, the immigrant were treated with greater severity than the well-connected or the native." He continues, "Having kith and kin was a sign of respectability, which in turn was rewarded by more lenient treatment."[8] In Manosque, this was certainly true. No Manosquin judge ever tortured a native. The fact that Margarida, a recent immigrant to Manosque, could establish her honorable life is a testament to the degree to which her family had successfully integrated into the local scene. It must inevitably also have spoken to her unimpeachable reputation. Part of the scandal of her trial was that so many people believed her innocent. This was evidence that the community valued her honor highly. Raymon's accusations against someone so clearly respected by the local women, and men, must have rung loudly in people's ears. He sang out of key from the rest.

Just as torture was rare in Manosque, so too was corporal punishment. Manosquin historian Rodrigue Lavoie found 10 cases of corporal punishment between 1289 and 1300.[9] By the fourteenth century, though, these occurrences had all but disappeared. Between 1340 and 1403, only five people paid for their crimes with their bodies. The later medieval court much preferred to collect fines from offenders. It did not lightly cut off limbs; mutilate tongues, noses, or ears; or brand convicted criminals. Though this may appear surprising, given popular notions on the brutality of medieval justice, it fits with what historians have found. To make a broad generality, the later Middle Ages were a relatively bloodless period for secular courts, at least when compared to those of the early modern era. Once the Reformation began, justice became "rougher," to borrow the phrase from two Renaissance historians.[10] There is no question that punishments inflicted on bodies increased as nation-states developed, as justice became centralized and less local, and as Europeans became caught up in confessional politics.

Had Margarida been convicted of poisoning her husband, her fate would have been left entirely up to the judge, and she may well have faced execution

---

7 The emphasis is mine. See Julian Pitt-Rivers, *The Fate of Shechem or the Politics of Sex: Essays in the Anthropology of the Mediterranean* (Cambridge: Cambridge University Press, 1977), 21.

8 Daniel Lord Smail, "Common Violence: Vengeance and Inquisition in Fourteenth-Century Marseille," *Past and Present* 151 (1996): 50–51.

9 Rodrigue Lavoie, "Les statistiques criminelles et le visage du justicier: justice royale et justice seigneuriale en Provence au Moyen Age," *Provence historique* 29 (jan.–fév–mars 1979): 15.

10 David Chambers and Trevor Dean, *Clean Hands, Rough Justice: An Investigating Magistrate in Renaissance Italy* (Ann Arbor: University of Michigan Press, 1997).

or corporal punishment, but we cannot know for certain what penalty he would have ascribed. Killing another person, remarkably, was entirely unregulated in the town's otherwise comprehensive penal agreement. When the inhabitants sat down with their seigneur in 1235 to negotiate the charter that governed delicts (minor offenses) and crimes and fixed appropriate punishments, they remained completely mute on killing. Since this was so, they also offered no local legal guidelines to differentiate between what we would consider deliberate killing (murder in most modern Western jurisdictions) or accidental killing (manslaughter). Even more surprising, the court almost never prosecuted killing. Margarida's poisoning case is one of only a small sample that saw the court prosecute a suspected killer. There are only 11 trials for killing out of the 1,600 I studied. Three began as assault cases, but the victim subsequently died and the judge escalated the charge. Many more cases alleged intended murder, but this phrase is problematic. Court scribes often wrote that someone attacked someone else, deliberately and with intent to kill. This was partly legal formula. Often, the formula concluded that the offender would have committed murder had he or she not been restrained by some bystanders. It was also part of the honor game: public displays of bravado or other forms of posturing helped maintain or augment honor. It was a popular game, and important in the town's honor exchange market, but it was also a game that almost never led to death.

Margarida's trial is unique among the few other inquests for killing in two important ways. First, its charge does not involve a violent crime, and, second, the alleged mode of killing is highly gendered. Poison or magic, her alleged weapons, were both thought to be feminine tools. Honest men were more direct in their use of force. Raymon, by calling Margarida a sorceress or poisoner, slandered her feminine honor. He implied she was weak, pathetic, and sly. All the other cases that involve killing involved men who killed other men by means of force. In one, for example, an assassin beat a Jew to death in front of his synagogue. Another involved a botched robbery of a wealthy Jew. In short, all the other cases that involve a killing resulted from a physical assault between men.

Unlike the gendered nature of the supposed offense, the appearance of the doctor, a man who tended bodies, in a murder trial is not unusual. Doctors appeared as expert witnesses in six of the 11 prosecutions for killing.[11] What is unusual is that in Margarida's case, Vivas Josep, the physician, seems to have been brought in by her family and not by the court. Normally, judges requested expert testimony to help them render accurate verdicts in cases that involved criminal death.

---

11 Steven Bednarski, "Crime, Justice, and Social Regulation in Manosque, 1340–1403," Ph.D. Thesis (Université du Québec à Montréal, 2002), 285, in particular Table 4.7.

There is a way to inscribe Margarida's story into a history of gendered bodies. An historian interested in doing this would necessarily consider the gendered nature of honor and how men and women evaluated one another through the honor exchange. This in turn would lead to an exploration of the law's assessment of personal honor. Torture, the judicial exploitation of bodies to determine veracity, plays its part in this analysis, as does a consideration of potential corporal punishments and even feminized forms of bodily assault. Finally, the involvement of a physician shows the connection between justice and intimate knowledge of bodies. Here, too, we see another way to divert a story of interpersonal tension. Margarida's story could equally have been told as one that shines light on multiple aspects of the history of men's and women's bodies.

For the purposes of my microhistory, this entire context supports how the court determined that Margarida was indeed a good and honest woman. Her legal character was unimpeachable, and this consensus, coupled with the doctor's evidence, compelled Judge Rebolli to render an innocent verdict. Margarida may have been proven to be a good person, but subsequent records allow us to see other aspects of her personality. In the coming pages, I argue that the vindicated Margarida next went on the attack. Observe how I use the documents to build a case for her character to argue that she was proud, courageous, and strong. Keep in mind that this is my historical assessment. Determine whether and to what extent it is an accurate and fair portrayal or a problematic distortion.

4.4 An Honest Widow's Pension?

The archives contain a number of subsequent litigations involving Margarida and Raymon. In general, they are in a poor state of conservation, are out of chronological order, and are highly repetitive.[12] None of this is unusual. Still, even from jumbled sources a story emerges that allows me to know—or to think I know—what happened after the judge declared Margarida innocent.

Six months after the criminal case ended, Raymon continued to do his best to ruin Margarida. Though his efforts in criminal court had failed spectacularly, Margarida was in a vulnerable situation socially and financially. She had her brothers to support her, but she was now a young widow. It remained to be seen whether she could find a new husband. In the meantime, she had limited means to support herself and was a drain on her family's resources. She, thus, with her brothers' support, set out to defend her interests. At some point, they approached

---

12 For these reasons, they make poor and confusing editions and I have chosen not to append them below. Instead, I provide Latin quotations and footnote relevant archival locations.

Raymon and his siblings for a share of the inheritance. When Raymon refused, they took him to court.

In a civil suit dated 2 August 1395, Margarida petitioned the court to order Johan Damponcii's heirs to grant her a widow's pension, called in Latin an *alimentum*.[13] The *alimentum* had its roots in ancient Rome as a form of public welfare. In the first century BCE, Roman politicians implemented a system of free grain for the poor. By the time of Julius Caesar and Augustus, this system had become costly, and later emperors sometimes offered subsidized, rather than free, grain. By the start of the second century, the Emperor Hadrian implemented an *alimentum* system that was essentially state-sponsored welfare for Italian widows and orphans. His scheme disbursed monetary allowances, food, and even educational bursaries to the needy. This was the ancient origin of the *alimentum*.

Several parts of the Digest, that crucial volume of the Roman emperor Justinian's Code of Civil Law, discuss legacies, the special forms of inheritance that testators, people who made wills, could bequeath. Among these special legacies is another sort of *alimentum*, a private or personal *alimentum*. Private *alimenta* were bequeathals left by the deceased to provide sustenance to vulnerable heirs. In that respect, the private *alimentum* followed the same general purpose as the more ancient public *alimentum:* both were forms of social security. The private *alimentum* was a way for families to provide a pension to their loved ones after a primary provider died. It could take the form of food, clothing, or cash equivalents and could be paid out in installments until a child attained his or her majority, or even for life. They could also be left to other vulnerable relatives besides children.[14]

Since Johan died intestate, he did not bequeath a specific *alimentum* to Margarida. This did not prevent her, in August 1395, from seeking the *alimentum* for one year on the grounds that she was "in the state of widowhood, and had mourned, still mourns, and intends to mourn for one complete year, until the anniversary of her husband's death, as is customary for honest women."[15] In essence, Margarida claimed to be in a period of ritual widowhood, one that prevented her from seeking sustenance from another man. Custom, she felt, required her husband's estate to provide for her during that time. Laying a stake on Johan's estate in this manner was a particularly effective strategy. If it succeeded, she gained a portion of

---

13 This civil suit is also stored in ADBDR 56 H 936 unfoliated. It begins with the water-damaged title "*In causa alimentorum Margarite [de Portu . . .] contra heredes et bonorum decetero. . . .*"

14 *Digest* 34.1. For an overview on legacies, see David Johnston, *Roman Law in Context* (Cambridge: Cambridge University Press, 2004), 46–47.

15 ADBDR 56 H 936 unfoliated reads "*cum ipsa Margarida vitam vidualem ac honestam servet servaverit ac servare intendat per anum completum adie obitus dicti condam Johannis ut sua interest et est consuetum per mulieres probis . . . .*"

Raymon's inheritance and material support for one year. She also received further vindication of her honest reputation. As a young marriageable woman, her honor and good name were her currency in the world, and this was a wise investment that would bring financial gain while simultaneously bolstering symbolic capital. Who could fault her for not attending her husband's funeral if she mourned so properly and for so long? In addition to bringing sustenance, the widow's *alimentum* would settle any lingering doubts about her honor while allowing her a public ritual of devotion. Of course, there is also the possibility that her actions were purely sincere, not merely tactical or theatrical. Most likely there were elements of both behind the move.

Margarida's brother, Peire, chaplain and priest, presented her request for the *alimentum*. Raymon responded in court and asked for time to consult legal experts. The judge refused him. Raymon, in a pique, informed the court that there were no adequate legal experts in Manosque to advise him and that the time frame imposed by the judge was sufficiently tight to "throttle justice." He filed an immediate appeal.

At that point, common sense prevailed and the parties met out of court to explore options. Two of the heirs agreed to pay Margarida their share of the *alimentum*. On 25 August, Peire Rebolli, the judge of first instance against whom Raymon had filed his appeal, urged Raymon to stop his bickering. Rebolli said to Raymon, "Come to an agreement about the *alimentum*, since you are the only one of Johan's heirs not to have agreed to it."[16] The agreement to which Rebolli referred seems to have been brokered by one of Margarida's supporters, a man who was possibly charged with overseeing her legal as well as financial well-being, the notary Nicolau Attanulphi. Attanulphi and his supporters first persuaded Peire Rufferii, who was married to one of Margarida's former sisters-in-law, Beatritz, to put money down toward an *alimentum* payment. Rufferii and Attanulphi agreed to place the pension in trust with the brothers minor, Franciscans who maintained a monastery in Manosque. Rufferii deposited wheat, spelt, oats, wine, and one frank with them on behalf of his wife, Beatritz. He did this with the caveat that if, in future, a court decided that Margarida was not owed an *alimentum*, then she must repay Beatritz in cash. Judge Rebolli, the judge from the original criminal case, was present and reminded Raymon of all this. He watched Raymon capitulate and voluntarily place one hand upon the Gospels, the other upon his chest, and swear to pay his share of the *alimentum*.

---

16 ADBDR 56 H 936 unfoliated, ". . . *Petrus Rebolli dixit dicto magistro Raymundo Gauterii prevaleret quod concorderetur de omnibus et de alimentis et de omnibus aliis, quia omnis alii heredes dicti condam Johannis Damponcii se concordaverunt preter vos* . . . ."

But Raymon lied. Despite his public oath, he was canny and withheld his share of the deposit. Once the parties separated, Raymon re-evaluated his options. Part of his hesitation may have been a concern that Margarida would ask for more support later on. He may have known, as a trained notary, that the ancient Roman jurist Ulpian had opined that if a testator did not impose a time limit on a legacy, then it should be granted for life.[17] Whether Margarida and her brothers knew this, or intended to make a subsequent request for support at a later date, is lost to time. Regardless, for whatever reasons, Raymon decided to renege on his oath and appeal the decision. In the meantime, he withheld the money from Margarida.

Two months later, in November 1395, the judge of first appeals, Fortunat Reynaudi, entertained Raymon's appeal on the grounds that Margarida was technically unable to have sued for her *alimentum* since she was a legal minor. In order to act in court, people had to have reached a certain age. Raymon told the court that, by all appearances, Margarida was less than 25 years old, the full age of majority in Roman law.[18] He argued that since she was a minor, she should not have been allowed to bring suit against him and that he should not be liable for any of the expenses resulting from her *alimentum* lawsuit.

The age of majority was more complex in Roman law than it is today since, for the ancient Romans, there were three stages of minority. Young children, those under the age of seven, were *infantes,* infants. Children between seven and puberty were *impuberes,* youths. Romans set the official age of puberty at 14 for boys and 12 for girls. These ages were fixed and not necessarily grounded in personal biological development. Infants and youths required special care under law and were subject to the power of their fathers or, in the absence of fathers, tutors. People between legal puberty and age 25, however, were considered *puberes,* adults. But though adult, *puberes* were still technically legal minors. They did not attain full legal majority until their twenty-fifth birthday. Adult *puberes* (people between 12 or 14 and 25) had many of the freedoms of older men and women but still required some legal oversight to protect their interests. They were not subject to tutors, like infants and youths, but special curators, caretakers, or guardians could protect their property.

Margarida responded to Raymon's objection by calling it "frivolous" and stating that she was a legally emancipated woman who had attained her majority. She told the judge she was about 15 or 16 years old (*ipsa sit mulier sui juris et maior anorum XV vel XVI*). She also endorsed all the actions taken on her behalf by her procurators, especially Johan de Selhono. Finally, she told the court about

---

17 *Digest* 34.14.
18 *Codex* 6.45.5.

the agreement Attanulphi made on her behalf with the three heirs to pay her an *alimentum*. This was the crux of her defense: Raymon and the others had already promised to pay the *alimentum*. Raymon had no business appealing the case since the out-of-court settlement bound him.

The judge was perplexed, not knowing Margarida's exact age nor having known there had been a prior out-of-court settlement to pay her a pension. He asked Margarida her precise age. She, in good medieval fashion, swore she did not know exactly. This was probably an honest response and not game playing, though it may have been. Margarida was old enough to marry. Raymon had never raised that objection about her union to his dead brother. People in the Middle Ages, however, had a different sense of time. They remembered important life events relationally. Someone was born in the summer that people saw a comet in the night's sky, which was 10 harvests ago. Someone else was born the winter of the pestilence, which was now 18 years past. For the bulk of the human population, age was approximate and largely dependent upon recollection and observation. Raymon knew this and, seizing upon the evidence of Margarida's young face, demanded that the judge ask her brothers for sworn proof of age since, as her closest living relatives, they were most likely to know.

The judge also asked Raymon whether he had agreed to pay the *alimentum* privately. On this point, Raymon dissembled: It was so long ago! Who can remember? Those witnesses she brings forth are talking about an event that happened ages ago! I question their memories, too! Eventually, the appellate judge was forced to summon the other men present at the agreement. Attanulphi, Margarida's defender, swore Raymon had promised to pay the *alimentum*. Eventually, so did Rufferii, who was married to Raymon's sister, Beatritz, who said he was "content to pay the *alimentum* through the agreement on condition that, in case it was not required by law, he would receive it back."[19] Even Rebolli, the judge in the original case, testified that Raymon had sworn in his presence to pay the *alimentum*.

The appeals case dragged on thanks to Raymon. He raised procedural objections at every turn. First, he protested loudly when the appeals judge was called away on business and subrogated the court's subvicar to serve as vice-judge in his absence. Raymon questioned the subvicar's competency. He then objected to Margarida's defense (*patrocinum*) on the grounds that he suspected its veracity. The subvicar told him that if he truly had such serious doubts about the truthfulness of her claim, then he should submit a formal libel against her. He did not. Next Raymon objected whenever Margarida appeared in court to respond to

---

19 "*Petrus Rufferii contentus erat dictum alimentum solvere cum pacto quod eo casu quo de jure non deberentur quod illud ^quod^ solveret de ipsis alimentis reciperet deberet . . . .*"

questions on the grounds she was too young to answer them. The judge found this objection "frivolous and inane" (*frivolem et inanem*). Raymon then disappeared for a spell. This forced the court to go through the lengthy process of issuing three formal public summonses for his return. When he eventually reappeared, he explained he was kept from returning to Manosque because of the dangers of the road (*ob quodam propter viarum pericula*). To stall further, he withheld documents necessary to the trial. At one point, he presented the claim that since Margarida was not pregnant or breastfeeding, and since she had abandoned his brother for a month, he should be absolved of having to pay her a shilling. He added that she should pay his legal expenses. Throughout all these delays and protests, the judge grew impatient. The transcript conveys his frustration through notations in which he stated he wanted the parties to conclude their arguments so that he might render sentence in a timely manner.

All of this resulted in an appeal that lasted far longer than it should have. Raymon notified the lower court of his intention to appeal on 5 August. The parties reached their informal settlement later that month. The appellate judge heard opening arguments for the appeal on 16 November. The case continued throughout the autumn and winter. In February both sides were exhausted and strained financially. They agreed to submit their dispute to two arbitrators, masters Johan Autrici and Jacme Simonis. But here Margarida dissented. She had had enough.

At the thought of handing her case over to two new arbitrators, Margarida balked. She appeared in person before the appeals judge and threw herself on his mercy. She protested the abandonment of the formal legal case and uselessness of the whole process. She implored the goodness of his office, saying she was merely a poor woman and that these things had proven very expensive to her. She asked him, once and for all, simply to pass sentence.

This plea did not sit well with Margarida's procurator, Johan de Selhono. In a surprising break with his client that signals the limits of Margarida's legal agency in all this, he also appeared before the judge. He requested "once, twice, three times, and many times that Margarida observe that which he, Johan, promised and swore in her name, namely to attend her so that Johan Autrici and Jacme Simonis know about this case." Basically, he wanted the judge to order Margarida to heed his counsel.

She would not. Margarida responded that she would not do what he wanted, since she did not trust the two men commissioned to determine her fate. She said "their knowledge was greatly turned to her detriment" (*Quia vertitur cognitio dictorum comissarorum in magnum dampnum ipsius Margarite*). The judge, faced with this break in Margarida's side, announced he would proclaim a sentence at vespers. Sunset was as dramatic a time as any to settle this duel.

The empty space left by the court notary for the judge's sentence remains blank to this day. For whatever reason, the judge did not rule. Worse, though the records are damaged and badly disorganized, a faded and water-stained date suggests that in April the parties were still presenting arguments. Raymon protested that by that time, Margarida's witnesses were giving testimony about the agreement to pay her *alimentum* that allegedly took place "eight or ten months earlier."

This appeal, which began in August and carried over at least until April, contains no resolution or verdict. Whether Margarida succeeded in obtaining her *alimentum* or whether Raymon succeeded in preventing her from drawing a pension from his family remains unknown. More holes in history. What is known is that Margarida and her faction were dogged, if not always united, in their struggle against Raymon. Equally evident is the extent to which Raymon was willing to draw things out to prevent her from ever seeing a shilling of support from her dead husband's estate.

4.5   Margarida's Defamation Suit

In February 1396, the same month that both parties agreed to seek arbitration in the *alimentum* suit, Margarida's faction attempted a parallel litigation against Raymon. No doubt the two suits are connected, simultaneous strategies aimed at a common purpose: to seek social and financial redress from Raymon for wrongs inflicted upon Margarida.

On 23 February 1396, Margarida did not rely on lawyers or male relations to make her case. She appeared before Judge Rebolli at terce, the third hour of prayer for monks and other medieval religious. Terce was first thing in the morning for the court, the start of the new business day, around 9:00 a.m. in our terms. There she was, at the earliest possible hour, standing newly vindicated before the judge who had exonerated her. Her presence, in person, is important, because it speaks to her resolve. The court record notes that she appeared before Rebolli "with the consent, license, and authority of master Nicolau Attanulphi, notary, and Johan de Selhono, her procurator."[20] These men were empowered still to act on her behalf, but still she spoke in her own voice, not through theirs.

Over several days, Margarida demanded that the court summon Raymon to respond to a set of accusations. Despite repeated summonses by the court *nuncio* and his trumpet, Raymon did not appear. Eventually, Margarida expressed her frustration in the form of a personal objection, noting the costs she incurred by repeatedly appearing with counsel and demanding that the judge declare Raymon

---

20 ADBDR 56 H 936 unfoliated dated 23 February 1396, "*ymo cum concensu licentia et auctoritate magistri Nicolay Attenulphi notarii et Johannis de Selhono curatoris.*"

contumacious. This form of guilt *in absentia* brought a steep fine since it implied contempt of court. At one point, in the midst of Raymon's summonses, Margarida also submitted a paper schedule. That document, copied carefully into the court's transcript, explains her case against Raymon.

Margarida's schedule, drawn up by one of her male supporters, alleged character defamation. It said that Raymon Gauterii, her deceased husband's uterine brother, "with audacity and wickedness, had greatly defamed her, inflicted a grave injury upon her reputation, given a serious wound to her good name. Through insinuations and denunciations, he had denigrated her in court, saying she was an impious woman who had murdered her husband through sorcery or poison."[21] These insinuations, her schedule stated, led the court to launch a humiliating criminal investigation against her. To compensate for the damage done to her reputation and the loss to her patrimony, she sued Raymon for the enormous sum of 350 gold florins, which included her court costs. She urged the judge to avoid a formal libel suit and to impose instead an immediate tax upon Raymon.

Raymon disappeared. This is good indirect proof of his isolation in the community, if not his guilt. At one point, the judge located a former lawyer who had represented Raymon and asked whether that man intended to defend Raymon in this new matter. The lawyer, an old ally of Raymon's, pled ignorance and declined. Later, Raymon's son, Little Johan, arrived in court to say his father was out of town at that moment. The boy nevertheless requested copies of all the records to bring to his father. Margarida cried foul. Once again, without using an intermediary, she spoke directly to the judge in her own voice and on her own authority: "This boy cannot be heard in court!" she protested. "He is a child, seemingly younger than 15!" Margarida learned from her adversary and turned Raymon's tactics against him. This was a valid appeal, the very same one Raymon had attempted against her in her *alimentum* suit. Again she pressed the judge to condemn Raymon *in absentia*, stating that he was hiding in a place called Lunio and was unlikely to return for the trial. And then the record stops suddenly.

---

21 ADBDR 56 H 936 unfoliated, a page beginning with the date, Saturday 26 February, under the heading *"Tenor dicte cedule loco libelli preducte,"* literally reads: *"Raymundum Gauterii notarium dicte ville fratrem uterinum dicti condam Johannis que dictum magistrum Raymundum sua audacia et malicia presumptive motus et in magnam diffamationem et atrocem injuriam nec non in maximam lesionem laudabilis nominis et fame ipsius Margarite et ejus ^boni^ nominis denigratione dictam curiam informavit ejus* [crossed out: *que*] [crossed out: *nu*] *clamoribus precendentibus contra ipsam Margaridam et informationes quam plurias ad modum denunciationis dedit in ipsa curia contra eandem Margaridam quod ipsa Margarida tanquam mulier neque et impia repentive? mitendo interficere dictum ejus maritum fachioris quam plures parare debuit ipsi marito suo et pocula illicita et venona eidem dare ipse Johannes dies suos extremos clausit et mortem subiit corporaliter."*

Three years later, the transcript resumes. Some things had changed, others remained the same. A note from May 1399 indicates that the defamation suit was still, shockingly, pending. Margarida was fierce and determined, Raymon slippery as ever. He had avoided her defamation suit for 39 months. In the meanwhile, she had remarried, proof that her life carried on despite problems with Raymon. By 1399, the court scribe called her "Margarida de Portu, wife of Antoni Barbarini and widow of Johan Damponcii." But even a supportive new husband and family could not advance her case. Though better integrated into the Manosquin landscape than ever before, legally at least, she was stalled. There are no statistics that track how long the average civil suit lasted, but this one appears to have dragged on abnormally. The court, noting that the matter was "from a very long time ago" (*dudum*), issued fresh summonses for Raymon.

At last the villain returned. Instead of answering Margarida's accusations, he played the legal scholar: "I deny that Peire de Portu is Margarida's procurator, and, if he is, let him produce an official document attesting to his legal powers" (*magister Raymundus Gauterii negare dictum dominum Petrum esse procuratorem dicte Margarite . . . [et] petit . . . instrumentum publicum*). Margarida, the record tells us, immediately proved and ratified the oaths sworn by her brother confirming him as her legal counsel. Raymon shifted tactics. He still refused to respond to Margarida's charges and instead claimed the entire process was on shaky grounds, since, if she lost, she would be unable to cover his court costs. This, he said, was a very weighty and costly litigation (*sit magni ponderis et expensis*). He refused to proceed until Margarida provided sufficient sureties that she was able to cover the costs. Margarida, he pointed out, was, after all, a poor woman with no possessions in Manosque (*sit pauper et nulla possideat bona in villa Manausce.*) The judge agreed. Undeterred, Margarida offered up her new husband, Antoni Barbarini, and her supporter, the notary Nicolau Attanulphi, as guarantors. They swore upon the Gospels to abide by all the responsibilities imposed by canon and civil law. Raymon still groused, "Nicolau Attanulphi owns nothing in Manosque!" Worse, "all the wise old men of Manosque know the public rumor of how Nicolau Attanulphi sold or alienated 50 gold *scuti* from his wife's dowry."[22] This was a very serious offense. Husbands received dowries from their wives at marriage and, according to Roman law, were responsible for maintaining or, when possible, growing them. Dowries were meant to be married women's financial safety nets should disaster strike. If women were widowed, dowries were a

---

22 ADBDR 56 H 936 unfoliated " . . . *quod pro quinquagentis scutis aurei ipse magister Nicolau non restitueret uxor sue bona dotalia que vendidit et alienavit et hoc est publicosum et famosum per antiquos homines ville Manuasce.*"

means of support. If not, they were designated as protected wealth destined for a woman's children. Historian Julius Kirshner has shown that in late medieval Italy, courts even allowed some wives to sue their husbands to regain independent control of their dotal wealth. Everywhere dowry culture existed in the northwestern Mediterranean, courts of Roman law took seriously the problem of husbands squandering wives' dotal assets.[23] If Raymon were correct, and Attanulphi had no possessions and was desperate enough to spend his wife's dowry money, then this was good grounds not to allow him to stand surety for Margarida.

For a time, Raymon's tactics succeeded, but this would not last. The judge, after insisting that Margarida prove she could afford the potential costs of this lawsuit, surprised Raymon by demanding the same of him. If she were to offer guarantors, so must he. Margarida's brother, Peire de Portu, leapt at this. "Notwithstanding the frivolous objections alleged by master Raymon" (*non obstantibus exeptionibus frivolis per ipsum alegatis*) about Attanulphi, which Peire and Margarida intended to disprove, they asked the lord judge to compel Raymon to provide his own guarantors and to respond to the libel. Peire pushed on: "out of reverence for the lord judge . . . I present Rixenda, wife of Johan Barbarini, the deceased father of Antoni Barbarini, Margarida's new husband."[24] Margarida, ever adept at drawing people to her cause, had convinced her new mother-in-law to offer her wealth up as surety to satisfy Raymon's demand and force him to respond to her charges. Raymon tried a similar tactic against the mother-in-law, claiming Rixenda owned nothing in Manosque except her dowry. Having had enough, the judge called in three prominent local men. He made them swear upon the Gospels and asked them, point blank, whether master Attanulphi, Antoni Barbarini, Margarida, and Rixenda could together offer sufficient guarantees to cover a cost of 100 gold scudis. The local dignitaries all swore that this group was more than sufficient. Antoni Suavis, the lord judge, finally insisted that Raymon appear the following Saturday with his own guarantors and prepared to respond to Margarida's charges. Failure to do so would lead Suavis to declare Raymon contumacious, in contempt of court and subject to strict judicial penalties.

Some of the greatest frustrations in working with archival records are the gaps. I could find no resolution to Margarida's defamation case. The record simply stops at that point. Did Raymon ever appear with guarantors and respond to the

---

23 Julius Kirshner, "Wives' Claims against Insolvent Husbands in Late Medieval Italy," in *Women of the Medieval World: Essays in Honor of John H. Mundy*, ed. Julius Kirshner and Susanne F. Wemple (Oxford: Basil Blackwell, 1985), 256–303.

24 ADBDR 56 H 936 unfoliated "*ob reverenciam ipsius domini judicis licet non teneatur de jure iterato cautionem dare et cavere ad quod faciendum obtulit et presentat Ricenda uxor Johannis Barbarini condam patris Anthonii Barbarini mariti Margarite antedicte . . . .*"

charges? Did Judge Suavis accept his guarantors? Did Raymon find another tactic to stall, or did he once again flee to Lunio? We will never know.

Though the narrative rupture annoys, Margarida's three-year actions against Raymon are telling. They prove beyond a doubt the extent to which this young woman was able to integrate herself into the Manosquin social fabric and draw supporters. Any taint from her criminal trial—a fact she emphasized in her defamation suit—or any stigma from her infirmity, or even Johan's death, did not prevent Antoni Barbarini from marrying her. Nor did these things prevent her from forming such a good relationship with Barbarini's mother that Rixenda was willing to place her dowry on the line to support Margarida's claim. The libel suit confirms what was only suggested in the criminal case: Margarida was young, but she was strong, supported, and liked. She was also resourceful and fearless. Though she had the support of her brothers and a lawyer in court, she often chose to speak for herself, even raising objections in her own voice.

None of this is surprising to historians who read records from this time and place, but all of it is out of line with how most people think of medieval women. Popular conceptions wither when held up to the light of historical scrutiny. Premodern women, though in many ways players in a patriarchal world, were not disempowered. Certainly, they had to worry about sexual, legal, and financial matters in a manner different than young men. But a young woman like Margarida, from a humble background, still had considerable space in which to move, think, act, and speak. One of the main differences between men and women was the way they accessed wealth.

Though neither Margarida's attempts to obtain damages for slander nor her attempts to win a pension convey an outcome, her story is not entirely without a conclusion. Deeper excavations in the archive allow us to know a little more about the life and times of this woman once accused of using magic or poison to kill her mate.

CHAPTER FIVE

Pieces of a Life

"Good humour is the health of the soul, sadness its poison."
—*Lord Chesterfield (1694–1773)*

5.1   Archival History

It is a happy irregularity, supported by diligent excavations, that I know something of what became of Margarida de Portu after her time in court. This is usually impossible. I have read thousands of criminal and civil cases and am almost never able to see the protagonists, except sometimes from the most limited of glimpses, beyond their surviving historical "moment." I keep a list of interesting individuals in the hopes of stumbling across additional traces of their lives in the archives. For years, for example, I have tracked the midwife Bila Fossata. She testified for Margarida, but she plays a more prominent role in another trial I studied elsewhere, and she made occasional appearances in court.[1] I know she was an important public figure, and I suspect her life story could illuminate the role of public midwives in the later Middle Ages, a topic in desperate need of elaboration. Despite my best efforts, I have no idea who she was or how she lived. Bila's story is typical and truncated. Margarida's is not.

This chapter demonstrates the benefits and limitations of a particular historical methodology, archival investigation. Just as there are many different theoretical approaches that guide historians, each informing the questions they ask, and different

---

1 Bednarski, *Curia,* 96–97 *et passim.*

genres of historical writing, so too are there a variety of working methods. Historians develop different methods to gather their evidence and explore, elaborate, prove, and promote their arguments. Some historians study midden or garbage remains to recreate diet and food sources, others look at coin deposits to recreate trade routes. Emerging technologies sometimes open up new methodological avenues. Today, for example, environmental and medical historians retrace the routes of pathogens, such as bubonic plague, through physical evidence stored in skeletal tooth pulp. The vast majority of historians, however, study written primary sources, that is, the texts left behind by past societies. Even then, techniques vary since not all texts are of a uniform sort; the method of collecting and accessing source data depends upon the source. The techniques of manuscript history, the study of handwritten books stored in libraries, differ from those of epigraphy, the study of inscriptions on stones or monuments, and both require skills and techniques that are distinct from archival investigation.

Archival investigators, microhistorians among them, face a particular challenge since their texts are often less well organized, less thoroughly cataloged, and far more numerous than, say, individual manuscripts. In Paris, to use a famous example, everyday written records from the late Middle Ages are stored in boxes stuffed with loose papers. Historians who study such texts spend months sifting through the sheets, making notes of interesting texts. From there, they begin to formulate a topic of inquiry. Or they must sift through box after box in search of a single type of document or reference. Only sometimes do they find what they require. In the south of Europe, in Provence and Italy, there are no boxes. There, medieval notaries and clerks bound their everyday records into books called cartularies or registers, whose contents vary widely. For Manosque, Margarida's adoptive home, some notarial registers are collections of every single contract or act drawn up by an individual man over a period of time; others are collections of contracts and acts drawn up by several men. In no cases do registers contain thorough tables of contents, indices, or subject headings. The research task of the medieval microhistorian who wishes to extract data from the registers is to sift and to note.

Archival investigation is slow and tedious, although it has been made easier, in large part, thanks to computers. For my book on criminal trials, I read roughly 1,600 court records. I compiled a database that listed all common features (accused person's name, sex, profession, place of residence, charges, verdicts, witnesses' names, sex, professions, etc.). Ninety per cent of the trials I processed were repetitive and anecdotally uninteresting to my study. From my cumulative database, however, I was able to generate criminal statistics: how many men committed assault, how many women stole, how many Jews denounced crime, and so on. Whenever I encountered a trial of potential interest, I transcribed it fully in

Latin into my word processor and made notes in English. By the time I completed my study, my word processor file was nearly 900 pages long and fully searchable. This method took years. Very gradually, it allowed me to transform single uninteresting pieces of data into relevant information. More importantly, it helped me make connections: to see trends in judges' sentences, identify repeat offenders, deduce gendered patterns of behavior, and reconstruct networks of solidarity and relationships between people and groups. I slowly made connections because of my methodology.

A similar method, reading through hundreds of pages of everyday records in search of references to people in her circle, offers an epilogue to Margarida's tale.[2] This method shows that the de Portu family name appears not just in court records but also in municipal council deliberations, taxation records, and private notarized acts such as dowry contracts and final testaments. Individually, these references offer little of immediate interest. Compiled together, they paint a limited picture of how things went for Margarida after her protracted quarrel with Raymon. If not for the survival of this additional information, the rest of Margarida's story would, as is far more usual, remain lost. Thankfully, that is not the case. The cumulative evidence available through supplemental archival records affords me a unique opportunity. For once, my narrative has a conclusion.

Even in writing Margarida's conclusion, though, I make choices. Not all of the information I can extract from municipal council records, notarized testaments and dowry contracts, or tax records, fits comfortably with the story I wish to tell. Ultimately, narrative form constrains as much as it liberates. To conclude Margarida's tale, I focus on the state of her family in the second half of her life. While the documents allow for other sorts of inquiries, I consciously set them aside. Absent from my narrative conclusion is an analysis of the extant data on tax rates, which provide indications about the levels of wealth for the men in Margarida's circle. Had I wished to conduct a comprehensive survey of the taxation records, I could have used this information to locate Raymon and Johan in relation to other ratepayers. This seemed to me unhelpful to Margarida's conclusion. Similarly, the archival records provide insights into habitation patterns and integration that do not fit easily with my tale. I could have used them to study how immigrants settled into new homes. The late-fourteenth-century archival records for the de Portu family identify members as being "from Beaumount," that alleged place of scandal, to recall Raymon's phrase. In the first decades of the fifteenth century, however,

---

2 I am deeply endebted to Andrée Courtemanche, who conducted much of the preliminary archival excavation and compiled a dossier of notes on the de Portu, Gauterii, and Damponcii clans. She generously shared it with me for the purpose of this book.

the records begin to identify the de Portus as "inhabitants of Manosque" and, eventually, to identify their children as coming purely "from Manosque." Within two generations, the de Portus successfully integrated to become local citizens. They cleansed themselves of alterity's stain and of the suspicion associated with foreigners. Since this is only of tangential interest to Margarida's tale, I chose not to pursue a study of migration and integration. Finally, the Manosquin municipal council's deliberations record which members of the de Portu, Gauterii, and Damponcii families were elected to local government. Council status indicated some degree of community support and respect. It might be interesting elsewhere to show how levels of wealth and community integration related to political office. I do none of these things here. Instead, I proceed to relate how I believe the archives preserve aspects of Margarida's later life and death.

5.2   Beyond Court Records

After trials came different kinds of labors. Margarida had five babies, four girls and a boy. Even epilepsy and a celibate first marriage did not prevent her from having children. Her daughters—Catarina, Joveneta, Johanna, and Bartolomea— grew up with a strong maternal role model, a woman surrounded and supported by family. Her son they called Johan. It was a common enough name but one that also paid quiet tribute to the former husband whose heart stopped that day in 1394 and whose family had defended her against one of its own. Johan paid a different tribute to the other man who had shaped her life when she first came to Manosque by following in the path chosen by his Uncle Peire. Margarida's brother was a deacon when Raymon accused her of poison and sorcery, and he sheltered and protected her in a religious cloister. Later in life, he took full vows to become a local priest. It was only fitting that Margarida's only son, like her brother, should lead the life of the cloth.

The father of her children was Antoni Barbarini, her second husband. He took her in, provided for her at the height of her conflicts, and helped battle Raymon. Antoni and Margarida were married at least by 1398, that is, within a few years of Raymon's accusations of poison and sorcery. They grew their family until, by 1428, Antoni had passed away, leaving Margarida once again a widow. Her second marriage lasted over 30 years and left her far more secure than her first. By the time she was widowed the second time, Margarida was a mature woman with access to stable assets. There was neither need nor want for her ever to marry again. And so she did not.

Old age did not soften her resolve and, even as a widow in her fifties, she lost none of her spirit. In 1428, she and her son Johan, the priest, sued another family member in civil court.[3] The quarrel was again over money. Margarida's ire was this time directed against a son-in-law, Johan Martini, who had married Bartolomea. Mother and son worried that Martini was squandering matrimonial assets that Margarida and her dead husband had invested in the young couple. They argued in a civil suit that Martini should protect the family patrimony, not endanger it. Ultimately, the case was handed over for arbitration to four men: the vicar of St. Sauveur Church, a priest of the priory of Villemus, a local syndic, and a notary from Digne. Johan did not trust his mother's interests to laymen and made certain there were two fellow clerics to decide the matter.

There were other heartaches, too, not the least of which was the loss of two brothers. Margarida was one of at least seven siblings, but it was her brothers who kept special watch over her. Her defender in the poison case, the priest Peire de Portu, she lost in midlife. Peire's testament of 1415 notes that he was then of unsound body (*egra corpore*). This notation in itself is no guarantee that he died immediately thereafter; people did recover from illness. But it is likely that he perished around that time, given the absence of any subsequent references and of a later testament. He asked to be buried in the graveyard of the Church of St. Sauveur, where other priests were laid to rest. Like all good priests, he bequeathed money for his funeral but also a florin to pray for the souls in purgatory and another for a mass. To a nephew, not Margarida's son but rather their brother's, he left a blue shirt and his breviary. This little prayer book was a gift should the boy follow him into the priesthood. If not, Peire asked that the breviary be sold and the money used for masses for his soul. He acknowledged he owed 20 florins to Sister Maria, his relation, the Clarissan nun who had also helped shelter Margarida from the court 20 years earlier. Peire the priest and Maria the nun were cousins as well as co-religionists and helped each other out from time to time. Peire left some grain to Margarida and Guilhema, his sisters, and canceled their debts with him. He also left Margarida his red robe. To his brother, Bartomieu de Portu, he left his dark-haired workhorse. He named his brothers, Guilhem, Onorat, and Bartomieu, equal co-heirs to the rest of his estate. Missing from the list was his remaining brother, Ugo, who almost certainly had predeceased him. By mid-life, therefore, Margarida had outlived two of her brothers. She lost a third, Onorat, by 1442.

Due to their difference in age, Margarida almost certainly also outlived her tormentor, Raymon. At the time of her criminal trial, she was a young woman of about 16 years of age, Raymon much older. He was already practicing as a notary

---

3 The civil suit is in 2885 fo. 84 dated 10 June 1428.

34 years before the criminal trial,[4] which means he was already well into his fifties when he accused Margarida of murder. We can only wonder how she felt,
outliving him, knowing she breathed, ate, and laughed, while he lay cold and buried. Was there satisfaction to be had there? Perhaps. When exactly Raymon died
remains a mystery, though if he were about three decades older than Margarida,
then he must surely have predeceased her by many years. Raymon did make a testament, but he redacted it four years before Johan, his half-brother, dropped dead
of a heart attack. This early and incomplete testament of 1390 survives. From it,
we learn the name of the Gauterii patriarch, another Guilhem. He sired Raymon,
Catarina, and Beatritz, but not their brother Johan. The siblings, recall, shared
a mother and not a father. So we may surmise that their mother remarried after
Guilhem Gauterii's death. Raymon's testament does not, alas, name the mother
whose blood flowed through all four siblings' veins. It does mention Raymon's
wife, Matheuda, and their son and two daughters. It names Matheuda executor
over all Raymon's goods, so long as she remain a widow, and requires that she
make an inventory of his possessions. It also provides for their daughters and
requires Matheuda to oversee an endowment until their son reached the age of 25
and then to provide from it an annual salary. Out of filial devotion, Raymon asked
to be buried next to his father. Finally, he requested that a religious donation be
made from his estate, in the form of sacks of wheat, to redeem the sins he had
committed in life. He instructed his executors and heir that, if they were merciful,
they would in no way attempt to alter that religious donation. If they did so, he
warned, God's wrath would descend upon them.[5] Even as a young man contem-
plating his ultimate days and the state of his eternal soul, Raymon was vengeful.

The archives show that Margarida reached a ripe old age, outlasted loved ones
and rivals alike, and remained strategic to the very end. This ordinary woman,
who observed young the chaos caused by an intestate death, wisely dictated her
own testament on 20 August 1450.[6] If Margarida were, as she claimed, 16 when
Raymon accused her of poisoning Johan, then she was about 72 years old in 1450
when she recorded her last wishes, an extraordinary lifespan for a woman of
this time.

---

4 Archives départementales des Alpes de Haute Provence (henceforth simply ADAHP), Series 2 E,
   register 2840 dated 17 November 1360 has Raymon serving as procurator for a woman named
   Laura, the wife of Ugo Barbe.
5 ADAHP 2 E 3805 fo. 38 v. dated 14 August 1390. The warning reads *Ita quod si esset carestia[ra]
   nullo modo herede mei mitigare possint dictam donam neque valeant et si contrarium facerent ira
   Dei veniat super eis.*
6 The testament is in ADAHP 2 E 2896 unfoliated dated 20 August 1450.

At the end of her life, Margarida de Portu contemplated the importance of home and family. She asked to be buried not in her natal village beside her ancestors, nor with her first husband, but in her second husband's tomb in the cemetery beside the Church of St. Sauveur. Antoni had stood by her under trying circumstances and had given her children and security. It was fitting she should ask to be laid to rest beside him. At the time of her testament, her children were likely all still alive, a blessing to any parent. To her daughter Johanna, she bequeathed 10 florins and some clothes; to her daughter Bartolomea, she left five florins and some other things; to her daughter Joveneta, she gave five florins and a green dress. The document containing her testament is damaged in part, but she also made a gift to one other daughter, either her remaining natural child, Catarina, or perhaps a woman named Alriasia. Alriasia was her second husband's daughter by a previous marriage, in which case it was a kindness for Margarida to remember her as her own. In all other matters, Margarida's son Johan, by then a prior of nearby Villemus, was her heir. A notary drew up her testament in the presence of several witnesses in her son's house in Manosque in a cozy little room that looked out onto the street (*in domo . . . domini Johannis Barbarini in parva camera supra carreria*). Thanks to references scattered in the archives, we know that Margarida lived a very long life and died in her seventies surrounded by family and friends.

5.3   Conclusions: Detoxifying the Past?

Though I have, at times, invoked narrative voice to lend color to my account of Margarida's life, the tale I constructed is founded upon certain historical events. It is still a constructed story—almost certainly different from Margarida's lived experiences, forever lost. Still, the tale is most certain when it comes to its points of biography: Margarida de Portu was a common townswoman who survived two husbands; several childbirths; a debilitating physical illness; repeated court actions; accusations of murder, sorcery, and poison; imprisonment; and all the usual dangers of life in the fifteenth century, contagious disease and warfare chief among them. The life story I built around these facts is not what we might expect. Its outcomes fly in the face of what we know, or think we know, about life in the fifteenth century. Scholars and popular culture place particular emphasis on this turbulent, repressive, and misogynistic era. After all, around the time that Margarida stood accused by powerful men of killing her husband through occult methods, Christian intellectuals launched the witch-hunts. The infamous *Malleus Maleficarum,* the Hammer of Witches, first published in Germany in 1487, circulated widely throughout Europe within a generation of Margarida's death. That book, quite literally, would ignite fires that would spread throughout the continent. But Manosque circa 1400 was still medieval and not yet affected by growing concerns about religious hegemony and diabolism.[7] And, even if violence, fear of alterity, and misogyny were all typical features of late medieval society, they were not inevitable or omnipresent. Margarida's case, thus, is a useful reminder that other attitudes could still prevail. In many ways, her life, seemingly exceptional, was actually quite normal. In Manosque circa 1400, an innocent woman, though strange and alien, could still rely on family and friends for support and success. She could act with them to defend her good name, to build a life, and to prosper.

Just as Margarida's tale instructs on the benefits of family support, it also tests their limits. Raymon misjudged these limits when he attempted to ruin Margarida. He learned to his peril what it meant to be without family support. His own kith and kin worked against his cause in court, choosing Margarida over him. This shows that membership in a family did not necessarily guarantee unanimity. The collapse of Gauterii support, and the development of the de Portu coalition, a veritable story in opposites, emphasizes the ties that bound medieval people for good or for ill.

Beyond this broad lesson, one that emphasizes the importance of community and networks of solidarity, and that instructs about the limits of agency and the need for support, Margarida's tale has much to offer about everyday life at the dawn of the Middle Ages. Through neighbors' voices, we hear a young girl and her older husband squabble, laugh, and eat together. Beneath the table, a dog brushes their feet and begs for scraps, which he finally laps up in a sticky, garlicky wooden bowl. In Margarida's own voice, we hear a girl lay stake to feminine vulnerability: fear and weakness of strong men who would drag her from her hiding place in the cloister; shame and anguish at missing her new husband's funeral; self-loathing at her physical infirmity. Whether true sentiment or clever ploy, the plausibility of these claims rings true to how medieval women maneuvered social spaces. In Margarida's Manosque, we also hear women gossip. There, they passed rumors back and forth as currency and speculated about one another's intimate lives. How else did a judge know to ask Margarida about her sex life with Johan? He heard, like everyone else in Manosque, including the Jewish physician, that things were amiss in the boudoir. This was life in a small town where everyone knew everyone else's business. This level of communal monitoring was not all bad, though. Through it, Margarida managed a difficult illness, her supposed *morbum caducum*. Neighbors kept watch over her, and even her husband acknowledged it was better for her to return to her natal village so her brothers could mind

---

7 Courtemanche and Bednarski, *"De l'eau."*

her than to have her collapse near the kitchen fire. In Margarida's Manosque, those same communal monitors scoffed when Raymon accused her of abandoning Johan and stealing from his home. Instead, they told what they had seen and heard. So close was their watch over Margarida that they could itemize what she was carrying and what she was wearing when she left Johan's house. Though we cannot study a photograph of the streets she walked, we feel the eyes upon her back as she moved. The scent of the ginger she cut for Johan to carry in his pocket to ward off chest pains trails behind her. It wafts through history and imagination to lend proximity to a distant time.

The court records that frame Margarida's tale extend its utility far beyond everyday life and convey lessons about legal culture. Through them, the historian monitors legal tactics, ploys, and formulae. Stuffed in the registers are the paper "schedules" filed by an angry notary. Squeezed between the lines of dense, spidery Latin words are phrases and principles of law transmitted by ancient Roman jurists to medieval lawyers. In the court's lists of creditors, we read how medieval law, like modern and ancient law, defended economic interests. In an inheritance dispute between uncle and siblings, we ascertain the rules governing the legitimate transmission of wealth. In Margarida's quest to obtain her *alimentum,* we understand one mechanism medieval society put in place to support single women. Throughout all this legalese there echo forms and traditions that persist still today and provide institutional links between ancients, medievals, and moderns.

The law is not the only institution reflected in Margarida's tale; medicine and governance play prominent roles. First, we must consider the level of knowledge brought by Vivas Josep to her cause. His expertise at surgery and physic overrode any potential anti-Semitism or racial mistrust that may or may not have existed in late medieval Manosque. In his testimony, the learned doctor quoted medical authorities to convey the impressive extent of his knowledge and training. Though framed in the language of classical humoral theory, the doctor's diagnosis of Johan's heart attack measures the depths and limits of medieval medical knowledge. Likewise, Raymon's assault on Margarida underscores a fundamental and sudden breakdown in governance structures that, though startling, were temporary and reparable. Raymon's ability to convince judge and preceptor alike to seek an opinion in favor of illegal torture is telling. In the end, all his political influence spent, Raymon's machinations failed. Through the traces of his ploys, though, we see how seigneurial lordship was supposed to work and how it did, in fact, work.

All of this illustrates the close relationship between the micro and the macro and between provable facts and probable realities. Through glimpses into a constructed tale of a single woman's life story, we see at the same time the exceptional and the normal, the small and the large. I have tried here to show both while underscoring process and, to use an apt metaphor, by tipping my hand. I sifted, strained, and unpacked narrative to allow for as pure and frank an analysis of the tale as possible. In the end, I leave it to the reader to consider the merits of historical investigation and storytelling. I have done my best to spell out the paths I took while probing the records of Margarida's life in order to build a story. In reading it, you must balance the near and familiar against the distant and foreign, and consider my choices carefully, to assess for yourself the usefulness and shortcomings of history writ small.

Family Trees

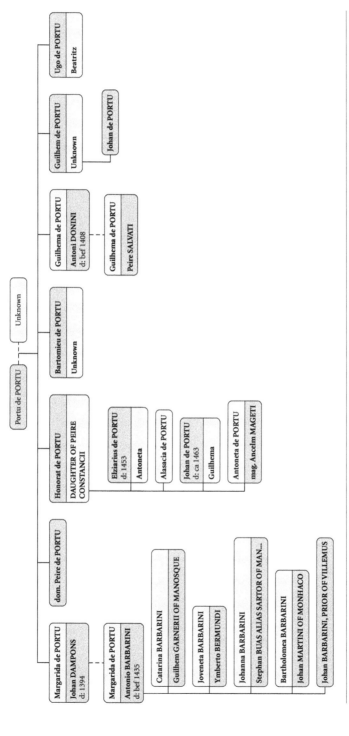

FIGURE A.I: *The de Portu family of Beaumont and Manosque*

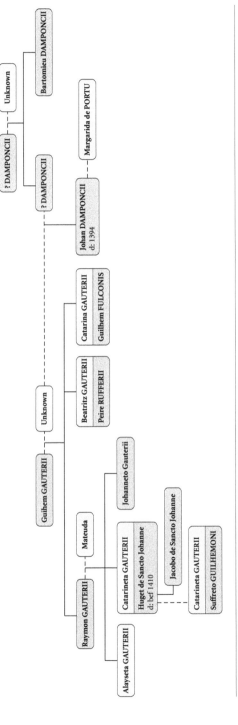

FIGURE A.2: *The Gauterii and Damponcii families of Manosque*

APPENDIX II

Transcription of Criminal Inquest

ADBDR 56 H 1001 ff. 32–60, begun 16 October 1394

The spirit of this book is one of methodological transparency. It seems important, therefore, to present the core document in its full form alongside the analysis. What follows, however, is the *working* transcription used to write this book. It was never my intention to publish a formal scholarly edition of Margarida's inquest. Instead, I hope to show actual process: this is the level of transcription necessary for me to do the sort of work required by this book. The transcription still contains errors; there are words I could not decipher from the originals (due to physical damage or ambiguous paleographical abbreviations), and there are likely errors in the Latin (due to my own linguistic gaffes or those of the original scribe). Still, I hope this transcription is useful to show the level of preparation carried out by historians before they begin to write. I also hope it is of interest to more advanced students and teachers who wish to confirm, debate, or refute my analysis. The text appears verbatim to the original, except where an indent indicates an unbroken line in the original.

> [f⁰32] Contra Margaritam filiam de Porti
> de Porti condam de BelloMonte uxoremque Johannis
> Damposii condam de Manuasca et omnes
> alios universos et singulos qui de sub-
> scriptis ope opere consilio vel favore modo
> quolibet poterunt culpabiles reperiri.
>
> [In the margin:]
> Factum est instrumentum

absolutionis pro
parte dicte Margarite.

Anno incarnationis Domini, millesimo ccc^{mo} ^nonagesimo^ iiii^{to} et die veneris
sextadecima mensis octobris. Quoniam si nocentes condigna
pena non flecteret prostrata subcumberet justicia et malorum
perversitas turbato ordine bonorum paciencia subiugaret,
suadet et enim ratio ob maleficia penas solui quia non
frustra institute sunt potestates Regis jus cognitionis
virgule carnificis arma militis disciplina dominantis
pariterque severitas [*corrected from:* servitas] boni patris ymo ipsorum
    singula suos habe[n]t
modos, causas, rationes et utilitates apertas non transgressorum
exemplaris ulcio fit ceteris indictio delinquendi quia alii
eorum exemplati correctione preterita et si non virtutis
amore saltem pene formidine prosilire[1] ad similia merito per-
timescunt pena enim delinquencium occulos racionis apperit
quos culpe cessitas[2] clauserat et ipsius pene metu ma-
chinantes transgredi alapsu revocate pietatis. Sane
quia vulgaris fama sic aures curie Hospitalis ville Manuasce
[*crossed out:* propu] propulsavit et clamoris frequencia sic celebre ipsius
officium excitavit quod absque scandalo dissimulari non potest
nec sine exemplo destabili abstinere quin ad inquirendum procedat
cum tanta fama loco accusacionis succedat, idcirco ex
officio curie Hospitalis dicte ville Manuasce mandato quippe
nobilis et circumspecti viri domini Petri Rebolli jurisperiti judicis
dicte curie proceditur ad inquirendum contra supradicta [sic]
Margaritam filiam de Porti de Porti de BelloMonte uxorem-
que Johannis Dampocii condam de Manuasca ac omnes alios et
singulos qui de infrascriptis ope opere consilio, auxilio vel fa-
vore modo aliquo poterunt culpabiles Reperiri super eo videlicet
quod dicta fama et clamoribus propulsantibus eius aures ad
ipsius audienciam est noviter deductum, et specialiter magistri
Raymundi Gauterii fratris dicti Johannis Dampocii condam deffuncti

[f⁰32 v.] qui contra dictam Margaritam causa suspicionis coadjuvando
curiam predictam aliquos titulos accusatorios dedit

---

1 to rush towards a course of action; used with *ad*
2 *cessitas* = *caecitas* ?

et dicte curie obtulit, quod prefata delata sue salutis
eterne inmemor tanquam mulier nequam et impia omni
malignitate plena divinum et temporale judicium minime
concernens, cuius iniquitas malicia et electa superbia
amor vel timor dominicus non dominavit hostis antiqui
nequissimi subgestionibus adherens, non verens quam grave
et destabile est creaturam humanam ad ymaginem Dei
formatam, et insuper eius maritum cui per thorum matri-
moniale sponsata extiterat propter falsam et dolosam subgestionem
in eius anima dampnabile detrimentum morti tradere repentine
et insuper propter fachuras sive venena, cum plus sit
veneno st[r]ingere quam gladio perhimere. Hodie in presenti titulo
contenta et descripta, dicta delata nequiter erudita animo
Luciferario [*crossed out:* imp]inbuta a[r]te impia et maligna. Et
de mane [*crossed out:* certa hora] circa horam prime ipsius diei
   qua hora
Johannes Dampocii maritus dicte delate bibere seu comedere
consueverat et demum extra ire et laborare, eidem Johanni
eius marito debuit ministrare ac preparare aliquod ma-
lignum poculum seu ferculum seu alias pravas et
pessimas fachuras quod vel quas in dicta potacione
matutina eidem Johanni marito suo ipso incio comedere
seu bibere fecit. Et ipsis per ipsum sumptis et receptis
incontinenti extra villam Manuasce causa laborandi ivit
et Recessit. Et adveniente hora terciarum ipsius diei dictus
Johannes Dampocii maritus dicte delate, tanquam multum gravatus
et senciens dicta venena sibi data eidem nocere et non
plus ^ea^ ferre posse ad presentem villam Manuasce reddiit et
in domo sua supra lectum se posuit. Sic et taliter quod
causantibus supradictis malignis poculis seu ferculis venenosis sive aliis fachuris per dictam Margaritam supra delatam
eidem Johanni eius marito datis et abeuratis? Christo reddens Spiritum
Sanctum in domino in dicto loco predicto in eius camera et in
dicto lecto ab hoc seculo migravit et extremos suos dies

[f°33] clausit cuius animam paradisus pos[s]ideat et in gloria celesti
cum Christo semper Requiescat amen. In penas contra vene-
ficos et alias graves penas quas utraque jura prodeunt?
temere et miserabiliter incidendo.

Ad ipsius curie audienciam jam pervenerunt indicia subscripta:

I   Primo videlicet resultat indicium contra dictam delatam
quod inimiticie precedebant de ipsa delata contra dictum maritum suum propter quas ipsa recesserat apud BellumMontem
et ibi per spacium octo dierum et ultra steterat.

II   Item resultat aliud indicium contra dictam delatam
super eo videlicet quia dum ipsa delata venit de Bello
Monte non stetit in presenti villa Manuasce nisi per unam noctem
et in crastinum dictus eius maritus sanus et ylaris mortuus
fuit subito ut in dicto titulo continetur.

III   Item resultat aliud indicium contra dictam delatam super
eo videlicet quia ipsa Margaritam [sic] est de loco videlicet
de BelloMonte in quo loco talia scandala et similia multociens fieri sunt consueta. De quo est publica vox et
fama ubique.

IIII   Item resultat aliud indicium contra dictam delatam super
eo videlicet, quod ipsa de premisso excessu senciens se culpabilem pro eo quia dictus eius maritus mortuus erat, in
salva gardia ecclesie sive monasterii dominarum monialium
dicti loci se transtulit. Et demum ad ecclesiam Nostre Domine
in quadam camera ipsius clastre [sic] se posuit et latitavit.
Et ad domum dicti eius viri deffuncti pro suo honore
faciendo minime ire curavit.

[f⁰33 v]

V   Item resultat aliud indicium contra dictam delatam, quia
ipsa ut supra dicitur senciens se culpabilem de dicto
excessu credens non satis esse in loco tuto [*corrected from:* dicto]
      infra dictam
cameram ubi se prius posuerat infra dictam ecclesiam Nostre
Domine, in capella Sancti ^Anthonii^ se posuit pro eius securitate.

VI   Item resultat aliud indicium contra dictam delatam
Super eo quia adveniente die sabati que erat dies xvii

mensis octobris, qua die dictus Johannes eius maritus sepultus
fuit infra siminterium ecclesie Nostre Domine, ipsa delata existens
infra dictam ecclesiam in dicta capella, dicta delata ad
tumulum sive sepulturam dicti Johannis minime ire curavit
neque eundem flevit neque aliquem dolorem passa fuit neque alia
fecit que quelibet bona mulier pro suo marito deffuncto
facere tenetur ymo nil fecit sicut eundem nunquam cogno-
visset.

VII   Item resultat aliud indicium contra dictam Margaritam
supra delatam super eo videlicet quod cum mandato dicti domini
judicis dicta delata citata extitisset personaliter per Isnardum
Laurerie nuncium dicte curie infra dictam claustram ecclesie predicte
ut venire deberet responsum inquisitioni pretacte ac jus
et justiciam subitura sub pena c librarum, dicta inquam delata
[crossed out: dicta] in dicta curia tunc minime comparere curavit tanquam
senciens se de premissis culpabilem.

    Item quod de premissis est publica vox et fama contra dictam
delatam in dicto loco de Manuasce.

Unde ne huiusmodi criminis nequicia deffectu correctionis
digne prejudicialiter invalescat, Neve tantus fraus seu
dolus in et tantis maleficiis recalescat illis detur?
locus pestilensie pro medicina, Essurrexit enim

[f⁰34] supradicti domini judicis ac nobilium virorum domini Raymundi
Cornuti militis baiuli et Petri de Salensono clavarii
dicte curie recta intencio ad huiusmodi crimen cor-
rigendum; Et de omnibus incidentibus et emergentibus ex eodem
ac qui consilium, auxilium vel favorem supradicte delate
prestiterunt, contra dictam delatam audito clamore
predicto ^ad finem ne mala remaneant impunita^ et quia eius equalitas hoc
     merito exhigit
una cum me Hugone Bonilis notario dicte curie processum
et inquisitum fuit prout infra sequitur.

Anno quo supra et die veneris decima sexta mensis
[crossed out: novembris] octobris prefatus dominus judex precepit et

injunxit Isnardo Laurerie nuncio dicte curie presenti et
intelligenti quatinus citatum accedat dictam Margaritam supradelatam personaliter ad dictam claustram
ut hodie hora vesperorum in curia predicta et coram
dicto domino judice personaliter comparere procuret sub pena
c librarum responsura titulis inquisitionis contra ipsam
factis et formatis ac jus et justiciam subitura. Et
refferat, Quiquidem nuncius yens et paulo post
rediens retulit se dictam Margaritam personaliter
infra dictam claustram repertam citasse ad actum
et horam suprascriptos prout habuit in mandatis, ego
Hugo Bonilis notarius dicte curie hec hec [sic] scripsi et signo
dicte curie signavi. [*signed with seal*]

Ad quam horam vesperorum ipsius diei in dicta curia et
coram prefato domino judice pro tribunali sedente, comparuit providus
vir Petrus de Salensono clavarius dicte curie accusans

[f° 34 v.] contumaciam dicte Margarite supradelate personaliter citate
ut supra patet cuius contumacia exhigente petit
ipsam Margaritam iterato pro secunda dilatione ad id quod
supra citari.

Et dictus dominus judex dictam Margaritam supradelatam
non comparentem contumacem reputavit in cuius contumacia
precepit et injunxit dicto Isnardo Laurerie nuncio dicte
curie presenti et intelligenti quatinus citatum accedat dictam
Margaritam personaliter ad dictam claustram aut ibi
ubi personaliter reperietur ut die crastina in vesperis
in dicta curia et coram dicto domino judice personaliter comparere
procuret responsura inquisitioni contra eam facte et omnibus
emergentibus ex eadem ac jus et justiciam subituram [sic]
sub pena cc librarum et refferat.

Ad quam diem crastinam hora versperorum ipsius diei que est
sabati xvii mensis octobris dictus Isnardus Laurerie nuncius
curie jam dicte retulit dicto domino judici michique notario
infrascripto personaliter citasse supra dictam Margaritam uxorem

condam Johannis Dampocii ad id quod supra ad presentem [*crossed out:*
 dicte et]
horam vesperorum prout habuit in mandatis. Ego qui supranotarius
hec scripsi et signo dicte curie signavi. [*signed with seal*]

Et ibidem et incontinenti facta dicta relatione
in dicta curia et coram prefato domino judice pro tribunali
sedente comparuit dictus clavarius nomine dicte curie accusans contumaciam dicte Margarite supradelate personaliter
citate ut supra patet et minime comparere curantis
cum contumacia exhigente dicto nomine petit ipsam
ut moris est licet citari deberet pro tercia dilatione publice
preconizari juxta formam dicte curie.

[f°35] Et dictus dominus judex, quia parum prodesset humilitas
humilibus si contumacia contumatibus non noceret
igitur dictam delatam non comparentem contumacem
reputavit in cuius contumacia precepit et injunxit
Hugoni Javelle nuncio [*crossed out:* dicte curie] et preconi publico
dicte curie presenti et intelligenti quatinus per presentem
villam Manuasce et eius loca soluta publice sono tubete
sonitu preheunte preconizationem faciat subscriptam et
refferat.

Videlicet

Mandamentum est magnifici viri domini Hospitalis
et Manuasce preceptoris et sui baiuli quod Margarita
uxor condam Johannis Damposii habitatrix Manuasce accusata
in dicte curie Hospitalis ville Manuasce de morte mariti
sui prout in titulo inquisitionis contra eam formato continetur citata bina citacione et in
nulla ipsarum comparere curando infra xviii dies proximos
perhemptorie et precize in dicta curia comparere procuret
responsum^titulis^ inquisitionis contra ipsam factis ac jus et justiciam subitura sub pena c marcarum argenti
fini.

Die lune xix mensis octobris, supradictus nuncius
et preco publicus dicte curie retulit dicto domino judici
michique notario subscripto se dictam preconizationem
ut moris est fecisse et divulgasse prout habuit
in mandatis. Ego Hugo Bonilis notarius dicte curie hec
scripsi et signo dicte curie signavi. [*signed with seal*]

[f⁰35 v.] Dicta die, magister Raymundus Gauterii frater ute-
rinus supradicti Johannis Dampocii condam constitutus
in presencia nobilis et circumspecti viri domini Petri
Rebolli jurisperiti judicis dicte curie Hospitalis ville
Manuasce et coadjuvando ipsam curiam et pro informacione ipsius curie contra dictam Margaritam supra
accusatam tam nomine suo proprio quam omnium amicorum
dicti Johannis Dampocii condam exhibuit et presentavit
quandam papiri cedulam tenoris subsequentis.

Tenor dicte cedule
talis est prout ecce:

Resultant indicia subscripta contra Margaritam
uxorem Johannis Dampocii.

I   Et primo dicta Margarita cotidie blasfemabat
et maledicebat coram pluribus gentibus que matrimonium inter ipsam et dictum Johannem tractaverat.

II   Item eciam dicta Margarita quando videbat dictum
suum maritum de visione ipsius dicti mariti sui
tristabatur dicendo quod ipse erat plorator et
tristis homo et semper dicebat malum de dicto
marito suo.

III   Item eciam dicebat coram pluribus gentibus quod in
brevi ipsa revertetur ad Bellum Montem.

IIII   Item duabus vel tribus vicibus ipsa volebat ire ad Bellum
Montem nisi fuisset residencia³ diaconi fratris sui
cui dyacono respondebat quod nisi ipsam dimiteret ire

---

3 residencia = resistencia ?

[f°36] ad Bellum Montem ipsa faceret dedecus omni et causam
de quo omnes sui amici essent irati. Qui dyaconus
eidem respondit minando "Per Deum ego verberabo te
tantum quod malum tibi veniet"; dicendo coram dicto
dyacono quod male gratibus suis dictum deffunctum
in maritum sibi dederant et quod ipsa nichil faciebat
hic.

V   Item eciam dicebat quod nisi ipsa iret ad Bellum
Montem ipsa non posset deliberari aliquo modo.

VI   Item quod suam raupam nupcialem extra hospicium dicti
mariti sui de tribus septimanis et ultra non [*crossed out:* stetit]
tenuit in dicto hospicio sui mariti.

VII   Item ad Bellum Montem ivit et portavit secum
tria paria caligarum et tria paria socularium
et in dicto loco stetit per octo dies.

VIII Item eciam omnia jocalia que habebat portavit
ad dictum castrum de Bello Monte.

IX   Item quod sero illo quo venit de Bello Monte, dicta
Margarita non applicavit in domo mariti sui
ymo jacuit in domo dominarum monialium.

X Item in crastinum bene mane surgens de dicto monasterio dixit cuidam fratello suo parvullo quod diceret
marito suo ut daret sibi pecunias pro emendo
menudetos; qui Johannes deffunctus respondit quod nolebat
comedere menudetos.

[f°36 v]

XI   Item illo mane fecerunt viaticum cum allio.

XII Item facto et decocto dicto viatico ipsa venit
ad punctum pro faciendo paraxides et fecit paraxidem marito suo.

^XIII Item ponere in decoctu neque facere paraxides dicta
Margarita temporibus retroactis numquam consueverat
facere neque volebat comedere cum marito suo.^

XIIII Item facta paraxide per dictam Margaritam et comesto
viatico per dictum maritum suum eundo ad ferraginem
nobilis domine Anthonete Savine prope portale supremum
dum affuit in fonte Albete idem Johannes deffunctus dixit
famulo suo "tota lingua mea michi ardet. Qui dyabolus fecit viaticum?" Qui famulus respondit quod nesci-
ebat et dum affuit in dicta ferragine nobilis domine
Anthonete ibidem seminavit unum selhonum et ut dicit
famulus suus aliquociens revertebatur totus niger aliquociens totus rubeus.

XV Item ut [*crossed out:* dixit] dicit dictus famulus, ipse incepit
tremere totus dicendo sibi quod magnum malum habebat
in corde et in ventrelho cui deffuncto dictus famulus
dixit "Vos tremitis totus et estis niger in facie,
recedatis ad villam."

XVI Item incontinenti dictus deffunctus venit ad villam
tremendo et quodam modo carens visu et dum
affuit infra suum hospicium in lecto neque loqui
seu movere potuit suam personam ymo incontinenti
tradidit spiritum et suos dies ultimos clausit.

Supplicatur igitur pro parte amicorum dicti deffuncti.
Magnificenciam et dominationem vestram instanter et

[f°37] instantissime multis precibus exoramus ut de tanto ex-
cessivo perfidio ac nequissimo facinore quod cum
poyson interficere et destruere naturam humanam
eo quod sumus certi quod vos estis equa libra hac justicia
in mensura et vindictam facinorum justicie temporalis
quare premissis attentis et consideratis dictam magnificenciam vestram lacrimando requirimus dictam
Margaritam cum effectu capi faciatis et saltim
eandem poni in loco tuto infra dictam ecclesiam in compe-

dibus ferreis reponi et ibidem eandem precipere
custodiri tam per dictam vestram curiam quam expensum
dicti deffuncti ut cultum justicie augmentetur
ut habetur in phasinista? veritas de terra orta est, et
justicia de celo prospexit. Et predicta, amici [*crossed out:* dictus]
dicti deffuncti omnia supradicta dicunt humiliter
lacrimando per viam intimacionis seu informationis
dicte vestre curie et non aliter parati se offerentes
dicti amici cum juvamentum? dicte vestre curie dictam mortem
prosequi pro posse. De quibus si necesse fuerit petunt
eis fieri publicum instrumentum et publica instrumenta.

Sequntur deposiciones testium

Testis: Anno et die quibus supra. Billa Fossate testis pro informacione
dicte curie recepta juravit ad Sancta Dei euvangelia per ipsam
sponte corporaliter tacta dicere et meram fateri veritatem
super hiis in quibus fuerit interrogata. Et primo super contentis in dicto inquisicionis titulo ipso prius sibi lecto et
dato intelligi in vulgari eius juramento dixit se nichil
scire de contentis in eo.

Item fuit interrogata super primo indicio post titulum veniente;
que suo juramento dixit se nichil scire de contentis in eo, nisi

[f⁰37 v.] tantumquod pridie ipse Johannes Dampocii eidem loquenti dixit
    quod
maladicta esset persona que posuerat malum inter
ipsum [bis] Johannem et eius uxorem. Et quod ipse tale
malum habebat sicut ipsa.

Item fuit interrogata super secundo indicio, que deposuit
medio eius juramento se scire auditu quod ipsa Margarita
venerat illo vespere ^de Bello Monte^ et in crastinum verum fuit quod
    dictus
Johannes maritus dicte delate mortuus fuit.

Item super tercio indicio, dixit se audivisse dici ut in eo
continetur; et fama ipsum locum sequitur de contentis
in eo.

Item, fuit interrogata super contentis in quarto indicio,
dixit verum fore quod dicta Margarita erat in domo
Anthonete Olivarie supra unum lectum in quo steterat propter illud morbum caducum quod habuerat prout alie mulieres asserebant, et venit quedam monaca
vocata soror Maria; que monaca est de Bello Monte
habitatrix tamen monasterii Sancte Clare de Manuasca. Et eidem
loquenti dixit quod duxerent dictam Margaritam ad monasterium predictum super eius lectum quod et fecit.
Et demum venit frater dicte Margarite qui est dyaconus Nostre Domine et eandem Margaritam simul cum Sanxia
uxore Moneti Sarelherii duxerunt ad claustram Nostre
Domine in quadam camera dicti diaconi et eam ibidem posuerunt.

Item fuit interrogata cur dicta Margarita recesserat ad
dictam ecclesiam Nostre Domine dixit quod non alia de causa quod
ipsa sciat sed propter minas quas faciebat eidem Margarite magister Raymundus Gauterii quia eam accusabat
de morte dicti mariti sui.

Item fuit interrogata dicta testis si audiverat dici antequam
ducerent dictam Margaritam ad ecclesiam an ipsa Margarita esset culpabilis de morte mariti sui, vel si erat
fama quod ipsa dedisset fachuras sive venena aliqua
dicto eius marito propter quas ipse subisset mortem, dixit
eius juramento quod non s[c]it aliqua de predictis; nisi quod magister

[f⁰38] Raymundus Gauterii dicebat et clamabat dum dictus
Johannes eius frater mortus fuit quid hoc fecit; et
multa alia dicebat clamendo de quibus non recordatur.

Item fuit interrogata super quinto indicio [bis], dixit
eius juramento de contentis in eo se nichil scire.

Item fuit interrogata dicta testis super contentis in
sexto indicio, dixit eius juramento se nil scire de contentis
in eo quia erat tunc temporis infra presentem curiam arrestata. [crossed out: erat]

Item fuit interrogata super viii indicio, septimo omisso,
[*crossed out:* dixit] si de predictis omnibus est publica vox et fama, dixit
quod de confessis per eam est publica vox et fama in loco Manuasce per
    eos scientes.
Pluribus interrogationibus sibi factis, dixit se nil aliud scire quam supra
confessa fuit.

Item fuit interrogata dicta loquens et diligenter examinata super
indiciis in cedula per magistrum Raymundum Gauterii producta
    contentis
et descriptis. Primo super primo indicio, dixit se nichil scire de contentis
in eo, sed bene audivit dici a Johanne Dampocii condam quod male
dictus esset qui eisdem fecerat malum, alia non.

Item fuit interrogata super contentis in secundo, tertio, quarto, et
quinto indiciis, que medio eius juramento dixit se nichil scire
de contentis in eisdem.

Item, super sexto indicio, dixit se nichil scire de contentis in eodem.

Item fuit interrogata super vii indicio, dixit eius juramento se nichil
scire de contentis in eo, et eidem Margarite non vidit portare
nisi sacularis [sic] [*crossed out:* quodq] quos portabat calciatos.

Item, super viii indicio, dixit se nichil scire de contentis in eo.

Item fuit interrogata super nono indicio, dixit eius juramento se
nichil scire de contentis in eo, nisi auditu dici.

Item, super x indicio, dixit se nichil scire de contentis in eo.

Item super xi indicio, dixit se nichil scire, nisi quod audivit dici ab
ipsa Margarita. Et ipsa dixit quod illud potagium non fecit;
verum tamen eidem ^dixit^ quod de eodem comedat.

[f⁰38 v.] Item fuit interrogata super xii indicio, dixit se nichil scire
nisi auditu dici. Interrogata a quo illa dici audivit, dixit quod
a famulo qui secum morabatur.

Item fuit interrogata super xiii indicio, que eius juramento
dixit se nichil scire de contentis in eo. Tamen contrarium
dici audivit a famulo qui secum morabatur.

Item fuit interrogata super xiiii et xv indiciis, que dixit
eius juramento se nichil scire de contentis in eisdem.

Item fuit interrogata super xvi indicio, dixit eius juramento
se nichil scire nisi quod audivit dici quod ymo locutus
fuit ex post quod fuit in lecto. Pluribus interrogationibus
sibi factis, dixit se nichil ^scire^ quod supra deposuit.

Dicta die, Sanxia, uxor Moneti Sarelherii testis pro
informacione curie recepta juravit dicere et deponere
veritatem super hiis in quibus fuerit interrogata. Et primo
super contentis in dicto inquisicionis titulo ipso prius
sibi lecto et dato intelligi in vulgari et per ipsam ut
dicit bene intellecto, eius juramento dixit de contentis in
eo se nichil scire.

Item fuit interrogata super primo indicio, que eius juramento
dixit se nil aliud scire nisi tantumquod multociens
dici audivit a dicta Margarita existens in [*crossed out:* dicta]
carreria ante suum hospicium. Que dicebat quod propter
morbum caducum quod habebat ipsa non poterat
stare alacriter neque ut dicebat dicta Margarita
unquam habuerat illud morbum nisi ex post quod venerat ad presentem villam.

Item fuit interrogata super secundo indicio, dixit eius juramento
se nil aliud scire nisi quod dici audivit quod dicta
Margarita venerat illo vespere. Verum tantum est verum
quod in crastinum eius maritus mortuus fuit quia ipsa

[f⁰39.] loquens ipsum Johannem vidit mori. Et ipse Johannes multum
plangebat, dicendo quod cor sibi defficiebat et dicebat
dictus Johannes quod multum preparenter venerat de extra propter
malum quod senciebat quia timebat [*corrected from:* tremebat] ut non
    reciperet
vercundiam[?] per villam dum veniebat de extra.

Item fuit interrogata super tercio indicio que eius juramento dixit
verum fore ut in eo continetur. Interrogata quomodo scit,
dicit quia dici audivit.

Item fuit interrogata super iiii^{to} indicio, que eius juramento dixit
et deposuit ut testis precedens.

Item fuit interrogata super aliis indiciis, dixit et deposuit
ut precedens testis. Pluribus interrogationibus sibi factis,
dixit alia se nescire.

Item fuit interrogata dicta testis loquens et diligenter examinata super contentis in primo indicio dictorum indiciorum
in cedula per magistrum Raymundum Gauterii producta contentorum,
que eius juramento dixit se nichil scire de contentis in eo, nisi quod
audivit dici a dicto Johanne Dampocii loquendo cum eius
uxore, "sta alacriter," que Margarita eidem respondit quod
non poterat stare eo quia non habebat sanitatem.

Item fuit interrogata super secundo, tertio, iiii^{to}, quinto, sexto,
septimo et octavo indiciis, que respondit eius juramento
se nichil scire de contentis in eisdem.

Item fuit interrogata super nono indicio, eius juramento dixit
se nichil scire de contentis in eo nisi auditu dici.

Item fuit interrogata super x°, xi°, xii°, xiii°, xiiii° et
quintodecimo indiciis, que eius juramento dixit se nichil
scire de contentis in eisdem.

Item fuit interrogata dicta loquens super sextodecimo
indicio, que eius juramento dixit se nil aliud scire de contentis in eo
nisi quod eidem loquenti dixit in dicto lecto quod magnum dolorem
cordis paciebatur propter quod ipse multum preparenter venerat
et itineraverat per carreriam rectam ne acciperet verecundiam

[f°39 v.] Anno quo supra et die mercuri xxi mensis octobris.
Johannes Baudiment [*crossed out:* testis] de Roca Volcii testis pro
informacione dicte curie receptus juravit ad Sancta Dei

euvangelia per ipsum sponte corporaliter tacta dicere
et deponere veritatem super hiis in quibus fuerit interrogatus primo super titulo inquisicionis ipso prius sibi
lecto et dato intelligi in vulgari et per ipsum ut
asserit bene intellecto eius juramento dixit de contentis
in eo se nichil scire. Interrogatus si ipse morabatur cum
Johanne Damponcii condam, dixit quod sic pro bubulco.

Item fuit interrogatus super primo indicio immediate
post titulum sequentem, qui eius juramento dixit quod
aliquando irascebantur et aliquando ludebant
insimul; item eciam quod de voluntate eius mariti
dicta Margarita recesserat ad Bellum Montem
et hoc propter morbum quod habebat. Interrogatus
si ipse Johannes Dampocii condam habebat simile
morbum sicut ipsa Margarita, dixit quod illud
ignorat. Tamen dixit idem loquens quod dictus Johannes
deffunctus quolibet mane paciebatur dolore
cordis ut ipse deffunctus asserebat et ab eodem
dici audivit propter quem dolorem cotidie multum
mane bibebat et comedebat et eciam semper
portabat gingiber in cr—-ena? et de eo comedebat.

Item fuit interrogatus super secundo indicio, medio eius
juramento dixit verum fore ut in eo continetur
quia vidit ipsum Johannem eius magistrum mortuum et
quod dicta Margarita dum venit de Bello Monte
portavit tres pesias pellasorum.

Item super tercio indicio fuit interrogatus dixit contenta in
illo penitus ignorare.

[f⁰40.] Item fuit interrogatus super quarto indicio, dixit medio ejus
juramento se nichil scire de contentis in eo, quia ad huc
ipse erat extra in labore tunc temporis. Tamen dum venit
de dicto labore circa horam nonam non invenit dictam Margaritam ad eius domum, et eciam post dici audivit quod
ipsa erat in ecclesia Nostre Domine.

Item fuit interrogatus super quinto indicio, dixit quod illud dici
audivit quod ipsa est in capella Sancti Anthonii ac tamen non
eam vidit.

Item fuit interrogatus super sexto indicio, dixit eius juramento
quod contenta in eo penitus ignorat, quia ipse eo tunc iverat aratum in quadam terra Petri Rufferii. Et alia dixit
se nescire.

Item fuit interrogatus super indiciis in supradicta cedula
per magistrum Raymundum Gauterii producta contentis et
descriptis. Et primo super primo indicio dicte cedule, dixit
eius juramento se nichil scire de contentis in eo.

Item fuit interrogatus super secundo indicio dicte cedule, dixit
eius juramento se nichil scire de contentis in eo. Sed aliquando te-
nabant [sic] et aliquando ludebant insimul prout supra dixit.

Item fuit interrogatus super tercio indicio, eius juramento dixit
se nunquam contenta in illo audivisse.

Item fuit interrogatus super quarto et quinto indiciis eius
juramento dixit se nichil scire de contentis in eisdem.

Item fuit interrogatus super sexto indicio, dixit eius juramento
quod de voluntate eius mariti dicta Margarita dum ire
volebat ad Bellum Montem dictam raupam a domo sui
mariti extraxit et dum fuit in domo dominarum monialium
habuerunt consilium quod dictas raubas dimiterent infra
dictum monasterium pretimore gencium armorum.

[f⁰40 v] Item fuit interrogatus super septimo [indicio], dixit eius juramento
        contenta
in illo ignorare quia dum ipsa Margarita recessit ipse
loquens non erat presens.

Item super viii° [indicio], dixit eius juramento contenta in eo penitus
ignorare.

Item fuit interrogatus dictus testis loquens et diligenter
examinatus super nono indicio, eius juramento dixit verum
fore ut in eo continetur. Et quod dicta Margarita volebat
ire cubitum ad domum dicti eius mariti sed ipse Johannes
hoc noluit ymo eam remanere fecit in dicto monasterio
dicendo dominus Hugo Gardiloni "cubabit mecum". Interrogatus quomodo predicta s[c]it, dixit quia dici audivit
a dicto magistro suo deffuncto.

Item fuit interrogatus super x° indicio eius juramento dixit ^verum^ fore
ut in eo continetur.

Item fuit interrogatus super xi [indicio], eius juramento dixit contenta
in illo fore vera. Interrogatus quis preparavit potagium, dixit
medio eius juramento quod eius magister et ipse loquens et quidem
parvulus
vocatus Bartholomeus de Porti frater dicte Margarite. Et demum,
dixit quod cocto illo potagio dicta Margarita venit et
posuit de oleo infra dictam olam in presencia omnium ibidem existentium.

Item super xii [indicio] fuit interrogatus, eius juramento dixit verum
fore ut in eo continetur. Tamen dixit quod hoc fecit de precepto
mariti sui quia eius maritus dixit dicte Margarite "fac
nobis paradixes postquam venistis." Interrogatus si ipsa de illo
viatico comedit, dixit quod sic cum quedam filia Petri
Rufferii; item plus dixit id loquens absque aliqua inter-
rogatione, quod dum ipse magister suus comedit in scutela
sua adhuc remansit unum modicum de illo potagio et
illud dedit ad comedendum cuidam cani quem habebat.

Item fuit interrogatus super xiii indicio, eius juramento dixit
quod contrarium est veritas. Quod ymo ipsa Margarita semper

[f°41.] comedebat et consueverat comedere cum dicto eius marito
simul in una tabula et uno silserio, et eciam eidem semper
faciebat paraxidem et omnibus aliis.

Item fuit interrogatus et diligenter examinatus id testis
loquens super contentis in xiiii indicio ipso prius sibi lecto

et dato intelligi in vulgari. Dixit verum fore quod eius
magister tantum sibi dixit "'que la lenga li coya, dicendo sibi,
vos autres aves mal picat los ales' sic eciam fecistis
pridie quia ego inveni unum amindolum integrum infra
potagium." In aliis dum dixit "quis dyabolus fecit
viaticum?" Idem testis dixit quod non est verum quod sibi dixerit illud quoniam ipsemet magister suus bene sciebat quod
ipse loquens et eius magister et alter fecerant dictum potagium.

Item fuit interrogatus super xv indicio, dixit contenta
in illo nunquam dixisse. Bene dixit quod eius magister dicebat
quod videbatur sibi quod terra sibi defficeret subtus pedes. Et
tunc ipse se posuit subtus unum olivarium et ipse loquens
eundem coperit cum rauba [*corrected from:* raba] et dum ibi stetit per
    modicum
spacium ipse surrexit per se ipsum et ad villam recessit.

Item fuit interrogatus super xvi indicio et ultimo,
qui juramento suo dixit verum esse quod eius magister ivit
et recessit ad villam et resedendo idem Johannes eius magister cupiens transire per quendam parietem orti condam
Raymundi Guasqui quod nunc tenet magister Raymundi Gauterii
et assendendo per lapides hic circum circa existentes retro
cecidit magnum ictum super dictos lapides. Et ipse loquens
hoc videns voluit ire ipsum juvare, et dum fuit prope
eum, dictus Johannes, eius magister, surrexit et eundem lo-
quentem retrocedere fecit dicendo "vade et recede ad animalia" Et
ipse loquens ivit et recessit. Et pluribus interrogationibus
sibi factis, dixit se nil amplius scire quam supra deposuit.

[f⁰41 v] Et generaliter fuit interrogatus idem testis loquens et diligenter
examinatus si fuit instructus, doctus, avisatus neque aliter subordi-
natus ut deponeret prout et quem ad modum superius
deposuit. Dixit eius juramento quod non.

Item fuit interrogatus dictus testis si fuit sibi aliquid
datum, promissum vel aliter oblatum per aliquem propter quod
deposuerit prout supra continetur, dixit eius juramento
    quod non.

Item fuit interrogatus idem loquens et diligenter examinatus
si sperat habere comodum vel incomodum de depositis supra
per eundem nec si est de parentela aliquarum partium, dixit
eius juramento quod non.

TESTIS: Anno et die quibus supra. Constituta in dicta curia et
coram prefato domino judice eo pro tribunali sedente [*crossed out:*
      Baudi] Guillelma
Baudrigue vicina Johannis Dampocii condam testis pro
informatione dicte curie recepta juravit ad Sancta Dei
euvangelia dicere et deponere veritatem super his in quibus
fuerit interrogata. Et primo super primo [*crossed out:* indicis] titulo
et contentis in eodem ipso prius sibi lecto et dato intelligi
in vulgari, eius juramento, dixit se nichil ^scire^ de contentis in eodem.

Item fuit interrogata super primo indicio immediate post
titulum sequentem, que eius juramento dixit se nichil scire de contentis in eodem. Tamen dixit verum fore se audivisse
dici quod ipsa Margarita iverat apud Bellum Montem.

Item fuit interrogata super secundo indicio, que eius juramento, dixit quod
      ne-
s[c]iebat si venerat illo vespere tamen in crastinum audivit
dici et est verum quod dictus Johannes mortuus fuit subito ut
audivit. Et illo mane locutus fuerat cum eadem loquente
idem Johannes dicendo sibi quod sibi prestaret filiam suam.

[f°42] Item fuit interrogata super tercio indicio eius juramento dixit quod
      contenta
in illo ignorat fore vera, bene dixit quod audivit quod ipsa Margarita erat et est de Bello Monte, alia non.

Item fuit interrogata super iiii^to indicio indicio, ^dixit^ se nichil scire quia
tota ille die stetit in furno.

Item fuit interrogata super quinto [indicio], dixit se nichil scire nisi
auditu dici.

Item fuit interrogata super sexto [indicio], dixit se nichil scire. Tamen non
presens fuit dum dictus Johannes sepeliebatur, et ubi erat dicta Margarita
nescit.

Item fuit interrogata dicta loquens super indiciis in cedula
per magistrum Raymundum Gauterii producta contentis. Et primo
super primo, secundo et tercio indiciis, dixit se nichil scire de contentis
in eisdem.

Item fuit interrogata super iiii^{to} indicio, dixit se nil aliud scire
nisi quod semel ipsa Margarita volebat recedere ad Bellum Montem
nisi fuisset Honoratus Hospitalarii et Johannes Dampocii eius
maritus qui eam non dimiserunt recedere pro eo quia non
erat satis associata, ac tamen de voluntate eius mariti
recessit ad dictum locum.

Item fuit interrogata super quinto, sexto, septimo et octavo
indiciis, dixit se nichil scire de contentis in eisdem.

Item super nono [indicio], dixit se nil aliud scire nisi auditu dici.

Item fuit interrogata super x, xi, xii, xiii, xiiii, xv,
et xvi indiciis, dixit se nil scire de contentis
in eisdem quia ipsos conjuges non perseverabat.

[*Transcript interrupted by notation that six folios are out of order. I have
corrected the order here. The notation reads* istuc signum cadit / in ferius in
tali signo / et pone hic in vi folio.]

[f^{0}48 v]

TESTIS: Anno quo supra et die jovis xii mensis novembris. Beatrix
Rufferia [uxor Petri Rufferii et soror Johannis Dampocii] testis pro
        informatione dicte curie recepta ju-
ravit ad Sancta Dei euvangelia puram et meram fateri
veritatem super hiis in quibus fuerit interrogata. Et primo
super contentis in dicto inquisitionis titulo ipsa prius sibi
lecto et dato intelligi in vulgari medio eius juramento,
dixit se nichil scire de contentis in eodem.

Item fuit interrogata super primo indicio post
titulum sequentem, eius juramento dixit se nichil

scire de contentis in eodem quia numquam audivit aliqua
verba contensiosa inter ipsos. Tamen bene scit quod de
voluntate eius mariti dicta Margarita ivit ad
Bellum Montem.

Super secundo indicio, dixit verum fore ut in eo continetur.

Item fuit interrogata super tercio indicio, dixit quod verum
est quod ipsa Margarita est de Bello Monte ut dici audivit tamen ignorat alia in dicto indicio contenta nisi
auditu dici.

Item super quarto, dixit verum fore quod ipsa Margarita
habuerat morbum ibidem in domo sua dum eius maritus
in lecto erat et venit eius frater et eam extraxit de
dicta domo ubi eam duxit, nescit. Et eciam alique

[f⁰49] mulieres propter dictum morbum ipsam fretabant;
verum est quod ex post non fuit in domo mariti
sui.

Item fuit interrogata super quinto et sexto indiciis,
eius juramento dixit se nichil scire quia ipsa remansit
in domo dicti deffuncti.

Item fuit interrogata super indiciis in cedula
per magistrum Raymundum Gauterii producta contentis.
Et primo super primo et secundo indiciis, dixit se
nichil scire de contentis in eisdem.

Super tercio indicio, dixit verum fore ut in eo continetur, ut dici audivit ab aliquibus quorum nomina
nescit.

Item super quarto, dixit se nil aliud scire nisi quod
ipsa Margarita semel volebat recedere ad Bellum Montem
nisi fuisset suus maritus deffunctus et Honoratus
Hospitalarii qui eam retinuerunt.

Item fuit interrogata super quinto indicio,
eius juramento dixit se nil aliud scire nisi quod ipsa
Margarita dicebat quod numquam saneretur a morbo quod
habebat nisi iret ad Bellum Montem quia eius
fratres eam custodirent ne caderet in igne
sicut faciebat pretextu dicti morbi.

Super sexto indicio, dixit se scire quod semel quando
dicta Margarita ire volebat ad Bellum Montem
et fuit retenta per suum maritum et Honoratum
Hospitalarii ipsa tunc temporis extraxit suam
raubam nuptialem de domo sui mariti et eam por-
tari fecit per quendam puerum Jacobi Charentasii
admonasterium dominarum. Quid post fecit, nescit. Interrogata
de tempore, dixit quod circa xv dies antequam eius maritus Johannes
Dampocii moreretur.

Super septimo, dixit se nil scire de contentis in eo. Tamen bene scit
quod ipsa Margarita stetit in loco de BelloMonte per viii dies
vel circa.

[f⁰49 v.] Item super viii indicio fuit interrogata, dixit se nil scire de
contentis in eo.

Super nono [indicio], dixit se nichil scire nisi auditu dici.

Item fuit interrogata super x [indicio], dixit se nichil scire de contentis in eo.

Item super xi [indicio] fuit interrogata, dixit se nichil scire
de contentis in eo. Tamen ipsa Margarita posuit sal
et oleum infra olam ipsa loquente presente et vidente.

Super xii indicio, dixit se ignorare contenta in eo
quia incontinenti recessit a dicta domo.

Item fuit interrogata super xiii indicio, dixit
eius juramento quod ymo dicta Margarita faciebat cotidie
paraxides dicto marito suo et secum comedebat alacrum.

Super xiiii indicio, ignorat contenta in illo.

Item fuit interrogata super xv [indicio], dixit quod audivit dici
a famulo dicti deffuncti quod ipse in arata revertebatur
niger; alia nescit.

Item fuit interrogata super xvi indicio, [*crossed out:* fuit
interrogata] dixit eius juramento quod ipsa loquens ipsum
deffunctum invenit in lecto et eidem loquenti ^dixit^ quod ipse
numquam habuerat talem dolorem cordis sicut nunc
habebat. Et incontinenti ipsa loquens dixit dicte
Margarite quod iret quesitum de ovis ad domum
dicte loquentis. Et dum venit, invenit ipsum Johannem
mortuum. Interrogata si eidem dixit quod haberet suspicionem
in aliquo nec in sib arris? nec contra aliquem,
dixit quod non.

[text returns to the point where it left off, six folios earlier]

[f⁰42]
Anno quo supra et die lune nona mensis novembris in curia
Hospitalis ville Manuasce et coram nobili et [*crossed out:* religioso v]
circumspecto viro domino Petro Rebolli jurisperito judice dicte curie
constitutus Petrus de Porti dyaconus frater Margarite de Porte
supradicte. Et eidem domino judici exhibuit et presentavit

[f⁰42 v] quandam papiri cedulam petens, postulans et requirens
ut in ea continetur, et nichilominus peciit ipsam in
presenti processu describi et inseri.

Tenor dicte cedule
talis est

Constitutus Petrus de Porti de BelloMonte ut frater et
conjuncta persona Margarite relicte Johannis Damposii
de Manuasca ante presenciam nobilis viri domini Petri Rebolli jurisperiti judicis ordinarii curie Hospitalis ville
Manuasce dicens et exponens nomine quo supra
cum querela, quod cum aliter, videlicet xx die mensis

octobris proxime lapsi, aliqui ex afinibus dicte Margarite petierunt copiam aliquorum titulorum contra
Margaritam eandem oblatorum ut patet quodam mandato
scripto manu magistri Hugonis Bonilis notarii dicte curie
quod exhibet et producit in quo quidem[4] mandato extiterit per eumdem dominum judicem responsum quod paratum se offert idem dominus judex tradere et assig-
nare copiam dum tamen sit completus processus
si tamen comode et de jure eidem copiam tradi et assignari debeat. Igitur cum dicta Margarita
vexetur laboribus et expensis et disturbiis contra Deum
et justiciam salva reverencia et plus de facto
quam de jure ob deffectum habitionis copie eiusdem supra pe-
tite. Et aliter minime possunt purgari indicia si que
quod absit et non credit dictus exponens contra
Margaritam eandem resultent.

Et cum citra requisicionem de qua supra sit
mencio fuerit eidem domino judici opportu[n]um facere
compleri dictum processum quod si fecerit dictus exponens ignorat pro parte dicte Margarite.

[f⁰43] Ea propter instanter et reverenter requirit dictus exponens
vos prefatum dominum judicem quatinus dignenum [dignemini?] eidem
exponenti nomine quo supra tradere et tradi facere
et assignari copiam supra petitam et diem congruam
assignari et facere per notarium dicte curie assignari copiam
predictam tociusque processus cum de jure copia non sit
deneganda, alias est locus appellacionis quare petit dictus
exponens nomine quo supra et ut supra et que supra.

Cum summa pericia vestri ^dicti^ domini judicis minime ignoret quod fere
et omnes afines et amici dicti Johannis Dampons ipsam Margaritam excusent nullamque se dicant habuisse seu
habere suspectionem contra eandem, licet magistri Raymundus
Gauterii aliquas minimus veras informaciones salva

---

4 Could be *quidam*

reverencia et citra injuriam cuiusquam false ut percepit
dictus exponens dederit dicte curie contra eandem que minime
probare potest ymo nonnulli afines dicti condam
Johannis Dampons quibus conabatur idem magister Raymundus
fortificare producta per eundem contra Margaritam predictam
ipsam Margaritam de contentis in ipsis falsis et false
prepositis titulis, salva reverencia et citra injuriam ut
supra eandem Margaritam continue excusarunt et nunc
excusant prout vos dominus judex extiteritis plenarie
informatus.

Quare premissis attentis et consideratis, dictus exponens
dicto nomine petit et requirit instanter et reverenter
ut supra et que supra vestrum dicti domini judicis officium
propter ea benigne implorando cultu justicie de cuius vestri
predicti domini judicis pericia sufficiencia et legalitate
pars dicte Margarite cum ea que petit juste petit plenarie considit requirendo nichilominus vos dictum dominum
judicem quatinus ex vestri incumbenci officio inspicere dignemini processum cause ipsius ut deliberare et parcendo

[f⁰43 v.] parcium actricis et ree laboribus et expensis lacius
et citius valeat vestra sentencia pericia quod justum
fuerit concedere et assignari jubere ut supra petitur.

Et presentem cedulam et mandamentum de quo in eadem fit
mencio petit de verbo ad verbum dictus exponens nomine quo supra inseri et describi in pede processus et de
presentacione presentis cedule et mandamenti et tenore eorun-
dem una cum responcione et ordanicione vestri domini judicis
velsive [sic] petit dictus exponens dicto nomine sibi fieri
si et quando opus fuerit et habere voluerit publicum instrumentum.

Et dictus dominus judex volens deliberare super petitis et
requisitis premissis et contentis in precedenti cedula
ad audiendum eius deliberatam responsionem si ei fuerit [written as
    fuiter] opportu-
num diem sabati pro termino assignavit.

Actum in terelho supra lapidem ubi sedebat pro tribunali presentibus
Petro Cornuti et Rostagno Fabri de Manuasca et Daniele
Chaberti.

Tenor mandamenti de quo superius fit
mencio sequitur in hunc modum

Anno incarnationis Domini millesimo ccc^{mo} nonagesimo iiii^{to},
die martis vicessima mensis octobris. In curia Hospitalis
ville Manuasce et coram nobili et circumspecto viro domino
Petro Rebolli jurisperito judice dicte curie ordinario pro
tribunali sedente, constitutus Laugerius Montaguti consangui-
neus Margarite de Porte de BelloMonte uxoris Johannis
Dampocii condam de Manuasca et Anthonius Donini cog-
natus dicte Margarite et ut conjuncte persone ipsius Margarite
et cum ad eorum audienciam jam pervenerit et plenarie
sunt informati quod magister Raymundus Gauterii notarius de Manuasca nomine suo et omni amicorum Johannis Damposii
condam, dicte curie exhibuit et presentavit pro informacione
ipsius curie aliquos titulos iniquos contra Margaritam predictam
accusatam de morte mariti sui indebite et injuste. Salva

[f°44] ipsius curie reverencia, et ut possint iniquitatem et ma-
liciam dictorum titulorum expellere et anullare petunt
igitur benigne et instanter requirunt suplicando
dicto domino judici ut eisdem vellit et dignetur dare
et concedere copiam titulorum et omnium per dictum
magistrum Raymundum seu alios amicos dicti Johannis
deffuncti productorum contra et adversus Margaritam
predictam cum ipsa nullo modo culpabilis criminis
predicti existat. Et dictus dominus judex audita et
intellecta suplicatione seu requisicione dictorum Laugerii
Montaguti et Anthonii Donini eisdem respondit quod processus ipsius cause nondum est completus et ipso facto
et completo paratum se offert si comode nec de jure
fieri potest copiam ipsius insolidum vel in parte
eisdem dare et concedere prout justicia suadebit. De
quibus omnibus dicti suplicantes pecierunt mandamentum.

Ego Hugo Bonilis notarius dicte curie hec scripsi et signo dicte curie
signavi.

Ad quam diem sabati supra per dictum dominum judicem assignatam
que est dies xiiii mensis novembris, comparuit dicta
Margarita de Porte personaliter citra revocacionem
omnium procuratorum suorum; nec non et Petrus de Porti eius
frater et pecierunt ut supra idem Petrus peciit videlicet
eis tradi et concedi copiam tocius processus, et terminum
congruum ad dicendum et allegandum contra.

Et dictus dominus judex attendens et conciderans quod hac die
presenti dicta Margarita comparuit in judicio judice cedendo
pro tribunali subitura jus et justiciam de intitulatis contra
eandem, et quia dicta Margarita copiam tocius processus
contra eandem factum peciit et requisivit, ideo ad deffencionem

[f⁰44 v.] ipsius et ad purgationem dictorum titulorum si de jure potue-
ruit se deffendere ad dandum allegaciones juris
super omnibus intitulatis et in dicto processu contentis
copiam eidem consentiit assignando eidem xviii
dierum terminum ad habendum consilium et ad
tradendum juris allegaciones ut supra et alios titulos reprobatorios si voluerit dare a copia processus habite, prius et ante omnia dicta Margarita
delata diligenter examinata et interrogata super titulo
inquisicionis contra eandem facto et aliis indiciis contra eandem
    resultantibus
prout et sicut de jure convenit.

Sequitur deposicio supradicte
Margarite presentis de premissis accusata.

Anno quo supra et die veneris xiii mensis novembris.
Constituta in curia Hospitalis ville Manuasce personaliter
Margarita relicta Johannis Dampocii condam de Manuasca
ante presenciam circumspecti viri domini Petri Rebolli jurisperiti judicis dicte curie ordinarii presentibus videlicet
nobili et religioso viro domino fratre Raymundo

Cornuti milite baiulo dicte curie, nec non et nobili
viro Petro de Salensono clavario dicte curie ac me
Hugone Bonilis notario eiusdem curie parata subire
jus et justiciam in presenti curie et obtemperare mandatis domini judicis antedicti petens et requirens
prout alias sepe et aliter extitit pro sui parte requisitum copiam processus et titulorum et omnium quorum
interest quibus juridice, et consulte possit et valeat
purgare si que contra eandem resultent judicia.

Et incontinenti ad inquirendum cum dicta Margarita
supra de premissis excessibus principaliter accusata supradicti
dominus judex baiulus et clavarius simul cum me Hugone
Bonilis notario dicte curie processerunt prout sequitur.

[f°45]
[in the margin:] Cum non confiteatur nec per testes
fide dignos in ali-
quo non convincatur
merito a presenti
inquisitione et
ab omnibus intitu-
latis contra eandem
tanquam ingno-
cens [sic] absolvatur.
[signed:] Petrus Rebolli

Principalis: Dicta die, dicta Margarita supra principaliter accusata
     perso-
naliter constituta coram supra nominatis dominis judice,
baiulo et clavario et me notario predicto stans
coram eisdem sine compedibus et sine aliqua liga-
tura ferrea nec cordarum sine vi metu aut formidine tormentorum monita et diligenter interrogata
per dictum dominum judicem, super primo titulo ipso prius sibi
lecto et dato intelligi in vulgari, suo juramento omnia et
singula in ipso contenta et contra se intitulata
negavit penitus et per omnia fore vera. Item fuit

interrogata per dictum dominum judicem medio suo juramento
si illo mane ipsa prepaverat sibi potagium, dixit
eius juramento quod non, neque sibi ivit austum? vinum sed
ipsemet eius maritus hoc fecit. Interogata si sibi
fecit scutelam, dixit quod sic et cuidam famulo
suo et cuidam alie parvule. Interrogata eius juramento
de quo patagio [sic] erat, dixit quod erat factum cum
amindolis siculis et alhis et oleo. Interrogata qua
hora erat, dixit quod circa horam prime. Interrogata
per dictum dominum judicem si ipsa loquens cum dicto eius marito comedit, dixit eius juramento quod ipsa comedit cum
quedam parvula que ibi erat circa duas hophas tantum
et non plus comedere potuit quia erat nimis
mane. Interrogata per dictum dominum judicem si ipsa aliquid
posuit in scutela sui mariti propter quod ipse sumeret dictam
mortem ut in titulo continetur, eius juramento dixit quod non.
Interrogata si alibi nec in ovis nec in vino aliquid
posuit propter quod ipse maritus suus sumeret dictam mortem,
dixit suo juramento quod non. Interrogata quid post fecit dictus Johannes
eius maritus, dixit quod ivit extra causa laborandi cum
eius famulo. Interrogata si ipsa loquens cum aliquo suo amico
vel amica vel aliis habuerat consilium vel auxilium vel aliud

[f⁰45 v] tractatum propter quod ipse maritus suus subiret dictam mortem,
dixit eius juramento quod non. Interrogata si quando dictus Johannes eius
     ma-
ritus venit de extra villam si sibi dixit aliquid, dixit eius juramento
quod nil aliud sibi dixit nisi quod senciebat magnam ama-
ritudinem in corpore et cor sibi defficiebat. Interrogata
si eam dictus Johannes eius maritus eam carnaliter cognovit,
dixit suo juramento quod non quia quando erat juxta ipsam in lecto
multum fortiter tremebat taliter quod cum ipsa appropinquare
nec habitare poterat illa de causa. Interrogata si scit nec
dici audivit quod aliquis eidem Johanni marito suo portabat
iram nec rancuram, dixit suo juramento quod non.

Item fuit interrogata dicta Margarita per dictum dominum
judicem medio suo juramento super primo indicio post titulum sequentem. Que respondit suo juramento contenta in illo
nullo modo fore vera nam eidem marito suo magnam

amiticiam portabat. Interrogata si ipsa unquam dixit
illis qui matrimonium duxerant vel aliis quod maladicta esset dies qua ipsa sumerat dictum Johannem Dampocii
in eius maritum quia male gratibus suis hoc fecerat.
Dixit suo juramento quod non sed bene dixit quod maladicta esset
dies et hora qua ipsa nata erat. Et hoc dicebat propter
morbum caducum quod habebat, quia dixit quod ex post
quod venerat ad presentem villam et conjuncta erat cum
dicto Johanne Dampocii illud morbum habuerat et non
ante. Interrogata qua de causa ipsa iverat ad Bellum
Montem, dixit quod propter dictum morbum quod habebat pro
spaciendo et de voluntate dicti eius mariti ivit, videlicet
una die veneris et in die jovis sequenti ipsa ad presentem villam reddiit, ideo quia maritus suus eidem
mandavit unam litteram ut venire deberet per quandam
filiam Arnaudi Cantelani de Bello Monte.

Super secundo indicio fuit interrogata, que dixit contenta in
illo fore vera tamen non culpa sui mortuus est.

[f°46] Item fuit interrogata super tercio indicio, que eius juramento dixit
verum fore ipsam esse de Bello Monte, et semel fuit
quedam mulier ibidem que tamen non erat de dicto loco oriunda
ut dici audivit que semel illud scandalum fecit ex quo
penam subiit temporalem ut audivit dici.

Super iiii indicio interrogata, dixit medio eius juramento verum esse
ivisse ad monasterium dominarum monialium Sancte Clare usque ad
januam tantum; et post modum ivit ad cameram fratris
sui que erat infra claustram Beate Marie. Interrogata qua de causa
recesserat de domo mariti sui ad dictas ecclesias, dixit
quod propter miserias quas sibi faciebat magister Raymundus Gauterii
qui eidem dicebat "foras, foras quia tu interfecistis fratrem
meum." Et eciam propter illud morbum caducum quod ibidem in
hospicio suo habuerat bis dum eius maritus morte vexabatur,
et alique probe mulieres ipsam portarunt extra hospicium
dicti eius mariti videlicet ad domum Anthonii Olivarii et [*crossed out:* eius
frater dyaconus voluit quod ipsa iret ad suam cameram ubi
morabatur ad] ibi stetit per modicum spacium. Et post venit

quedam monaca vocata soror Maria eius consanguinea et
eam fecit ^ire^ ad eorum monasterium cum aliquibus mulieribus
quarum nomina ignorat. Et eius frater dyaconus voluit
quod ipsa iret ad suam cameram ubi morabatur ad clastrum
Nostre Domine et cum eodem recessit ad cameram predictam.

Item fuit interrogata super quinto indicio, que medio eius
juramento dixit verum esse ut in eo continetur, ivisse ad dictam
cappellam tamen illuc ivit pretimore domini Manuasce preceptoris
quia timebat ne ipsam extraxeret de facto de camera in
qua erat ante.

Super sexto indicio fuit interrogata, que medio eius juramento
dixit verum esse non ivisse ad dictam sepulturam ex eo

[f⁰46 v] quia erat sola et nullam societatem habebat. Tamen satis flevit
et doluit.

Item fuit interrogata super vii⁰ indicio, que eius juramento dixit
verum esse se non ivisse ad dictam curiam licet citata
extitisset quia eius frater hoc noluit tamen si voluisset
libenter ivisset pro se excusando.

Item fuit interrogata dicta loquens et diligenter examinata
per dictum dominum judicem super primo indicio aliorum indiciorum
in cedula per magistrum Raymundum Gauterii producta contentorum.
Que eius juramento dixit se nil aliud dixisse nisi quod de mala
hora ipsa fuisset nata. Et hoc dicebat propter morbum
quod paciebatur non aliter. Cetera in eo contenta negavit
fore vera.

Super secundo indicio fuit interrogata, medio eius juramento que negavit
contenta in illo fore vera et quod falso modo fuit sibi
allevatum.

Super tercio indicio, negavit se umquam dixisse verba in eo
contenta et quando ivit ad dictum castrum de Bello Monte
hoc fecit de voluntate eius mariti ut supra dixit.

Item fuit interrogata super iiii^{to} indicio, que eius juramento dixit
verum esse quod semel ire credidit ad dictum locum
de Bello Monte. Tamen eius maritus hoc noluit quia non
habebat bonam comitivam.[5]

Item fuit interrogata dicta delata super quinto indicio, que eius
juramento negavit omnia in ipso contenta fore vera et numquam
illud dixisse. Interrogata per dictum dominum judicem attento quod generaliter negavit dictum titulum eam interrogavit quomodo
intelligebat illud verbum: "Deyluirar an propter maritum,
maritum an propter morbum," dixit quod numquam protulit illud
verbum verbum [sic]. Tamen dixit quod si esset in Bello Monte quod eius
fratres eam custodirent ne caderet in igne quia sepissime in eo cadebat propter morbum quod habebat.

[f°47] Super sexto indicio, dixit eius juramento quod illa die qua recessit
        apud
Bellum Montem ipsa extraxit quandam raubam suam nupcialem
de voluntate mariti sui pro se illuc parando et dum revenit
ipsa portavit xviii massanos canapi[6] et tres pullos.

Item fuit interrogata super septimo indicio, que eius juramento dixit
se non portasse nisi unum par caligarum et aliud par sa-
cularium in tibiis et pedibus calciata; et non plus.

Super octavo indicio, medio eius juramento fuit interrogata, que dixit
se non portasse ad dictum locum de Bello Monte nisi unam
zannam de suis jocalibus quia non plus habebat. Et illam [sic] reddiit.

Item fuit interrogata super nono indicio, que eius juramento dixit
verum esse ut in eo continetur. Tamen ibidem jacuit de
voluntate eius mariti.

Super x^{o} indicio fuit interrogata, medio eius juramento que negavit
omnia contenta in illo fore vera.

5 *meaning "good company"*
6 massanos = bundles?; canapus = Fr. *chanvre*, or hemp

Item fuit interrogata super xi° indicio eius juramento, dixit quod eius
    maritus
et suus famulus fecerunt dictum viaticum cum alhis
et amindolis. Interrogata quomodo scit, dixit quia eum invenit
paratum et nullus alter erat tamen in ola posuit oleum
in presencia uxoris Petri Rufferii sororis dicti deffuncti.

Super xii° indicio eius juramento dixit verum esse ut in eo continetur. Et hoc fecit de voluntate et precepto mariti
sui, et quia illud facere consueverat.

Item fuit interrogata super xiii indicio, que dixit quod est falsum
contenta in illo quia secum semper comedebat et paraxides
faciebat.

Super xiiii° indicio fuit interrogata que medio eius juramento dixit
se nichil scire de contentis in eo.

Item fuit interrogata super xv° indicio, que dixit se nichil scire de
contentis in eo.

Item fuit interrogata super xvi indicio et ultimo, que eius juramento
dixit se nil aliud scire de contentis in eo nisi quod ipsa et uxor

[f°47 v] Petri Rufferii iverunt ad lectum eius mariti et eum
invenerunt supra lectum. Et eisdem dixit quod habebat "lo cor
sclatat." Interrogata si ipsa erat infra hospicium quando eius maritus
de extra venit, dixit quod non quia iverat in incaria [sic] pro emendo
decondolis (cordolis ?). Et post modum ivit quesitum de ovis ad domum Petri Rufferii de precepto sue [sic] uxoris. Et pluribus interrogationibus sibi factis, dixit se alia nescire et plus confiteri
noluit.

Et ibidem Hugo et Guillelmus de Porti fratres dicte Margarite et
Laugerius Montaguti de Bello Monte fidejusserunt omnes simul
et quilibet ipsorum insolidum pro dicta Margarita. Et cum juramento
etc. Et renunciaverunt jure de principale etc; Et promiserunt dictam
Margaritam presenti curie representare tociens quociens opus
erit et requisiti fuerint; et hoc sub pena centum
marcarum argenti fini. Quam promiserunt solvere curie presenti

casu quo ipsam non presentarent quandocumque requisiti fuerint.
Et eo casu quo unus ipsorum eam presentaret alii liberentur.
Et promitunt habere ratum et gratum omne id et quicquid
per illum factum erit. Et penam in qua ille se submitet
illam omnes alii promitunt habere ratam et solvere domino preceptori
casu quo in illa incidet.

Et nichilominus dictus dominus judex loco carceris et arresti
dictam Margaritam assignavit moraturam infra domum
dominarum monialium Sancte Clare de Manuasca ob reverenciam
et honestatem dicte mulieris licet casus non requirat et
hoc de expressa voluntate et licencia domini Manuasce preceptoris
que quidem Margarita promisit de inibi non exire suis pedibus
neque alienis sine licencia dicte curie; et hoc sub pena predicta.
De quibus dictus clavarius peciit instrumentum.

Actum in dicta curia in presencia et testimonio Jacobi Simonis, Rostagni
Fabri, magistro Nicolao Atenulphi et magistro Raymundo Guasqui
notariis de Manuasca.

Et me Hugone Bonilis, notario etc.

[f⁰48] Et post paululum et aliquod temporis intervallum dum
dicta Margarita fuit infra domum supradictarum dominarum
monialium, providus vir Raymundus Elerii subvicarius dicte curie
eidem Margarite imposuit penam centum marcarum argenti
fini de precepto supradicti domini judicis ut a dicta domo non
exeat suis pedibus neque alienis sine licencia dicte curie et
cum eadem fuerit concordata.

Actum ante portam dicte domus in presencia Rostagni Fabri, Johannis
Santoris et magistri Nicholay Atenulphi, notarii.

Et me Hugone Bonilis, notario.

Postque anno quo supra et die sabati xiiii mensis novembris.
Veniens ad presenciam nobilium virorum domini Petri Rebolli, jurisperiti judicis dicte curie pro tribunali sedentis, et domini fratris Raymundi
Cornuti militis baiuli, et Petri de Salensono clavarii eiusdem
curie ac mei Hugonis Bonilis notarii eiusdem, supradicta Marga-

rita de Porte mandato tamen et jussu supradicti domini judicis
causa eandem Margaritam iterandi et reaudiendi super contentis
in titulo inquisicionis contra ipsam facto et aliis indiciis contra mandatis seu formatis in presenti processu contentis et descriptis.
Et bene et diligenter interrogata et examinata per dictum dominum
judicem super eisdem ut decet, dicta Margarita medio tamen
eius juramento ad Sancta Dei euvangelia per ipsam sponte corporaliter
tacto dixit et respondit se alias in presenti curia super premissis
et contra eandem intitulatis fuisse et extitisse audita et
interrogata per eundem dominum judicem super quibus ipsa deposuit
omnimodo ut dixit veritatem tantum quidem deposicioni in omnibus
et per omnia de puncto ad punctum stare vult et intendit
nichil adito nilque remoto. Et per hanc presentem deposicionem illi deposicioni nullo modo derogare intendit
sed eam omnimodo pro posse confirmat et nil aliud dixit
se scire quam in eadem confessa fuit pluribus interrogationibus
sibi factis.

Et ibidem Hugo et Guillelmus de Porti eius fratres et Laugerius Montaguti pro eadem Margarita fidejusserunt per modum et formam

[f⁰48v.] quibus supra et sub pena ^predicta^. Et dictus dominus judex jussit
eam
reverti in domo dominarum monialium ut supra. Et ipsa promisit
de eadem non exire ut supra et sub pena predicta in
forma etc. Et sic actum recessit.

Actum in dicta curia presentibus Petro Valensie et Rostagno
Fabri de Manuasca et pluribus aliis.

[f⁰49 v, bottom]
Anno quo supra et die martis [*corrected from:* sabbati] xxiiii mensis
novembris
in dicta curie Hospitalis ville Manuasce et coram dicto
domino judice pro tribunali sedente. Comparuit Petrus de Porti
dyaconus frater dicte Margarite delate, et eidem domino judici

[f⁰50] exhibuit et presentavit quandam papiram
cedulam scriptam, quam legi et publicari petiit

per me Hugonem Bonilis notarium dicte curie indeque ipsam
in presentibus actis de verbo ad verbum inseri et describi
dicens, petens, protestans et requirens ut in
ea continetur cuius quidem cedule tenor sequitur
in hunc modum.

Tenor ipsius:

Constitutus Petrus de Porti de BelloMonte frater et ut
conjuncta persona Margarite relicte Johannis Dampons
ante presenciam nobilis viri domini Petri Rebolli jurisperiti judicis ville Manuasce dicens et exponens dicto
nomine quod cum tam idem Petrus quam alii sepe requi-
siverunt dicto nomine prout infra vel extra processum reperitur contineri quod est eidem domino
judici notum quod dicto Petro pro parte dicte Margarite
delate ut dicitur de nosse dicti Johannis eius viri ob
que seu quod inter cetera mandamento dicte curie ad reperiendum
veritatem qua de causa potuit presumi mors
dicti condam Johannis utrum subito voluntate divina
obierit seu aliter ob culpam alicuius fuit missus
et ductus magister Vivas Jozep medicus et surgicus
eo tunc visinus utrum divina voluntate aut culpa
ut supra expressatur obierit. Qui si dictus medicus
seu surgicus non deposuerit, quod pars dicte Margarite

[f⁰50 v] eciam deposuerit an ne, aut deposicio dicti medici
seu surgici scensa et descripta ad plenum ut in
talibus convenit fuerit. Quod eo casu quod per scensum
et clare eius deposicio scripta non fuerit vel idem
medicus non deposuerit quod penitus pars dicte
Margarite ignorat et justam causam habet
ignorare quod dictus medicus si non deposuerit
deponat. Que deposicio scribatur et inseratur
cum aliter non possit plene sive comode compleri
processus absque eo quod deposicio dicti medici in processu
reperiatur. Qua propter idem exponens instanter
et reverenter eundem dominum judicem requirit quatinus
dignetur cultu justicie et ut citius veritas reper-

iatur utrum dicta delata sit nocens vel innocens
delicti predicti. Et habita copia processus compleri valeat indicia si que contra eandem resultent consulte purgare eidem instanti copiam processus completi tradi
et assignari faciat suo loco et tempore opportunis et
ut citius poterit satis facto dicto medici ut est
moris per illum quem viam peritia videbit et justicia
suadebit. Que petit dictus exponens dicto nomine
fieri et concedi ut supra vestri dicti domini judicis
officium benique implorando et aliter non permitatis
processum quousque ut convenit completum fuerit
eidem instanti dicto nomine vel eius dicte delate
parti assignari

[f⁰51] Et dictus dominus judex visa et intellecta cedula
et contenta in eadem respondit fore esse paratum
audire super contentis in dicta cedula dictum magistrum
Vivas fizicum et surgicum et tanquam expertum ad talia
peragenda jubens nichilhominus eundem citari ad
diem crastinam ad hoc ut juridice consciencia dicti domini
judicis plenarie sit informata et de dicta Margarita delata possit et valeat justicie complementum
minstrari.

Et ibidem et incontinenti retulit Isnardus Laurerie
nuncius dicte curie eidem domino judice adhuc pro tribunali
sedenti michique notario infrascripto se citasse dictum
magistrum Vivas Jozep judeum medicum, fizicum ad instanciam
[bis] dicti Petri de Porti, personaliter repertum ad
diem et actum quibus supra prout habuit in mandatis ego Hugo Bonilis notarius dicte curie hec scripsi
et signo dicte curie signavi. [*signed with seal*]

Ad quam diem crastinam que est [*crossed out:* martis] mercuri
xxv mensis novembris, magister Vivas Jozep judeus
medicus, fizicus et surgicus de Manuasca personaliter
constitutus coram supra nominato ^domino^ judice meque notario
infrascripto pro sua relacione facienda de premissis et in
supradicta cedula petitis, contentis et descriptis. Qui

juramento suo per eum corporaliter prestito super
litteris ebraycis more judayco, dixit verum fore se pridie

[f⁰51 v] non est diu, mandato tamen et jussu supradicti
domini judicis accessisse una cum eodem domino judice et me
notario infrascripto ad domum Johannis Damponcii condam
ad videndum dictum Johannem Damponcii qui dicebatur
mortuus esse subito. Et pro inspiciendo signa et menbra [sic] sua utrum posset cognoscere qua de causa mortuus
erat. Quemquidem Johannem invenit in lecto mortuum,
et omnia sua menbra [sic] inspexit, et specialiter menbra [sic]
faciei sicut sunt labie, occuli et lingua et color
vultus nec non et supra ventrilhum. Et eciam manus
et uncule, et utrum crini capitis de facili traherentur.
Et post modum peciit gentibus de domo dicti Johannis
si dictus Johannes de illa die aliquid comederat et quid comederat. Que eidem medico responderunt quod ipse Johannes illo
mane comederat antequam iret ad aratam de potagio facto cum
alhis et amindolis; et post paululum revenit de arata ut
sibi dixerunt; et dixit gentibus suis quod ipse habebat magnum
dolorem cordis et incontinenti mortuus fuit. Et eciam
idem medicus eisdem peciit si vomerat. Qui eidem responderunt quod sic. Et ipse cupiens videre quid vomerat et
illud cognoscere non potuit ^eo^ quia gentes illud trapida-
verant cum pedibus in terra. Et quia fuit sibi preceptum
per dictum dominum judicem ut supra ut videret si cognosceret
aliqua signa in eo an esset mortuus de poyson an ne,
quiquidem medicus cupiens suam relacionem ad effectum perducere
dicit quod secundum artem medicine et illud quod ipse cognosce-
rat in eo, ut sequitur: Primo dicit quod sunt multe
species poysonum prout ponit liber Albucosin [Albucasis] in capitulo
de poysons; qui dicit quod las poysons dividuntur in tres
partes; prima in rebus inanimatis prout sunt in metalis
et aliis similibus;

[f⁰52] alie sunt in rebus vegitativis prout in erbis et aliis que
nascuntur a terra; et alie sunt in animalibus venenosis et
adhuc subdividuntur in duas partes quia quedam
sunt nature frigide et alie calide. Et ideo dicit quod signa

non sunt similia nec de uno esse. Et quia dictus medicus non potuit videre illud quod vomerat quia in illo
quasi cognosci posset prout scribit Vicena [*Avicenna*] in quarto
libro in la fen sexto. Que dicit que quis potest cognoscere la
poyson in hoc quod quis vomit videndo ad occulum; et
quia idem medicus illud non vidit non potest cognoscere,
quod sit mortuus de poyson. Et prout sibi videtur sunt
aliqua signa comunia et magis principalia in poysonis
prout dicit Vicena in quarto libro in la fen sexto quod
omnis persona que biberit poyson debent sibi enflare
labie et lingua et occuli sibi debent grossari et quodam
modo exhire multum extra caput. Et quia ipse non invenit labias inflatas nec linguam nec occulos grossos
nec aliquam nigritudinem in ungulis nec in aliqua
parte sui corporis dixit idem medicus in eodem non
vidisse aliquod signum poysonis. Et pro sui veritate
fundanda, et ad probandum predicta dixit quod
viso quod dictus Johannes comederat illo mane viaticum
factum cum alhis, et quia speriensia sive natura
alhium est quod habet de cassare omne venenum prout dicit
lo Circasitans in libro suo super capitulo de alhis qui dicit
quod bibere alhios decassat omne venenum, et alibi Galianus
dicit ^in libro Bone Digestionis^ quod lac et alhi et vinum et acetum
    et sal decas-
sant venenum de omni causa venenosa que venit in
corpore humano. Et plus dicit Galianus in quarto libro
De Regimine Sanitatis, alhi est medicina que habet decassare

[f⁰52 v] omnem ventositatem et eam fondit, et minuit omnem
comescionem, et ideo ipsam appellat idem Galianus
triacla? [*ink smeared*] de villan. Et visis dictis rationibus et capitulis
loquentibus de proprietate alhium ad decassandum venenum,
Et viso et audito quod ipse Johannes de potagio alhium
illo mane comedit, dixit quod propter illam speriensiam
ipse nullo modo mori debuit de veneno. Item eciam
ad corroborandum predicta dixit dictus medicus
quod ipse invenit de alliis [sic] infirmitatibus de quibus multociens gentes illas habentes subito moriuntur prout
est quidem morbus vocatus sincopus, ut dicit Galianus

in tercio decimo capitulo De De [sic] Tecerop Pentit [De
    Therapeuticorum]
quia quando venit dictus morbus sincopus est plus quam
periculosum et est socius mortis et cum ea iungitur
et sunt consocii ut supra. Item plus dicit alibi Galianus in primo De Agaloquen quod ille morbus sincopus
devastat ^spiritum^ [*corrected from:* speciem?] vite subito. Item dixit
    idem medicus
se invenire alium morbum qui vocatur aplunnatisia [*epilepsy*]
quod vulgariter nuncupatur morbus caducus, quod gentes
illum habentes interdum subito moriuntur prout stabit
Vicena in libro tercio capitulo quinto de la fen primier
dixit quod ille morbus la plenniancia(?) est morbus
qui subito venit et subito recedit et aliquando
quis eum habet ita fortiter quod ex eo mortuus remanet
et prout eidem medico narratum fuit per aliquos ut
ipse asserit quod dictus Johannes uxorem virginem duo menses
sunt elapsi vel circa duxerat cum qua nullo modo
carnaliter jungere potuit seu copulare, et pro eo multociens illo ardore se inflamavit et sibi ipsi generavit

[f⁰53] malaenconia⁷ quia non poterat complere eius volutatem
cum eadem. Sic quod mala enconia est de accidentalibus
animatis quare potest esse quod ex eo dictus Johannes mortem
subiit, prout scribit Galianus in primo De Agaloquen
accidens animal con es fort engendia sincopus,
et mala enconia eciam generat sincopus quia
trahit intus frigus et congilat calorem et eum scingit.
Sic quod humores intrant infra corpus ^cum calore^ et sufocat
calorem, ideo una mala enconia fort adus la
mort. Et posibile est et esse potest quod propter
mala enconia quam ipse Johannes habuit de predictis
se congregavit aliquis humor prope cor de quo
humore eciam exivit aliqua sinusitas que se applicavit cordi que mutavit compleccionem cordis prout scribit Galianus qui per speriensiam ad occulum
vidit illum humorem, et prout alibi scribit
Vicena in tercio libro en la fen undecimo in capitulo

---

7 melancholy

de infirmitatibus cordis quod multociens reperitur in
illis partibus prope cor [*crossed out:* de quo humore] aliquis humor
qui quando crescit destringit cor et tunc homo mo-
ritur. Et dixit idem medicus quod posibile est quod propter
dolorem quem dictus Johannes passus fuit ut prefertur
subito mortuus est. Item eciam dixit dictus medicus
quod absque aliqua comescione seu potacione veninoza
possunt [*corrected from:* potest] generari aliqui humores venenosi in
corpore
humano qui generantur de epulentis et poculis cor-
ruptis ut dicit Galianus in libro De Teterop pentit, quod
epule et poculi corrupti generant et devastant

[f⁰53 v] corpus humanum sicuti poysones. Et dicit Vicena alibi
in libro primo en la fen primier in doctrina quarta
in primo capitulo quod potest generari aliqua species
coleris que similatur poyson et illa generatur
de utendo et continuando specibus ^accutis^ alhis et porris
et illa vocatur zenengarit vulgariter nuncupato
"verdet" quia quasi habet colorem de veridet. Et dicit
Vicena quod ista species coleris est ^plus calida et^ peior omni aliarum
et plus mortificabilis et quasi est de substancia
de poyson. Item dicit Ysac in suo libro vocato
Febres dIsac in capitulo de tersana quod si natura
corporis humani est fragilis ita quod non possit proicere
dictam coleram extra interficit sine dubio gentes.

Et visis et diligenter inspectis capitulis supra
allegatis et per suos magistros in talibus expertos
descriptis et viso dicto Johanne mortuo et ipso palpato
ut decet dicit idem medicus et concludit se non
invenisse in eo juxta cursum medicine aliquod
signum propter quod debuerit mori de poyson. Que
omnia predicta Ego Hugo Bonilis notarius dicte curie
scripsi et signo dicte curie signavi. [*signed with seal*]

[f⁰54] Anno incarnationis domini millesimo cccᵐᵒ nonagesimo iiiiᵗᵒ et
die mercuri xxvii mensis januarii fuit producta et ostensa
quadam papiri cedula, nobili et circumspecto viro domino
Petro Rebolli jurisperito judici curie Hospitalis ville Manuasce

pro parte Margarite uxoris condam Johannis Dampons pro suis
    deffensionibus
producta et ad eius innoscenciam declarandam et ostendendam
cuius quidem cedule tenor talis est ut ecce.

Tenor dicte cedule talis est

Cum Margarita de Portu delata in curia Manuasce de morte
viri sui sit ex ipso processu ^absolvenda^ ut clare patet tam per
    deposiciones
testium productorum pro parte curie quam per testes numeratos per
Raymundum qui partem facit contra ipsam nec non jurium allegaciones fuerint producte pro parte ipsius ex quibus clare apparet
ipsam omnino fore absoluendam ad ostendendum eius veram
innoscenciam et ad confondendum aliquia judicia contra ipsam
    Margaritam
oblata aliqua dicentur et ad informationem domini judicantis
consciencie.

Et primo super illo judicio qui continet ipsam Margaritam
fore de BelloMonte in quo loco scandalum tempore retroacto
accidit de morte aliquorum qui mortui fuerant ex vereno,
dicitur inde nullo modo illud contra dictam Margaritam resultare
quoniam non est bona consequencia quod si unus est malus quod omnes
    sint
mali ut nobis clare patet. Nam si unus ex discipulis Jhesu
fuit prodictor et malus ut est nobis notum de Juda proditore
non sequitur quod omnes alii apostoli quorum fidem nos christiani
tenemus fuerint proditores nec mali, quoniam confitemur illos
omnes fore sanctos et benedictos, nec ipsum castrum de BelloMonte
fuit melior arca Noe[8] in qua inter octo viri [sic] fuit unus reprobus
vel melior[9] domo Abrae cui fuit dictum eisse ancillam
et filium eius,[10] ut habetur xl vii[a] d. c; quantum et sic in

---

8 Noah's ark
9 A reference to Genesis 9:21–23 in which the eight passengers of the Ark are named (Noah, Shem,
   Ham, Japheth, and their wives). Ham had the unhappy pleasure of seeing his 600-year-old father,
   Noah, naked and drunk. His brothers were more dutiful and covered their father's nakedness without looking upon it. In punishment, Ham's son Canaan was cursed by Noah.
10 Genesis 16, which tells the story of Abraham's coupling with his wife Sarah's maidservant, Hagar
   the Egyptian. The product of this union was Ishmael.

casu nostro demum si aliquod per singularem pravam personam
scandalum in ipso loco evenit illa talis persona que talia comisit
fuit ut decebat corporaliter punita ut est manifestum
et tale grave malum non remansit impunitum, que corporalis
pena est et fuit et esse debuit et est ipsi Margarite
et omnibus scientibus in sempiternum tenorem et exemplum, nam cum
ipsa Margarita sit racionabilis mulier et prudens, si talia
attentare voluisset quod absit secura esset talem pati penam
sicut et alia que est sibi in exemplum, nam similia attentantibus
simili pena punirentur quare non est presumendum ipsa
Margarita talia comisisse, Et voluntarie detrimento et morti
corpus suum subisse. Denum non est presumendum ipsa Margarita
tale crimen comisisse que ex bona progenie et honesta est
ipsa Margarita et que ab ipsa progenie ulla scanda [*for* scandella ?]
    numquam provenerunt
nam bono peraguntur sive que sunt bona incohata principio ut habetur ita
    que
infra c. principatus et quantum ad illud ista sufficiant.

[f⁰54 v.] Item in oppositum inde dicentis ipsam Margaritam fugam rapuisse
dicuntur Sequencia videlicet ipsam Margaritam nullam fugam
rapuisse per quam contra [*crossed out:* al] eandem possint aliqua notari
    quoniam
post transitum accidentis et adhuc per ipsum confilicta
morbi caduci quo dicta Margarita eodem instanti detenta
fuit soror Maria monialis affinis sua dictam Margaritam
secum duxit ut a dicto malo seu morbo conflicta. Etalibi
ipsam Margaritam duxisset ipsa monialis si voluisset
cum dicta Margarita non esset causante morbo conpos
sui ut constat per deposiciones testium productorum per illum
qui contra dictam Margaritam facit partem et sic non potest
dici vel debet fugam rapuisse nam qui rapit fugam
proprio motu recedit ergo non est sibi imputandum quoniam
non est imputandum [*for* imputandus?] actus nisi voluntati ut xvᵃ que
    infra
c. non est. Demum ipsa Margarita non erat in hospicio
proprio vel viri sui ymo in alieno ut constat per processum
et per deposiciones testium productorum et per dictam monialem
fuit ducta dicta margarita ad cameram fratris sui
ut in suo proprio quoniam ut propriam domum ipsam cameram

habebat et habere debebat; quoniam non haberet alibi in presenti
villa reffugium vel affines nec ipsa monaca voluit eam
ducere ad hospicium mariti sui propter minas quas Raymundus
Gauterii faciebat eidem de morte fratris sui et ad evitandum
scandalla que eveni possent et quia corpus sive cadaver
viri sui erat adhuc in ipso hospicio quod si vidisset
dicta Margarita pre dolore posset p[r]ostrari a dicto morbo
et accidere scandalum de morte ipsius Margarite. Demum
ubicumque ipsa Margarita fuisset esset sibi licitum recedere
quoniam dominus preceptor dixit quod probatur quod ubicumque
     reperrisset
illam extraxisset et quia mulier est timens et
fragilior conditionis et debilioris potissime carente
amicis in dicta villa Manuasce, posset dubitare quin ipse dominus
preceptor de facto non incurrisset in personam ipsius
quod si fasseret ipsa Margarita leviter abugasset[11] Deum esse
in celum et potissime dixisset quod numquam cogitavit
fecisse. Demum non potest dici vel debet ipsa fugam
rapuisse nam posito sed non concesso ymo totaliter
negato quod ipsa Margarita recessisset et fugam
rapuisset hoc fecisset sencientem se culpabilem
de morte dicti viri sui; quoniam vir pretenditur mortuus
fuisse ex toxiquo vel veneno per ipsam Margaritam.
Et cum de contrario costet[12] per deposicionem magistri
Vivas Josep medici licentiati experti in arte sua et
sibi sit credendum qui medicus juxta artem medicine
deposuit et declaravit ipsum Johannem maritum dicte
Margarite non fore mortuum ex tosiquo vel veneno

[f⁰54 bis] non potest dici vel debet ipsam Margaritam fugam
rapuisse quia sine causa recesisset et sicpore ut?
non culpabilis de dicto crimine potuit ire quo voluerit
et sic est lex meliori modo interpretanda penes
dictam Margaritam et non dicendum fugam rapuisse
propter quam habeatur crimen pro confesso.

---

11 *For* abjurasset = abjuravisset
12 *For* constet

Cetera que in premissis desunt supleat peritia domini
judicantis et talia sufficiant cum per alias allegaciones et ex ipso processu ipsa Margarita sit
absolvenda et non in aliquo ut innoscens condempnanda
ut clarissime patet.

Anno domini millesimo ccc^mo nonagensimo iiii^to et die sabbati vi^ta
mensis febroarii. Comparuit Hugo de Portu de BelloMonte
ut frater et conjuncta persona dicte Margarite, dicens
et cum instancia requirendo nobilem virum dominum Petrum
Rebolli jurisperitum judicem ordinarium curie Hospitalis
ville Manuasce ut cum dicta Margarita taliter qualiter
et tacita veritate salva reverencia et citra [in]juriam
cuiusque delata detenta et arrestata diu existerit
et nunc existat prout dictus dominus judex merita
non ignorat et eciam quia propter fluxum temporis
potuerit compleri processus et discurere veritatem utrum sit
absoluenda vel condempnanda quod pocius probatur in processu
dictam Margaritam deberi absolui quam condempnari. Igitur
dictus Hugo dicto nomine humiliter benigne et instanter
requirit prefatum dominum judicem quatinus dignetur tempore
congruo dictam causam terminari, et super contentis et requisitis
minstrare dictam Margaritam absolvendo tamquam innocentem
jus et justiciam minstrare prout suo dicti domini judicis
incumbit officio parcendo sua benignitate illicitis laboribus
disturbiis et expensis et super petitis per eumdem dominum judicem
terminum congruum asseruit ad supra petita et requisiti et si neccesse
est et dicto domino judici videatur in causa huiusmodi suam sentenciam
diffinitivam proferri. Protestans nichilominus contra omnes et singulos
male incriminantis et denunciantes.

Et dictus dominus judex jussit ad se differri processum et ad deliberandum
super petitis et requisitis et ad inspiciendum veritatem contentorum
in processu eadem et ad terminandum causam si sibi videatur et [*crossed
out:* utrique]
parti [*crossed out:* ad] petenti ad se representandum coram eo de
terminum x dierum
pro termino assignavit.

[f⁰54 v. bis]

Die xvi mensis febroarii, dominus judex interrogavit magistrum
     Raymundum

Gauterii qui coadjutor ^curie^ fuit in presenti causa contra dictam
     Margaritam

medio eius juramento ad Sancta Dei euvangelia corporaliter prestito

si scit aliquas indicias nec aliqua resultancia contra ipsam Margaritam

exceptis aliis alias per ipsum datis, nec si intendit aliqua

alia contra eandem et pro informatione curie producere; nam ipse

dominus judex causam ipsam intendit terminare. Qui magister

Raymundus respondit se non fore paratum de presenti respondere

sed petit sibi assignari terminum ad id respondendum, protestando in
     omnibus

^et per omnia quod per alique^ que dixit seu dicet non intendit accusare de

predictis aliquam personam verumtamenet

^dum taxat pro ipsius curia informatione.^

Et dictus dominus judex ad respondendum per ipsum magistrum
     Raymundum

supra interrogat et ad exhibendum sive producendum omnia

que producere voluit contra ipsam Margaritam perhemptorie

et presise quinque dierum terminum pro termino assignavit.

Ad quam diem x supra per dictum dominum judicem, dictis partibus
     assignatam que est

martis xvi mensis febroarii Comparuit Hugo de Portu ut frater

et conjuncta persona dicte Margarite paratus audire deliberacionem dicti

domini judicis si quam induxerit proferendam juxta presentis diei
     assignatis.

Petens et requirens nichilominus benigne et cum instancia

ac instantissime prout supra peciit et requisivit protestans

ut supra fuit et est protestatus et contra quem supra fuit protestatus
     quam

protestacionem vult heri [haberi ?] in principio medio et in fine pro
     repetita

et facta videlicet contra omnes et singulos male intimantes et contra jus et
     justiciam

in presenti processu partem facientes.

Et dictus dominus judex dicit quod ipse fecit evocari magistrum
     Raymundum

Gauterii fratrem dicti deffuncti ad suam presenciam ^et interrogari eum
eius juramento^ [*crossed out:* cui sunt?] prestito
[*crossed out:* tamen? juramentum] si aliqua volebat indicia resultancia vel
    probaci-
ones alias dare contra dictam Margaritam pro informacione curie.
Et ut de eadem posset justicia minstrari et presens causa de-
terminari Quiquidem magister Raymundus hoc audito et intellecto
peciit sibi modicam dilacionem assignari super premissis Quiquidem
dominus judex eidem ^dilationem perhemptis et presise^ assignavit prout
    supra patet in suo decreto
et ideo non potuit de presenti deliberare. [*crossed out:* quam diem eidem]
Et ad audiendum eius deliberationem ut supra eidem parti comparenti
octo dierum termini pro terminum assignavit.

Et dictus Hugo dicte ordinacioni non consentit nisi si et inquantum
pro parte dicte Margarite esset causa copia tocius processus habuit pars
ipsius Margarite causa non sit idem magister Raymundus admitendus ad
superflua nec ad superfluas probaciones sive producciones que dicit
idem Hugo cum protestacionibus quibus supra.

Et dictus dominus judex ordinavit ut supra.

[f⁰55] Ad quam diem supra per dictum dominum judicem assignatam que
est dies jovis xxv mensis
februarii que succedit loco diei externe feriate juxta diei assignacionem
comparuit Hugo de Portu nomine quo supra petens instanter causam
    huiusmodi
terminari causa prefatus dominus judex semel bis, ter et pluries extiterit
    requi-
situs super quibus juxta mentem et seriem pretensi[?] processus et deffen
    tonum [sic]
super contentis in dicto processu productarum pro parte dicte Margarite et
jurium allegacionum petit juridice instanter et reverenter sentenciam ferri
et quod per ipsum non stat dicto nomine protestatur.

Et dictus dominus judex sedendo pro tribunali interrogavit magistrum
    Raymundum
Gauterii presentem fratrem dicti Johannis Damponcii deffuncti licet aliam
dilacionem habuerit perhemptorie et precise ut constat per acta an

partem facere intendat in presenti causa ac eciam si habet aliqua
indicia sive probaciones contra dictam Margaritam cum super toto
processu dictus dominus judex intendat justicie complimentum
minstrare et determinare prout ordo juris postulat et requirit
jubens ad maiorem cautelam citari alios parentes et affines
si qui sint ad diem crastinam in terciis si in presenti causa partem facere
intendunt.

[*in the margin:* d iii]

Et incontinenti, dictus magister Raymundus Gauterii frater dicti condam
    Johannis
Dampons presens protestatione prehita ut supra quod per aliqua que dixit
seu dicet in futurum non intendit accusare dictam Margaritam
seu alia quacumque persona, ac tamen pro ipsius domini judicis conscia
    informan-
da de certis indiciis contra dictam Margaritam manifest et tantum
manifestis que totaliter non indigent probatione loco et tempore ipsi
domino judici ostendendis. Petens et requirens prefatum dominum
judicem ut sibi concedere valeat copiam tocius processus in ea parte
in qua habere voluerit, causa alia eundem dominum judicem requisiverit
copiam tocius processus et minime habere potiit.

Et dictus dominus judex attento quod dictus magister Raymundus intendit
    aliqua
indicia de novo producere pro informatione ut asserit dicte curie eundem
admisit ad quod faciendum et producendum xv dierum terminum perhemptis
et presise eidem assignatum. Concedens copiam tocius processus vel in ea
    parte in
qua habere voluerit exceptis deffensionibus pro parte ipsius Margarite
productis.

[*in the margin:* totaliter contraduxit]

Et incontinenti dictus Hugo de Portu nomine quo supra non consenciit
    ^ymo^ alicui
ordinacioni de novo facte causa salva reverencia dicti domini judicis
ipse magister Raymundus sit minime audiendus [*crossed out:* ad audiendi]
    nec ad-

mitendus ad ea que petit, cum hanc? dilationem perhemptis et
presisam et non sit admitendus ad aliqua superflua producenda
cum ista sint superflua in presenti processu ut apperet liquide ex
ipsis. Protestans ut supra fuit et est protestatus et contra quem vel quos
quam protestacionem in principio medio et in fine vult pro repetita haberi.
Petens sibi fieri mandamentum de requisicione dicti magistri Raymundi.

Et dictus dominus judex ordinavit ut supra.

[f⁰55 v.] Et in crastinum quod est veneris xxvi mensis febroarii venientes
ad presenciam supra dicti domini judicis Beatrix uxor Petri Rufferii,
Catherina uxor Guillelmi Fulconis sororibus uterinis Johannis Danpons
quondam et Bertholomeus Dampons patruus dicti Johannis. Et eosdem
     dominus
judex interrogavit si sciunt aliqua indicia seu aliquos testis
nec aliqua intendunt probare ^ac producere^ contra Margaritam uxorem
     condam Johannis Dampons
de morte sui mariti accusata vel in ipso processu contra ipsam Margaritam partem facere intendunt. Quiquidem supra nominati
omnes unanimiter et concorditer responderunt dicto domino judici se
nullam partem facere vollentes in dicta causa nec fecerunt [*crossed out:*
     vult?] ^nec^ aliqua
producere intendunt vel produxerunt contra eandem, nec ipsam in aliquo
accusant seu intendunt accusare, ymo eam habuerunt et
hab[eb]unt pro bona et desenti et honesta muliere et proba.
De quibus Johannis de Salensono nomine dicte Margarite peciit
     mandamentum.

Anno quo supra, die veneris quinta mensis marcii comparuit in curia
Hospitalis ville Manuasce et coram domino judice supradicto Guillelmus
     de Portu
de BelloMonte ut frater et conjuncta persona supradicte Margarite
et eidem domino judici nomine quo supra exhibuit et presentavit
quandam papiri cedulam scriptam quam peciit in presencia dicti domini
judicis lcgi et publicari et in actis presentibus describi et inseri
petens postulans et requirens ut in eadem continetur.

Tenor dicte cedule
talis est prout ecce

Constitutus in curia Hospitalis ville Manuasce et coram vobis nobili
et circumspecto viro domino Petro Rebolli jurisperito judice curie
supradicte Guillelmus de Portu frater et ut conjuncta persona
Margarite de Portu uxoris quondam Johannis Dampons de Manuasca
delata in dicta curia de morte eius viri tacita veritate, salva
vestri domini judicis reverencia, dicit reverenter exponendo
quod cum in processus criminalis cause contra dictam Margaritam
Raymundus Gauterii notarius dicte ville faciat partem ut accusator
ut ex ipso processu clare patet et per vos dominum judicem

[f⁰56] ipsi magistro Raymundo post conclusionem et renunciacionem
    factam in
ipsa causa cum fuerit tacite conclusum et renunciatum
per consesionem copie tocius processus concesse parti dicte Margarite
pro suis defensionibus faciendis assignatus terminus perhemptorius
    quinque
dierum dicto magistro Raymundo ut si qua voluerit producere
vel dare contra dictam Margaritam et in ipso termino nichil
dixerit vel produxerit nec comparuerit ipse magister Raymundus.
Et post per vos dictum dominum judicem alius terminus fuerit
assignatus sive prefixus ipsi magistro Raymundo ad id quod supra
concedendo copiam processus, quod salva vestri domini judicis
reverencia minime facere debuistis rationibus predictis
et subsequentibus. Cum ipse magister Raymundus non comparuit
vel aliquid dicerit in termino quinque dierum sibi assignato
et prefixo nec contra ipsam Margaritam aliqua producerit,
sic nec esse debuit vel est audiendus nec ad
aliqua per eum postulata admitendus vel aliqua
copia ipsius cause sit vel fuit sibi concedenda cum de
jure caveatur. Quoniam accusator assignato termino nichil
dicente sic minime ut a jure traditor audiendus vel si accusator
non comparuerit in termino prefixo non est de jure amplius
audiendus in ipsa causa nec ad aliqua admitendus
ut in decretis habetur iiii.q. v. quis quid ^infra^et extra de accusationibus
[crossed out: et autem] c. licet in fine et c. qui accusare non possunt
l. uride forte ubi de crimine agitur [crossed out: extral?] de fide instru.? c. O.
et ff. dejure fiscil. ii. c. Senatus [crossed out: et] ff. quibus ex causis
maioresl. si cui c. i. [crossed out: et] ff. de indiciisl. si pretor
in fr. Quare attentis omnibus supradictis et allegatis

per ipsum Guillelmum dicit et instanter requirit ipse Guillelmus
nomine quo supra vos supradictum dominum judicem quatinus dignemini
dictum decretum seu assignacionem factam dicto magistro Raymundo
revocare, cum salva vestri reverencia eidem magistro Raymundo
assignaveritis terminum xv dierum ad producendum contra dictam
    Margaritam
concedendo copiam [*crossed out:* tocius] processus ipsi magistro
    Raymundo contra jus et justiciam
cum ut supra dictum est in primo termino sibi prefixo ipse magister
Raymundus non comparuerit vel aliqua producerit ut supradictum est

[f⁰56 v.] contra dictam Margaritam quod si secus fiat quod non credit
    protestatur
ipse Guillelmus nomine quo supra de deffectu justicie et juris
beneficio sibi denegato et de habendo recursum ad superiorem
per modum appellationis vel recursus seu aliter. De quibus una cum
responsione vestri domini judicis vel sibi petit ipse Guillelmus
nomine quo supra si et quando habere voluerit sibi fieri publicum
instrumentum.

Et dictus dominus judex ad audiendum eius deliberatam responsionem
super premissis si ei visum fuerit octo dierum pro termino assignavit.

Actum in teralho super lapide ante curiam ubi jus multociens
redditur per dictum dominum judicem.

Presentibus Guillelmo Castanihi, Bonifacio Peysoni et Petro
de Salensono.

Postque magnificus et religiosus vir dominus frater Johannes Sanini
    magnus Hospitalis
et Manuasce preceptor cupiens de dicta Margarita facere justicie complimentum minstrari secundum quod juris ordo postulat et requirit
volensque super premissis habere consilium peritorum ad cautelam licet
bonum habeat judicem et susficientem ad predicta per agenda copiam
tocius processus criminalis causa deffensionibus pro parte ipsius Margarite
    pro-
ductis et dubiis omnibus pro parte ipsius curie resultantibus desti-

navit venerabili viro domino Gaufrido Ganhomini in legibus licen[tiat]o
    curie Aquensis
mandando eidem per suas clausas literas ut bene et diligenter inspicere
habeat [*crossed out:* habeat] meritum ipsius cause et quod in eadem
decreverit secundum jus
sibi mandet. Quiquidem venerabilis vir dominus Gaufridus mandatis
    ipsius domini
preceptoris annuens, quod de eadem causa cognovit per suas clausas
literas in pede ipsarum suo nomine subscriptas et in eorum dorso suo
    sigillo
sigilatas eidem domino preceptori mandavit dirigendas quarum literarum
tenor sequitur incontenti.

Tenor ipsarum literarum et superscriptio
earundem

Venerabili et religioso viro domino fratri Johanni Sanini militi magno
et Manuasce preceptori eius domino reverendo.

Venerabilis et reverende domine recomandatione premissa, noveritis me
    vestras
literas recepisse duo effectualiter continentis unum videlicet super facto
    Margarite
filie de Porti de Porti delate quod debuit maritum suum poculo seu

[f⁰57] ferculo interficere secundum superfacto v florenorum vobis
    debitorum
per universitatem presentem cum erat obsidio ante castrum de Monte
Furono. Quantum ad primum dominatione vestre notifico me ad
plenum et cum deliberatione vidisse copiam tocius processus
inquisitionis et omni agitatorum pro parte ipsius Margarite
delate, super quo salvo jure cuiuslibet melius servientis
et sine allegationibus jure cum dominatio vestra et dominus judex
vester poterit videre per processum, michi videtur fore dicendum.
Primo, quod ipsa Margarita delata non potest ex debito sibi
imposito condemnari cum non convincatur nec ipsa fateatur
delictum ipsum comisisse. Item super alio quo pretendit non
possit pronunciari ad torturam vigore indiciorum resultantium

contra eam, michi ut supra viso dicto processu videtur dicendum quod
non.

Primo quia ad hoc ut quis veniat questionandus oportet
quod resultent indicia contra delatam verisimilia et talia quod ad
condempnationem non desit nisi sola confessio que indicia descripta
talia non consistunt in processu quia non fuga quia non constatis de
fuga ymo pocius de contrario nec alia indicia non sunt talia
nec verisimilia. Secundo, quia illa indicia non probantur ut constat ex
processu et indiciis non probatis ad actum pronunciationis
torture deveniri non potest cum eciam quia testes super indiciis
et titulo auditis pro parte curie deponunt pocius pro ipsa delata
quam contra et hoc fuit aliqui familiares et affines in quantum
pro parte curie fuerunt aprobati non potest curie contravenire;
quia testes pro utraque parte veritatem deponere debent.

Cum et quia ad probationem indicii requirit deposicio duorum testium
omni exceptione maiorum quia de periculo magno agitur juxta
decisionem glosarum et doctorum que hic videlicet in dicto processu in-
sunt neque consistunt ymo pocius probatur excusacio delate
ratione morbi ipsius et actorum subsecutorum et quod ex bonis
parentibus et quod bene se habebat comuniter vir et uxor et
quod potagium non paravit licet oleum posuerit presente marito
et aliis de domo que faciunt pro ipsa quia non deponitur
quod loco olei esset aliud poculum; et eciam quia ipsis praesentibus
quare ex his causis et aliis aparentibus per processum et de jure
procedentibus ipsa Margarita est absolvenda non obstantibus
quibuscumque conditionibus et opposicionibus per aliquem seu aliquos
affines mariti factis.

Et ita [*crossed out:* videtur] michi Gaufrido Ganhomini videtur de jure
[*crossed out:* faciendum] fiendum
salvo jure melius me sencientis et propterea predicta manu propria scripsi
et in testimonium premissorum hanc literam clausam sigillo proprio
sigillavi
scriptis Aquis die v marcii.

[f⁰57v.]
Ad quam diem octavam supra per dictum dominum judicem Guillelmus de
Portu
quo supra nomine supra proxime assignata que [*crossed out:* est] succedit

loco diei externe feriate propter festum Sancti [E]gregorii,[13] que dies
est sabati xiii, mensis marcii, comparuit in dicta curia et coram
prefato domino judice magister Nicolaus Atenulphi notarius procurator
assertus supradicte Margarite, et juxta presentis diei asserit paratus
audire deliberationem dicti domini judicis si quam duxerit proferendam;
et nichilominus petit sentenciam ferri in presenti causa prout sepe
et sepisse pro parte dicte Margarite extitit requisitum
de quibus sollempniter protestatur.

Ex adverso comparuit magister Raymundus Gauterii negans dictum
magistrum Nicolaum esse procuratorem et minime audiendum ad ea que
    petit.
Requirens de potestate quam asserit fidem facere [*crossed out:* respon]
    ante quam
ad alia procedatur respondendo nichilominus decreto prefati domini
judicis quando hiis diebus proxime lapsis prefixit terminum perhemptis
ipsi magistro Raymundo Gauterii fratri dicti condam Johannis Dampons ut
si qua produxere vellet ea produxisset infra xviii dies
quod ipse magister Raymundus minime facere potuit causantibus
    guerrarum
periculis et viarum discriminibus ymo pro habendo consilium suam
    diligenciam
fecit pro habendo quodam modo secur[i]tanciam ex qua ire posset
hinc inde pro habendo consilium super dicto processu quam
    secur[i]tanciam
totaliter habere requirit. Petens et requirens igitur dictus magister
Raymundus prefatum dominum judicem quatinus ^prout suo^ suo [sic]
    incumben[tem] officio sibi
dignetur dare aliam dilecionem infra quam ipse Raymundus valeat
ire hinc ad indegandum et habendum consilium super premissis.

Et dictus dominus judex non obstantibus exceptionibus frivole
proprositis et alleggatis per dictum magistrum Raymundum Gauterii et
aliis causis [*crossed out:* ipsum] animum ipsius domini judicis monentibus
attento quod dictus magister Raymundus unias seu plures dilaciones

---

13 Is the "e" crossed out before this name?

quod habuit perhemptas et presizas [*crossed out:* prout constat quod] diu
 lapsas
et in [*crossed out:* nulla in] termino ultimo minime comparere curavit, prout
constat per presentem processum, ideo dictum magistrum Raymundum ad
petita et requisita per eundem minime admisit, attento eciam
quod pro parte dicte Margarite petitur sentencia ferri pro condempnando vel
absolvendo, cum ipsa sit paupertina et non habeat unde se ali-
mentet et diu et longo tempore steterit inclusa et arrestata
per dictam curiam, et ideo omnibus attentis cupiens complimentam
justicie minstrare de dicta Margarita et causam abreviare ad
audiendum eius sentenciam deffinitiam condempnando vel absolvendo
diem jovis proxime que erit die xviii presentis mensis marcii ^ terciis^ dum
tamen non fuerit feriata eidem Margarite pro termino assignavit jubens
per alterum ex servientibus presentis curie eidem Margarite diem supra
assignatam seu statutam intimari et notificari, et inde relacionem
per dictum nuncium [*crossed out:* relacionem] fieri.

[f⁰58] Et ibidem [*crossed out:* et in continentem?] post aliquod temporis
 intervallum retulit
michi notario infrascripto Hugo Javelle nuncius curie predicte se
de precepto supradicti dominis judicis citasse Margaritam de Porte
delatam supradictam personaliter repertam in monasterio dominarum monialium ubi in arresto stat et eidem precepisse et intimasse ut
die jovis proxime terciarum hora compareat in presenti curia coram dicto
 domino
judice auditura suam sentenciam tam absolutoriam quam condempnatoriam
per dictum dominum judicem proferendam, prout habuit in mandatis. Que
scripsi ego Hugo Bonilis dicte curie notarius et signo curie signavi.
[*signed with seal*]

Postque die mercuri xvii mensis marcii convocatis ad presenciam nobilis
et circumspecti viri domini Petri Rebolli jurisperiti judicis curie Hospitalis
ville Manuasce videlicet discretis viris Isnardo Teralhi et Isnardo Samoelis
justifficatoribus in festo ephifanie proxime lapso per dominum Manuasce
 preceptorem
electis justam compositionem inhitam inter [*crossed out:* dictum dominum
 pre] Hospitalis [sic] et
dictam villam Manuasce ad consulendum dicto domino judici in causis
 non justificatis.
Et eosdem id dictus judex requisivit vigore [*crossed out:* prest] juramenti
 prestiti in

manibus dicti domini preceptoris et secundum eorum conscienciam
    quatinus eidem
domino judici consulere habeant bene juste et legaliter in sentencia ipsius
Margarite de intitulatis contra eandem proferenda et eorum veritatem
dicere habeant quid eis visum est de ipsa ^causa^. Qui quidem
    justificatores
visa prius et examinata inquisitione contra ipsam Margaritam facta
et visis dictis et deposicionibus testium pro parte curie productorum, nec
non et deffensionibus pro parte ipsius Margarite productis et dictis depo-
scicionibus [*crossed out:* su] testium super eisdem productorum, dixerunt
    medio eius
juramento eorum videre ^et secundum eorum consciencam et animam^
ipsam Margaritam nullo modo de intitulatis
contra eandem culpabilem fore et eam pocius esse absolvenda quam
condempnanda, retenta cognicione et ordinacione ipsius domini judicis.

Ad quam diem jovis in terciis supra proxime assignatis per dictum
    dominum
judicem que est dies xviii mensis marcii, in predicta curia
et coram predicto domino judice pro tribunali sedente satis faciendo
termino assignato, comparuit dicta Margarita personaliter citra revo[ca]-
cionem quamcumque petens instanter prout supra et sepissime
pro parte ipsius Margarite extitit requisitum in huius modi causa
criminali taliter qualiter salva reverencia et citra injuriam cuiusquam
contra eandem Margaritam incohatum[14] et deinde huc usque processum,
    sentenciam
ferri et quod per ipsam non stat humiliter et instanter et solempniter
protestatur, paratque est personaliter ad ipsam sentenciam proferendam
audiendam.

Sequitur preconisatio
vade inferius folio secundo
in tali signo
[*signed with seal*]

[f⁰58 v.] Sequitur sentencia diffinitiva
per dictum dominum judice[m] lata super
premissis, et est talis:

---

14 incohatam ?

Quoniam justi judices ad hoc constituuntur in urbe ut contra justiciam
nulli portant quin ymo modestos foveant innocentes absoluant
et puniant delinquentes nam aliter prostata quod absit subcumberet
ipsa justicia si innocentes condempnerentur et in adversum delinquentes
absolverentur, et propter ea justus judex ante occulos suos habere debet
sumam equitatem ut recte judicet [*corrected from:* judiget] delinquentes
     puniendo et
innossentes absolvendo, nam aliter innanum esset jus in civitate
esse nisi esset qui jus redderet et unicuique justiciam minstraret.
Et ideo constituti sunt ab eo per quem reges regirant et principes
regunt et principum potestates ut in virga equitatis et justicie
populum regant et sibi custodiant subditas naciones.
Tandem nos Petrus Rebolli jurisperitus judex curie loci de Manuasca
sedentes pro tribunali more maiorum in curia ubi jus redditur
viso pluries et diligenter examinato processu presentis inquisicionis
formato contra Margaritam de Porte de BelloMonte delatam de morte
Johannis Damponsii condam eius mariti visisque indiciis ac circumstanciis
et omnibus intitulatis contra eandem Margaritam delatam; ac eciam
omnibus tam pro pro [sic] parte curie quam pro parte dicte Margarite ad sui
deffensionem productis, allegatis et probatis; attento quod nullus
in dicto processu reperitur accusans, nilque validum eciam probatur
contra prefatam Margaritam ut liquide apparet per processum inquisicionis ob quod dicta Margarita juridice valeat condempnari
nullaque resultent indicia sufficiencia contra ipsam quibus de jure
procedi debeat ad torturam, attenta sua bona fama prout
in suis titulis deffensionalibus clare liquet et probatum extitit;
attento eciam quod nos predictus judex unacum aliis officialibus
curie predicte eciam nobiscum associato magistro Vivas Josep judeo phisico
et surgico et in talibus valde experto incontinenti clamore audito
quod ^casus^ sic acciderat ad domum dicti condam Johannis Damponsii
     accessimus
pro investigando et perquirendo se[15] quis erat culpabilis de nece dicti
condam Johannis. Quiquidem magister Vivas secundum artem suam dictum
     Johannem
sic deffunctum eundem propriis suis occulis nedum solum bis sed
quateret pluries et diversis horis diei nudum inspexit et
cum eius manibus tetigit et palpavit et in pluribus locis
et partibus sue persone. Quiquidem magister Vivas suo juramento super lege

---

15 *For* si ?

Mosayca per me judicem supradictum delato interrogatus quid novit
et quid videbatur sibi secundum artem medicine. Qui suo juramento respondit
quod non videtur sibi quod dictus condam Johannes fuisset mortuus ex
 toysico

[f⁰59] nec eciam aliquo veneno prout clarissime in sue deposicione
constat assignando causas et raciones. Que deposicio in dicto
processu per notarium presentis curie est descripta. Attentis
eciam omnibus de affinitate dicti condam Johannis deffuncti qui eciam
pocius dictam Margaritam delatam excusant quam accusent
preterquam magister Raymundus Gauterii frater dicti deffuncti condam
qui contra eandem delatam habuit suspicionem licet per judicem
predictum fuerint sepe et sepissime interrogati et requisiti
quos quascumque informaciones et indicia habuerent contra
predictam Margaritam delatam curie darent et assignarent
et super premissis plures dilaciones habuerunt et nil
probarunt prout constat per processum concideratis omnibus
et cum matura deliberacione pensatis, communicatoque
super premissis nobis consilio peritorum. Attento eciam [...]
Margarita delata non obstantibus quibus [...]
prepositis et obiectis contra eandem [...]

[*remainder illegble due to torn page*]

[f⁰59 v.] Sancte Cruci dicendo in nomine patris et filii et Spiritus Sancti
 amen.
Supra memoratam Margaritam delatam a meritis dicte inquisicionis
et omnibus et singulis in ea contentis contra eandem per nostram diffinitivam sentenciam absoluimus et absolutam in hiis scriptis hore proprio
pronunciamus per formam nostri decreti in margine dicte nostre inquisicionis propria manu nostra descripti. Cuius tenor talis est causa non
 confiteatur
nec per testes fidedignos in aliquo non convincatur merito a presenti
inquisicione et ab omnibus intitulatis contra eandem tanquam innocens
merito absolvatur. Pe[trus] Re[bolli] jubentes dictam inquisicionem de
cartulario curie in quo descripta est cancellari et penitus
aboleri.

De quibus omnibus dicta Margarita peciit instrumentum et instrumenta tot

[*remainder illegible due to torn page*]

Translation of Criminal Charges against Margarida de Portu

1.

[f⁰32] versus Margarida, daughter of Portius de Portu, deceased, of Beaumont, and wife of Johan Damponcii of Manosque, deceased, and each and every one of those who, concerning the following, aided through council or with some manner of assistance, wheresoever the criminals are able to be discovered.

2.

[In the margin:] The instrument of acquittal was made on behalf of Margarida.

3.

In the year 1394 of our Lord, Friday the 16th of October. For if the wicked should not bow under a worthy punishment, prostrate justice would succumb and the perversity of evils with the order of good disturbed would subjugate patience, and indeed reason urges that the punishment be paid for crimes, since the powers of the king are not established in vain: the right of the recognition of the rod, the weapon of the flesh, the discipline of the ruling soldier and equally the severity of the good father, rather each of them has their own manners, causes, reasons, and apparent uses. Do not let the indulgence of examples of transgressors be an indication to other evildoers, since through some of the examples of earlier correction, if not by love of virtue at least by fear of punishment, they are justly fearful of rushing to do similar deeds. Indeed, the punishment of the wicked appears before the eyes of reason which the blindness[?]¹ of fault had closed. And, by fear of that punishment, recall those machinations with lapsed

---

1 Or possibly necessity (*cessitas*)?

transgressions of piety. Truly, vulgar rumor beats upon the ears of the court of the Hospital of the town of Manosque. And, the abundance of protests, so frequent, rouses the office of that court, so that, without scandal, it is unable to be concealed nor withheld without a detestable[2] example, unless it proceeds to trial, since only rumor prevailed in the place of accusation. Therefore, by a mandate of the office of the court of the Hospital of the town of Manosque, indeed of the noble and circumspect man lord Peire Rebolli, skilled in law, judge of the court, it proceeds, for the inquiry against Margarida, daughter of Portius de Portu of Beaumont and wife of Johan Damponcii, deceased, of Manosque and each and every one of those written below who possibly appear guilty through works of council or aid or any manner of favor concerning that, namely that, with rumor and protests striking his ears it is deduced at last by the hearing of it and especially of Mr. Raymon Gauterii, brother of Johan Damponcii, deceased.

[f[0]32 v.] He made, in cause of suspicion against Margarida, certain accusatory allegations, aiding the court, and stated before the court that the aforesaid accused was unmindful of eternal salvation, as much a wicked woman, and fully impious in respect to all evils and giving little regard to divine and temporal justice. Her evil iniquity and pride chosen, love or fear of the Lord does not rule, following the most wicked suggestions of the devil. Not respecting how weak and shallow the creature of man is, formed in the image of God, moreover, she handed her husband, to whom she stands forth espoused through the matrimonial knot, on account of a false and harmful suggestion in her damnable soul, over to the defeat of death suddenly, and moreover, through the use of sorcery or venom, since venom is more painful to slay with than the sword. Today, contained and described in the present charge, how the accused was led evilly by the spirit of Lucifer, imbued with an evil and wicked art. On that morning, during the hour of prime of that day, at which hour Johan Damponcii, husband of the accused, was accustomed to drink and eat and then go outside and work, she was to serve Johan her husband and prepare a certain harmful drink or dish or some other wicked and evil sorcery that she would order for her husband Johan to eat or drink in the morning meal. And with that received and eaten, immediately he left the town of Manosque in order to work. And on the third hour of that day, the husband of the accused, Johan, both being heavily weighed down and realizing the venom was given to kill him, and not able to go on, returned to the present town of Manosque. He went home and got into his bed. In that way, with the deathly poison or venomous dish or other sorcery being given to him by Margarida the accused and ingested, returning to Christ,

---

2 *destabili* in ms. detestable = *detestabili*

giving his spirit to the lord, he left from that place, his chamber, his bed, from this world, and ended the remainder of his days. [f⁰33] May paradise take hold of his spirit, and may he always rest in the celestial glory with Christ, amen. In the punishment against poisoners and other heavy punishments that both laws produce, blindly and miserably meet.

4.

The following charges came before the hearing of this court:

5.

I. First, namely the charge against the aforesaid Margarida that states that fighting preceded between the accused and her husband, on account of which that woman had gone back to Beaumont and remained there for a period of eight days and beyond.

6.

II. Also, another charge against the aforesaid accused concerning that states that when the accused came from Beaumont she did not stay in the town of Manosque except for one night and, on the following day, her aforesaid husband, healthy and happy, had suddenly died as is written in the aforesaid allegation.

7.

III. Also, another charge against the aforesaid accused concerning that states that Margarida is of that place, Beaumont, where such scandalous things have become commonplace. About which, everywhere, there is a universal consent and knowledge.

8.

IIII. Also, another charge against the aforesaid accused concerning that states that the woman, knowing herself to be guilty regarding the abandonment of premises, doing that because her aforesaid husband had died, bore herself to that place into the safekeeping of a church or monastery of nuns. At length she put herself in the church of Our Lord and hid in a chamber of that cloister. Also, she took little care to go to the house of her aforesaid dead husband as she should have done for his honor.

9.

[f⁰33 v] V. Also, another charge against the aforesaid accused states that that woman, as is stated above, knowing herself to be guilty of the aforesaid flight, believing it not safe enough in that place, within the chamber mentioned previously where she had earlier put herself within the aforesaid church of Our Lord, moved herself to the chapel of Saint Anthony for her security.

10.

VI. Also, another charge against the aforesaid accused concerning that states that on the following Sunday, which was the 17th day of October, her aforesaid husband, Johan, was buried in the cemetery of the church of Our Lord while the accused remained within the aforesaid church in the aforesaid chapel. The accused took little care to attend the grave or burial of the aforesaid Johan. Neither did she weep for him nor suffer any sorrow nor do anything that any respectable woman would be expected to do for her deceased husband; rather, she did nothing, as if she had never met the man.

11.

VII. Also, another charge against the aforesaid Margarida, accused above, concerning that states that when, by the order of the aforesaid lord judge, the accused was summoned personally by Isnardo Laurerie, messenger of the aforesaid court, while within the aforesaid cloister of the church, in order that she should come to give a response to the examination and to aid law and justice under penalty of 100 libra, even then, the accused took little care to appear before the aforesaid court, although knowing herself to be guilty concerning the actions.

22.

[f⁰35 v.] On that day, Mr. Raymon Gauterii, uterine brother of the aforesaid Johan Damponcii, deceased, having stood in the presence of the noble and wise man, lord Peire Rebolli, skilled in law, judge of the court of the Hospital of the town of Manosque, both for the aiding of that court and for the information of that court against Margarida, the accused, as much in his own name as that of all the friends of the aforesaid Johan Damponcii, deceased, produced and presented a certain paper schedule with the following contents.

23.

The contents of the aforesaid schedule are as follows:

The following charges against Margarida, wife of Johan Damponcii, state:

24.

I. First, the aforesaid Margarida daily blasphemed and cursed before the many people who negotiated the marriage between her and the aforesaid Johan.

25.

II. Also, Margarida, when she saw her husband, was depressed concerning the appearance of her husband, saying that he was a whiner and a sad man. She always said bad things about her husband.

26.

III. Also, she said before many people that shortly she would return to Beaumont.

27.

IIII. Also, she had wished to go to Beaumont two or three times, except there had been resistance from her brother the deacon. To that deacon she responded that, unless he should permit her to go [f⁰36] to Beaumont, she would do a thing shameful to all and a crime about which all her friends would be angry. That deacon responded to her, admonishing, "By God I will whip you, as much as evil shall come to you." She said to the deacon that evilly they had given, with their thanks, the aforesaid dead man to her in marriage, and that she would do nothing at this time.

28.

V. Also, indeed she said that unless she should go to Beaumont, she would not be able to be free in any way.

29.

VI. Also, [she kept] her wedding dress outside the house of her aforesaid husband for three weeks and more; she did not keep [it] in the aforesaid house of her husband.

30.

VII. Also, that she went to Beaumont and took with her three pairs of boots and three pairs of socks and remained in that place for eight days.

31.

VIII. Also, she took all the jewels that she had to the aforesaid town of Beaumont.

32.

IX. Also that on that evening when she came from Beaumont, the aforesaid Margarida did not head to the house of her husband, rather she slept in a house of nuns.

33.

X. Also, the next day, rising early in the morning from the aforesaid monastery, she said to her little brother that she had told her husband to give her money for buying honeyed candies; Johan, the deceased, responded that he did not want to eat honeyed candies.

34.

[f⁰36 v] XI. Also, on that morning they made a meal with garlic.

35.

XII. Also, with the aforesaid meal prepared and cooked, the woman came at the time for making meals and made a meal for her husband.

36.

XIII. Also, on previous occasions, the aforesaid Margarida never made it a habit to be in the kitchen or make meals, nor did she wish to eat with her husband.

37.

XIIII. Also, with the meal made by the aforesaid Margarida and the meal eaten by her husband, going to the field of the noble lady Antonieta Savine near the upper gate, when that same Johan, deceased, came to the font of Albeta, he said to his servant, "My entire tongue is burning me. What devil made that meal?" The servant responded that he did not know, and when he came to the aforesaid field of the noble lady Antonieta, in that place he seeded one ridge[3] and, as his servant states, he turned completely black then completely red several times.

38.

XV. Also, as the aforesaid servant states, that man began to tremble all over, saying that he felt very ill in his heart and stomach. The servant replied to the deceased man, "You are shaking all over and your face is black, return to the town."

39.

XVI. Also, immediately the aforesaid deceased returned to the town, shaking and with some loss of sight. When he arrived in his own house, on his bed, he could not speak or move himself, rather he very quickly gave up his spirit and ended his final days.

---

3 *sellonus* = *selio*: ridge, strip of arable land

BIBLIOGRAPHY

Primary Sources

Archives départementales des Alpes-de-Haute-Provence (ADAHP). Series 2 E.

Archives départementales des Bouches-du-Rhône (ADBDR). Series 56 H.

Dutton, Brian, and Maria Nieves Sánchez, eds. *Bernardo de Gordino: Lilio de medicina. Fuentes de la medicina española*. Madrid: Arco / Libros, 1993.

Dyck, Andrew R., ed. *Cicero: Pro Sexto Roscio*. Cambridge: Cambridge University Press, 2010.

Kroll, Wilhelm, Paul Krüger, Theodor Mommsen, et al. *Corpus iuris civilis*. Dublin: Weidmannos, 1970.

Secondary Sources

Arnaud, Camille. *Histoire de la viguerie de Forcalquier*. Marseille: Étienne Camoin, 1874.

Anon. "Sex and Death in Renaissance Florence." *Reference and Research Book News* 25, no. 3 (Aug 2010).

Aubenas, Roger. *Étude sur le notariat provençal au Moyen Age et sous l'Ancien Régime*. Aix-en-Provence: Éditions du Feux, 1931.

Bakhtin, Mikhail M., and Pavel N. Medvedev. *Formal'nyi metod v literaturovedenii (Kristicheskoe vvedenie v sotsiologicheskuiu poetiku)*. Leningrad: Priboi, 1928. Available in English as *The Formal Method in Literary Scholarship: A Critical Introduction to Sociological Poetics*, trans. Albert J. Wehrle. Baltimore: The Johns Hopkins University Press, 1978.

Barker, Hannah Katherine. "Egyptian and Italian Merchants in the Black Sea Slave Trade, 1200–1500." Ph.D. Thesis, Columbia University, forthcoming 2014.

Bednarski, Steven. "Crime, Justice, and Social Regulation in Manosque, 1340–1403." Ph.D. Thesis, Université du Québec à Montréal, 2002.

Bednarski, Steven. *Curia: A Social History of a Provençal Criminal Court in the Fourteenth Century*. Montpellier: Presses universitaires de la méditerranée, 2013.

Bednarski, Steven, and Andrée Courtemanche. "Learning to be a Man: Public Schooling and Apprenticeship in Late Medieval Manosque." *Journal of Medieval History* 35, no. 2 (June 2009): 113–35. http://dx.doi.org/10.1016/j.jmedhist.2009.01.003.

Bednarski, Steven, and Andrée Courtemanche. "'Sadly and with a Bitter Heart'? What the Caesarean Section Meant in the Middle Ages." *Florilegium: Essays in Honour of Margaret Wade Labarge* 28(2011): 33–69.

Bellomo, Manlio. *The Common Legal Past of Europe: 1000–1800*. Washington, DC: Catholic University of America Press, 1995.

Bergeron, David. "Le prêt à crédit juif et chrétien à Manosque de 1303 à 1326." M.A. thesis, Université de Moncton, 2002.

Boswell, John. *Christianity, Social Tolerance, and Homosexuality: Gay People in Western Europe from the Beginning of the Christian Era to the Fourteenth Century.* Chicago: University of Chicago Press, 1980.

Boswell, John. *Same-Sex Unions in Premodern Europe.* New York: Villard Books, 1994.

Bourdieu, Pierre. *An Invitation to Reflexive Sociology.* Chicago: University of Chicago Press, 1992.

Bourdieu, Pierre. *Outline of a Theory of Practice.* Cambridge: Cambridge University Press, 2000.

Braudel, Fernand. *Civilisation Matérielle, Économie et Capitalisme, XVe–XVIIIe.* Paris: Armand Colin, 1976–1979. Reprinted in English as *Civilization and Capitalism, 15th–18th Centuries,* trans. Siân Reynolds. Berkeley: University of California Press, 1992.

Braudel, Fernand. *Écrits sur l'histoire.* Paris: Flammarion, 1977. Available in English as *On History,* trans. Siân Reynolds. Chicago: University of Chicago Press, 1980.

Braudel, Fernand. *La Méditerranée et le Monde Méditerranéen a l'époque de Philippe II.* Paris: Armand Colin, 1949. Available in English as *The Mediterranean and the Mediterranean World in the Age of Philip II,* trans. Siân Reynolds. New York: Harper and Row, 1972–73.

Braudel, Fernand. "Une parfaite réussite." Review of Claude Manceron, *La Révolution qui lève, 1785–1787.* Paris, 1979." *Histoire (Paris)* no. 21 (1980): 108–9.

Bresslau, Harry. *Handbuch der Urkundenlehre für Deutschland und Italien,* II, 2nd ed. Leipzig: Verlag von Veit & Comp, 1915.

Brown, Judith C. *Immodest Acts: The Life of a Lesbian Nun in Renaissance Italy.* New York: Oxford University Press, 1986.

Brucker, Gene. *Giovanni and Lusanna: Love and Marriage in Renaissance Florence.* Berkeley: University of California Press, 1986.

Brundage, James. "Sexual Equality in Medieval Canon Law." In *Medieval Women and the Sources of Medieval History,* ed. Joel T. Rosenthal, 66–79. Athens: University of Georgia Press, 1990.

Burke, Peter. "Introduction: Concepts of Continuity and Change in History." In *New Cambridge Modern History.* Vol. 13, ed. Peter Burke, 1–14. Cambridge: Cambridge University Press, 1979. http://dx.doi.org/10.1017/CHOL9780521221283.002.

Cappelli, Adriano. *Lexicon abbreviaturarum: dizionario di abbreviature latini ed italiani.* 6th ed. Milano: Hoepli, 1961.

Chambers, David, and Trevor Dean. *Clean Hands, Rough Justice: An Investigating Magistrate in Renaissance Italy.* Ann Arbor: University of Michigan Press, 1997.

Charvet, L. "Les serments contre la calomnie dans la procédure au temps de Justinien." *Revue des Etudes Byzantines* 8, no. 8 (1950): 130–42. http://dx.doi.org/10.3406/rebyz.1950.1025.

Cohen, Thomas V. "Bourdieu in Bed: The Seduction of Innocentia (Rome, 1570)." *Journal of Early Modern History* 7, no. 1 (2003): 55–85. http://dx.doi.org/10.1163/1570065033 22487359.

Collier, Jeremy. *An Ecclesiastical History of Great Britain, Chiefly of England, from the First Planting of Christianity to the End of the Reign of King Charles the Second.* Vol. 6. London: Printed for Samuel Keble, 1714.

Courtemanche, Andrée. "De Bayons à Manosque. Une expérience migratoire en Provence à la fin du Moyen Âge." In *Prendre la route. L'expérience migratoire en Europe et en Amérique du nord du XIVe au XXe siècle*, ed. Andrée Courtemanche and Martin Pâquet, 55–80. Hull, QC: Les Éditions Vents d'Ouest, 2001.

Courtemanche, Andrée. "Les femmes juives et le crédit à Manosque au tournant du XIVe siècle." *Provence Historique* 37 (1987): 545–58.

Courtemanche, Andrée. "The Judge, the Doctor, and the Poisoner: Medical Expertise in Manosquin Judicial Rituals at the End of the Fourteenth Century." In *Medieval and Early Modern Ritual: Formalized Behavior in Europe, China and Japan*, ed. Joëlle Rollo-Koster, 105–23. Leiden: Brill, 2002.

Courtemanche, Andrée, and Steven Bednarski. "De l'eau, du grain et une figurine à forme humaine. Quelques procès pour sortilèges à Manosque au début du XIVe siècle." *Memini: Travaux et documents* 2 (1998): 75–106.

Davis, Natalie Zemon. *Fiction in the Archives: Pardon Tales and their Tellers in Sixteenth-Century France*. Stanford: Stanford University Press, 1987.

Davis, Natalie Zemon. "On the Lame." *American Historical Review* 93, no. 3 (June 1988): 572–603. http://dx.doi.org/10.2307/1868103.

Davis, Natalie Zemon. *The Return of Martin Guerre*. Cambridge, MA: Harvard University Press, 1983.

De Vries, Jan. "Great Expectations: Early Modern History and the Social Sciences." In *Early Modern History and the Social Sciences: Testing the Limits of Braudel's Mediterranean*, ed. John A. Marino, 71–98. Kirksville, MO: Truman State University Press, 2001.

Derrida, Jacques. *Acts of Literature*. Ed. Derek Attridge. New York: Routledge, 1992.

Derrida, Jacques. *L'écriture et la différence*. Paris: Seuil, 1979. Available in English as *Writing and Difference*, trans. Alan Bass. Chicago: University of Chicago Press, 1978.

Derrida, Jacques. *Marges de la philosophie*. Paris: Editions de Minuit, 1972. Available in English as *Margins of Philosophy*, trans. Alan Bass. Chicago: University of Chicago Press, 1982.

Durkheim, Emile. *Les règles de la méthode sociologique. 1895*. Reprinted as *Rules of the Sociological Method*, trans. Steven Lukes. New York: Free Press, 1982.

Elliott, Dyan. "Bernardino of Siena versus the Marriage Debt." In *Desire and Discipline: Sex and Sexuality in Premodern Europe*, ed. Jacqueline Murray and Konrad Eisenbichler, 168–200. Toronto: University of Toronto Press, 1996.

Finlay, Robert. "The Refashioning of Martin Guerre." *American Historical Review* 93, no. 3 (June 1988): 553–71. http://dx.doi.org/10.2307/1868102.

Fischer, David Hacket. *Historians' Fallacies: Toward a Logic of Historical Thought*. New York: Harper Torchbooks, 1970.

Foucault, Michel. *Histoire de la sexualité*. Paris: Gallimard, 1976. Available in English as *History of Sexuality*. New York: Vintage Books, 1978.

Foucault, Michel. *Surveiller et punir: naissance de la prison*. Paris: Gallimard, 1977. Available in English as *Discipline and Punish: the Birth of the Prison*, trans. Alan Sheridan. 2nd ed. New York: Vintage Books, 1995.

Ginzburg, Carlo. *Clues, Myths, and the Historical Method*, trans. John Tedeschi and Anne C. Tedeschi. Baltimore: The Johns Hopkins University Press, 1989.

Ginzburg, Carlo. *Il formaggio e i vermi. Il cosmo di un mugnaio del '500.* Turino: G. Einaudi, 1976. Available in English as *The Cheese and the Worms: The Cosmos of a Sixteenth Century Miller,* trans. John and Anne Tedeschi. Baltimore: The Johns Hopkins University Press, 1980.

Ginzburg, Carlo. "Morelli, Freud and Sherlock Holmes. Clues and Scientific Method." *History Workshop* 9, no. 1 (1980): 5–36. http://dx.doi.org/10.1093/hwj/9.1.5.

Ginzburg, Carlo. *Stregoneria e culti agrari tra Cinquecento e Seicento.* Turino: Piccola Biblioteca Einaudi: 1966. Available in English as *The Night Battles: Witchcraft and Agrarian Cults in the Sixteenth and Seventeenth Centuries.* Baltimore: The Johns Hopkins University Press, 1992.

Ginzburg, Carlo, and Carlo Poni. "Il nome e il come. Scambio ineguale e mercato storiografico." *Quaderni storici* 40 (1979): 181–90. Available in English as "The Name and the Game: Unequal Exchange and the Historical Marketplace." In *Microhistory and the Lost People of Europe,* trans. Eren Branch, ed. Edward Muir and Guido Ruggiero, 1–10. Baltimore: The Johns Hopkins University Press, 1991.

Grendi, Edoardo. "Micro-analisi e storia sociale." *Quaderni Storici* 35 (Aug. 1977): 506–20.

Haskins, Charles Homer. "Orleanese Formularies in a Manuscript at Tarragona." *Speculum* 5, no. 4 (Oct. 1930): 411–20. http://dx.doi.org/10.2307/2848146.

Hobsbawm, E.J. "The Revival of Narrative: Some Comments." *Past and Present* 86 (Feb. 1980): 3–8. http://dx.doi.org/10.1093/past/86.1.3.

Hoogendijk, Francisca A.J. "Byzantinischer Sklavenkauf." *Archiv für Papyrusforschung und Verwandte Gebiete* 42, no. 2 (1996): 225–334. http://dx.doi.org/10.1515/apf.1996.42.2.225.

Hurlburt, Holly S. "A Review of *Lost Girls: Sex and Death in Renaissance Florence.*" *History (Historical Association [Great Britain])* 40, no. 2 (April 2012): 52–53.

Iancu-Agou, Danielle. "Les juifs et la justice en Provence médiévale: Un procès survenu à Manosque en 1410." *Provence Historique* 27 (jan.–fév. 1979): 21–45.

Isnard, M.Z. *Livre des privilèges de Manosque.* Paris: Honoré Champion, 1894.

Johnston, David. *Roman Law in Context.* Cambridge: Cambridge University Press, 2004.

Kirshner, Julius. "Wives' Claims against Insolvent Husbands in late Medieval Italy." In *Women of the Medieval World: Essays in Honor of John H. Mundy,* ed. Julius Kirshner and Susanne F. Wemple, 256–303. Oxford: Basil Blackwell, 1985.

Kuehn, Thomas. "Reading Microhistory: The Example of Giovanni and Lusanna." *Journal of Modern History* 61, no. 3 (Sept. 1989): 512–34. http://dx.doi.org/10.1086/468291.

Ladurie, Le Roy Emmanuel. *Montaillou, village occitan de 1294 à 1324.* Paris: Gallimard, 1975. Available in English as *Montaillou. Cathars and Catholics in a French village, 1294–1324.* London: Scolar, 1978.

Lavoie, Rodrigue. "La délinquance sexuelle à Manosque (1240–1430): Schéma général et singularités juives." *Provence historique* 37 (oct.–nov.–déc. 1987): 571–87.

Lavoie, Rodrigue. "Les statistiques criminelles et le visage du justicier: justice royale et justice seigneuriale en Provence au Moyen Age." *Provence historique* 29 (jan.-fév-mars 1979): 3–20.

Lee, Peter. "From National Canon to Historical Literacy." In *Beyond the Canon: History for the Twenty-First Century,* ed. M. Grever and S. Stuurman, 48–62. Basingstoke: Palgrave Macmillan, 2007.

Levi, Giovanni. "On Microhistory." In *New Perspectives on Historical Writing,* ed. Peter Burke, 97–119. University Park: Pennsylvania State University Press, 1991.

Lévi-Strauss, Claude. *Les structures élémentaires de la parenté*. Paris: Presses universitaires de France, 1949. Available in English as *The Elementary Structures of Kinship*, trans. James Harle Belle. London: Eyre and Spottiswoode, 1969.

Long, George. "Calumnia." In *A Dictionary of Greek and Roman Antiquities by Various Writers*, ed. Sir William Smith, 234–35. London, John Murray, 1895.

MacCaughan, Patricia. *La justice à Manosque au XIIIe siècle: Evolution et représentation*, Histoire et Archives, hors-série, 5. Paris: Honoré Champion, 2005.

MacCaughan, Patricia. "La procédure judiciaire à Manosque au milieu du XIIIe siècle, témoin d'une transition." *Revue historique de droit français et étranger* 76 (1998): 583–95.

MacCaughan, Patricia. "Les transformations de la justice au XIIIe siècle: l'exemple de Manosque (1240–1320)." Ph.D. Thesis, Laval University, 2001.

Magnusson, Sigurdur Gylfi. "What is Microhistory?" *History News Network*, accessed 17 July 2012. http://hnn.us/articles/23720.html#_edn4.

Michaud, Francine. "Crédit, endettement et patrimoine féminin à Manosque au milieu du XIIIe siècle." M.A. thesis, Laval University, 1984.

Michaud, Francine. *Un signe des temps: accroissement des crises familiales autour du patrimoine à Marseille à la fin du XIIIe siècle*. Toronto: Pontifical Institute for Mediaeval Studies, 1994.

Muir, Edward. "Introduction: Observing Trifles." In *Microhistory and the Lost People of Europe*, trans. Eren Branch, ed. Edward Muir and Guido Ruggiero, vii–xviii. Baltimore: The Johns Hopkins University Press, 1991.

Murray, Jacqueline. "On the Origins and Role of 'Wise Women' in Causes for Annulment on the Grounds of Male Impotence." *Journal of Medieval History* 16, no. 3 (1990): 235–49. http://dx.doi.org/10.1016/0304-4181(90)90004-K.

Murray, Jacqueline. "Twice Marginal and Twice Invisible: Lesbians in the Middle Ages." In *Handbook of Medieval Sexuality*, ed. V.L. Bullough and J. Brundage, 191–222. New York: Garland, 1996.

Pennington, Kenneth. *The Prince and the Law, 1200–1600: Sovereignty and Rights in the Western Legal Tradition*. Berkeley, Los Angeles: University of California Press, 1993.

Perfetti, Charles A., M. Anne Britt, and Mara C. Georgi. *Text-based Learning and Reasoning: Studies in History*. Hillsdale, NJ: Erlbaum, 1995.

Petkov, Kiril. *The Kiss of Peace: Ritual, Self, and Society in the High and Late Medieval West*. Leiden: Brill, 2003.

Pitt-Rivers, Julian. *The Fate of Shechem or the Politics of Sex: Essays in the Anthropology of the Mediterranean*. Cambridge: Cambridge University Press, 1977.

Roderigo, M.J. "Discussion of Chapters 10–12: Promoting Narrative Literacy and Historical Literacy." In *Cognitive and Instructional Processes in History and the Social Sciences*, ed. M. Carretero and J.F. Voss., 309–20. Hillsdale, NJ: Erlbaum, 1994.

Ruggiero, Guido. *Binding Passions: Tales of Magic, Marriage, and Power at the End of the Renaissance*. Toronto: Oxford University Press, 1993.

Schnapper, Bernard. "Testes inhabiles. Les témoins reprochables dans l'ancien droit pénal." *Revue d'histoire du droit* 33 (1965): 576–616.

Seixas, Peter. "What is Historical Consciousness." In *To the Past: History Education, Public Memory and Citizenship in Canada*, ed. Ruth Sandwell, 11–22. Toronto: University of Toronto Press, 2006.

Shatzmiller, Joseph. *La Famille juive au Moyen Age: Provence-Languedoc*. Paris: Centre nationale de la recherche scientifique, 1987.

Shatzmiller, Joseph. *Jews, Medicine, and Medieval Society*. Berkeley: University of California Press, 1994.

Shatzmiller, Joseph. "Les juifs de Provence pendant la peste noire." *Revue des Etudes Juives* 33 (1974): 457–80.

Shatzmiller, Joseph. *Médecine et justice en Provence médiévale: documents de Manosque, 1262–1348*. Aix-en-Provence: Publications de l'université de Provence, 1989.

Shatzmiller, Joseph. *Recherches sur la communauté juive de Manosque au Moyen Age, 1241–1329*. Paris: Mouton, 1973.

Shatzmiller, Joseph. *Shylock reconsidered: Jews, moneylending, and medieval society*. Berkeley: University of California Press, 1990.

Sheehan, Michael M. "*Maritalis affectio* revisited." In *Marriage, Family, and Law in Medieval Europe*, ed. James K. Farge, 262–77. Toronto: University of Toronto Press, 1996.

Smail, Daniel Lord. "Common Violence: Vengeance and Inquisition in Fourteenth-Century Marseille." *Past and Present* 151, no. 1 (1996): 28–59. http://dx.doi.org/10.1093/past/151.1.28.

Spence, Jonathan D. *The Death of Woman Wang*. New York: Viking Books, 1978.

Stearns, Peter N., Peter Seixas, and Sam Wineburg, eds. *Knowing, Teaching and Learning History: National and International Perspectives*. New York: New York University Press, 2000.

Stone, Lawrence. "The Revival of Narrative: Reflections on a New Old History." *Past and Present* 85 (November 1979): 3–24. http://dx.doi.org/10.1093/past/85.1.3.

Temkin, Owsei. *The Falling Sickness. A History of Epilepsy from the Greeks to the Beginnings of Modern Neurology*. 2nd ed., rev. Baltimore: The Johns Hopkins University Press, 1971.

Thompson, E.P. *The Making of the English Working Class*. London: Gollancz, 1964.

Turner, Victor. *The Anthropology of Performance*. New York: PAJ, 1986.

Turner, Victor. *Dramas, Fields, and Metaphors: Symbolic Action in Human Society*. Ithaca: Cornell University Press, 1974.

Turner, Victor. *The Drums of Affliction: A Study of Religious Processes Among the Ndembu of Zambia*. Oxford: Clarendon Press, 1968.

Turner, Victor. *The Ritual Process: Structure and Anti-Structure*. Chicago: Aldine Publishing Company, 1969.

Van Drie, Jannet, and Carla van Boxtel. "Historical Reasoning: Towards a Framework for Analyzing Students' Reasoning about the Past." *Educational Psychology Review* 20 (2007): 87–110.

Vauchez, André. *The Laity in the Middle Ages. Religious Beliefs and Devotional Practices*. Notre Dame: University of Notre Dame Press, 1993.

Ware, Caroline F., ed. *The Cultural Approach to History, Edited for the American Historical Association*. Port Washington, NY: Kennikat Press, Inc., 1940.

Wilson, Norman J. *History in Crisis? Recent Directions in Historiography*. 2nd ed. Upper Saddle River, NJ: Pearson, 2005.

Wineburg, Sam. *Historical Thinking and Other Unnatural Acts*. Philadelphia: Temple University Press, 2001.

Wineburg, Sam. "Making Historical Sense." In *Knowing, Teaching and Learning History: National and International Perspectives*, ed. Peter N. Stearns, Peter Seixas, and Sam Wineburg, 306–25. New York: New York University Press, 2000.

Winks, Robin W., ed. *The Historian as Detective: Essays on Evidence*. New York: Harper and Row, 1968.

INDEX